Torah Ethics of Interpersonal Relationships

MIDDOT LEDOROT

Torah Ethics
of
Interpersonal
Relationships

Rabbi Yakov Chaim Hilsenrath

KTAV PUBLISHING

URIM PUBLICATIONS
Jerusalem · New York

Torah Ethics of Interpersonal Relationships
Middot Ledorot
by Rabbi Yakov Chaim Hilsenrath

Copyright © 2021 Rabbi Yakov Hilsenrath

Typeset by Ariel Walden

Printed in Israel

First Edition

ISBN 978-1-60280-458-6

Urim Publications, P.O. Box 52287
Jerusalem 9152102
Israel

www.UrimPublications.com

Library of Congress Cataloging-in-Publication Data in progress.

Contents

Lech Lecha

VaYera

Shemot

VaEra

Bo

Yitro

Introduction

It is with a tremendous sense of humility and honor that we pen these words as an introduction to the writings of our holy father, Rabbi Yakov Chaim Hilsenrath, *Zichrono Livracha*. This *sefer* reflects not simply the printed word, but rather it embodies the passion and the love that our father exuded as a teacher of Torah with every breathing moment of his time in this world. Nothing gave him more joy, nothing gave him more energy, than to impart the wisdom and power of Hashem's word.

Our father was born in Nazi Vienna, raised in the immigrant Chassidic world of Williamsburg, and studied in the Yeshiva world of Lithuania. The life mission of "Rabbi Hilsenrath" was to change the world for the better by illuminating people's lives with his magnetic personality, contagious sense of humor, and most importantly, his ability to make Torah relevant and enjoyable.

From Wildwood to Highland Park, New Jersey one can still hear the echoes of "Our Rabbi." Living in a time and age when we yearn for role models for our children, our father stood above the rest. As strong as a lion, yet as soft as a teddy bear, our father gave solace and strength to his congregants throughout the mountains and valleys of the complicated cycle of life. Our father listened, and he listened, and he spoke.

Shabbos after Shabbos, Yom Tov after Yom Tov, people came to shul to be mesmerized by the manner in which our father wove a tapestry of the Weekly *Parsha* utilizing *Chazal*, current events, and the challenges of interpersonal relationships. Young and old knew the Rabbi was speaking *from* the heart *to* the heart, and the message remarkably hit its mark as if the words were tailored for each individual.

Our father treasured nothing more than to discover a hidden Midrash and to share its meaning with the world. How appreciated were those phone calls, "Do you have a minute, I just found a powerful *Chazal*." A Jewish bookstore was *Gan Eden*, and acquiring the latest publication of Midrashim was so much more than rubies and gold.

Our father's sweetest candies were his collection of antique Judaica. One by one, this collection was bound in leather. Rather than to protect and reinforce the fragile paper and binding, we believe that the binding process was to send a message to future generations, that one will behold nothing more precious than the transforming words of Hashem's Torah.

Our Shabbos Table was a lively mixture of *Divrei Torah*, *Zemiros*, dialogue and debate. Frequent guests drank from this well of spiritual inspiration, yearning to return for yet another dose of the Rabbi's and Rebbetzin's wisdom and "gastronomic delights."

Our father would have had limited impact upon his followers without his life's partner and guide. Our mother, the "Rebbetzin," rose from the ashes of Auschwitz, and not simply survived, she thrived. Her answer to her years of horror was to raise a family of honor. With indescribable inner strength and faith, her sole focus was to care for her husband, her children, and her greater family: the members of the community. Maintaining a balance of a public role and private life was a difficult one, but she did so with a sense of grace and dignity. Our mother shared our father's love of learning and she relished every word of Torah which our father taught. As a teacher, amongst our mother's favorite memories was her recitation of a *Dvar Torah* at the monthly Sisterhood meetings.

And partners they were; "The Rabbi and the Rebbetzin." One entity with one common mission, one common message. A life of Torah living and learning grants you spiritual heights and intellectual depths. A relationship with Hashem will solidify your relationship with your children, our People and our Land. The joy of Torah energizes the eternal happiness of life.

Our father was deliberate in his choice of words. He reveled in conjuring up the perfect word and delivering it at precisely the right moment. At the top of the list of these words was "quintessential," defined as "representing the most perfect example of a quality or class." Our father was the most perfect example of quality and class. Overt in his *Emunah*, private in his family life, embracing of people of all walks of life, our father's essence was to serve as a meaningful and relevant link from generation to generation for his children and for the Jewish People.

Our father merited to receive a family copy of his writings, and he presented a copy to each child and grandchild shortly before his passing. Towards the end of his life, he would often say that his decades of teaching would have been for naught, if he was not able to impart his life's mission to his own children, grandchildren, and great grandchildren. "Zaydee" was loving, and he was loved by each of his offspring. His dream was fulfilled.

We express our appreciation to Urim Publications. To Rabbi Johnny Solomon, a fine *talmid chacham*, who edited and translated numerous sections of the *sefer* with accuracy and beauty. To Mrs. Pearl Friedman, who oversaw the final stages of the editing process with acumen and skill. The expertise, patience and persistence of the publisher, Tzvi Mauer, yielded a *sefer* our father would be proud of.

To Shira (Hilsenrath) Murik for expending countless hours of proofing the various editions. Her focus on details, and her commitment to ensuring that her Zaydee's *sefer* would be just right, is remarkable.

Our holy mother, *Zichrona Livracha*, passed away on the 4th of Elul, 5780 – August 24th, 2020. A year before, we had taken the draft typeset version and the cover picture of the *sefer* you hold in your hands, and produced one copy for our mother. She would spend many a precious hour basking in the light that her husband of 61 years brought to the world. In the merit and blessed memory of our parents, may these words serve to elevate you to come closer to Hashem, to care more for His people, and to pass on the majesty and wisdom of His Torah for generations to come. *Middot Ledorot*, an everlasting tribute to our parents.

Rabbi Azriel and Chaya Heuman
Rabbi Baruch and Sima Hilsenrath
Philip and Rochelle Goldschmiedt
Michael and Aviva Rappaport

First Things First / בְּרֵאשִׁית

בְּרֵאשִׁית בָּרָא אֱ-לֹהִים אֵת הַשָּׁמַיִם וְאֵת
הָאָרֶץ: (בראשית א:א)

When G-d began to create heaven and earth.
(Bereishit 1:1)

Rabbi Yochanan began (with the following verse): "A house is built by wisdom" (Mishlei 24:3). A person must do three things in the way of the world, and they are: Build a house to live in, and plant a vineyard with which to support himself, and subsequently take a wife for himself and have children to be supported by them. And from whom do you learn this? From the Holy One, blessed is He. First, He built a house and established it, and He prepared all provision and food before humankind would enter the world. How [did G-d build a house first]? First He created the world, which is a house. How did He prepare all provision? He created domesticated animals, wild animals, birds, fish, plants and trees, which was the preparation of all provision. After He prepared the house and the means of sustenance, He brought in man, creating him and his wife. And man had children. And they established civilization in the "house." Therefore it says *Bereishit* (Bereishit 1:1) – *bet* (the second letter of the Hebrew alphabet which also means house) at the beginning. And similarly, the Torah began with *Bereishit*, as if to say *bet reishit* ("house first!"). It is all one matter.   (The Hidden Midrash, Bereishit – in the New Zohar, 4)

מדרש הנעלם בראשית בזוהר חדש ד

ר' יוחנן פתח "בְּחָכְמָה יִבָּנֶה בָּיִת" (משלי כד:ג). שלשה דברים צריך אדם לעשות בדרכי העולם ואלו הן: לבנות בית מושבו, וליטע כרם להתפרנס בו ואח"כ לקחת לו אשה ולהוליד בנים לפרנסם בהם וכו'. וממי אתה למד? מהקב"ה.

15

קודם בנה בית וכוננו, וזמן כל פרנסה והמזונות קודם שיבא אדם לעולם. היאך?
ברא את העולם בראש שהוא הבית, וזמן כל הפרנסה היאך ברא את הבהמות
ואת החיות ואת העופות והדגים הצמחים והאילנות שהם זימון כל הפרנסה
לאחר שהכין הבית והפרנסה הביא את האדם וברא אותו ואת אשתו והולידו
בנים ועשו ישוב בבית ועל כן נאמר "בראשית" בית ראש (כאשר תבין באותיות
– בראשית – תמצא בי"ת ראש) וכן התחילה התורה בראשית כלומר "בית
ראשית" והכל ענין אחד.

Rabbi Yochanan suggests a pragmatic approach concerning the
establishment of the single, most significant structure for civilization: the family. He begins by quoting Mishlei 24:3: "Through
wisdom a house is built." And how does he define wisdom? It is
in following the order of creation as the model for establishing a
family.

G-d introduced humankind into the world via a three-step
agenda. First, G-d created the world, the "house" or habitation
for humankind. Then G-d created the vegetation, fish, and animals with which humans were to be fed. Having thus prepared
both domicile and sustenance, G-d then created humans. That is,
only after the environment was hospitable and supportive to the
human family did G-d introduce human beings into the world.

This is a fascinating rabbinic observation regarding what
constitutes a responsible and mature social order. G-d did not
introduce the human family into the world until the world was
prepared to sustain this remarkable creation. Therefore, says the
midrash, do not establish a family until you are prepared to sustain it.

The Individual / בְּצֶלֶם אֱ-לוֹהִים

וַיִּבְרָא אֱ-לֹהִים אֶת־הָאָדָם בְּצַלְמוֹ בְּצֶלֶם
אֱ-לֹהִים בָּרָא אֹתוֹ זָכָר וּנְקֵבָה בָּרָא אֹתָם:
(בראשית א:כז)

And G-d created man in His image, in the image
of G-d He created him; male and female He
created them. (Bereishit 1:27)

Therefore Adam was created alone ... in order to proclaim the
greatness of the Holy One, blessed is He. For when a human being mints a number of coins using the same stamp, the coins are
all identical in appearance. Yet when G-d mints each human being
with the stamp used for the first human being, no single person is
identical to another. Therefore everyone is obligated to say "the
world was created for my sake."   (Mishnah Sanhedrin 4:5)

משנה סנהדרין ד:ה

לפיכך נברא אדם יחידי . . . ולהגיד גדולתו של הקדוש ברוך הוא, שאדם טובע
כמה מטבעות בחותם אחד – כולן דומין זה לזה, ומלך מלכי המלכים הקדוש
ברוך הוא טבע כל אדם בחותמו של אדם הראשון – ואין אחד מהן דומה
לחבירו. לפיכך כל אחד ואחד חייב לומר: בשבילי נברא העולם.

The Mishna articulates a fundamental principle of Torah: The
absolute value of every individual and the uniqueness of every
human being. No two people are alike.

How remarkable is the Talmud's view of humankind. Modern
science has demonstrated (with fingerprints and, more recently,
DNA) that, indeed, every single human has an absolutely unique
physical and biological identity. Even "identical" twins may be

17

distinguished one from another by their fingerprints and DNA "signatures."

The Talmud teaches that each person is unique and precious, and needs to consider him/herself worthy to the point that they may say "בשבילי נברא העולם/for my sake the entire universe was created" (Babylonian Talmud Sanhedrin 37a).

Obviously, this may lead to an exaggerated sense of ego, with destructive consequences; yet self-worth is a prerequisite for healthy motivation and serious aspiration. One must believe that serious goals can be achieved, that uncharted paths may be taken, and that the individual is capable of major contributions to society. Consider, for example, all the Children of Israel have accomplished from the days of Avraham and Sarah to this very moment.[1]

Our view of G-d changed the destiny of humankind. Our legacy of law and morality, the bedrock of Western Civilization, should add to our sense of self-worth. While humankind was yet in the dark and pagan world, when no sense of justice was applied to human society, when might, wealth and amorality ruled supreme – the Hebrew prophets spoke out for justice, truth, and peace. From Avraham the first Jew, to Nechemia the last prophet, the Torah is replete with the teachings and actions of individuals who made a difference.

---

1. The great chasidic master Reb Zushe taught that each person should carry two notes, one in each pocket. The first should read בשבילי נברא העולם – "for my sake the entire universe was created" and the other should read אנכי עפר ואפר – "I am but dust and ashes." These reminders would give the individual a balanced perspective on reality: Torah teaches the inherent potential of each human being, while also cautioning us that we are ultimately mortal.

Respect / כבוד חברו

וַיִּבְרָא אֱ-לֹהִים אֶת־הָאָדָם בְּצַלְמוֹ בְּצֶלֶם
אֱ-לֹהִים בָּרָא אֹתוֹ זָכָר וּנְקֵבָה בָּרָא אֹתָם:
(בראשית א:כז)

And G-d created man in His image, in the image
of G-d He created him; male and female He
created them. (Bereishit 1:27)

Whoever is honored through someone else's disgrace has no share
in the next world (eternity). (Midrash Bereishit Rabbah 1:5)

מדרש בראשית רבה א:ה
כל המתכבד בקלון חבירו אין לו חלק לעולם הבא.

Each human being is G-d's creation, a precious reflection of the
divine. The Midrash therefore considers כבוד חברו/respecting
your friend (i.e., any other human being), to be a paramount
value and sensitivity. We find a judgment of equal significance
in Pirkei Avot (*Ethics of Our Fathers*): המלבין פני חבירו ברבים אין לו חלק
לעולם הבא "Whoever humiliates another in public [*ba-rabim*] for-
feits all rights to eternity" (Pirkei Avot 3:11/פרקי אבות ג:יא). Quite
a harsh punishment. Virtually all rabbinic texts condemn, without equivocation, any word or act which may embarrass another
person. The word *rabim*/many, does not suggest a multitude.
Rather, *rabim* in this context suggests even a group of three; i.e.,
the speaker, the subject of the remark, and the listener. Thus we
must be very careful with our speech. Words are powerful and
at times may serve as weapons. Words may also heal, comfort,
and love. How we use the gift of speech determines, in part at
least, the kind of person we are. The Rabbis caution us: תן דעתך על

19

שיצא מפיך / שיצא מפיך/ "think before words leave your mouth" (דרך ארץ זוטא ג).
Thought should both guide and filter our words. A radical view is
introduced in a Talmudic text concerning ethical speech:

> Rav Dimi the brother of Rav Safra taught the following tradition:
> One should never speak of someone else's good qualities, for in
> speaking of that person's good qualities one will come to speak
> of his bad qualities. Some present a different version [of the tra-
> dition]: Rav Dimi the brother of Rav Safra became ill, and Rav
> Safra came to ask about him. Rav Dimi said to him: "I believe I
> am deserving of divine reward, for I have observed everything that
> the Rabbis have said." Rav Safra replied: "Have you observed 'a
> person should never speak of someone else's good qualities, for in
> speaking well of the other person, he will come to disgrace him'?"
> He replied: "I had not heard this tradition, but if I had, I would
> have observed it." (Babylonian Talmud, Arachin 16a)

ערכין טז:

תני רב דימי אחוה דרב ספרא: לעולם אל יספר אדם בטובתו של חבירו,
שמתוך טובתו בא לידי רעתו. איכא דאמרי: רב דימי אחוה דרב ספרא חלש על
רב ספרא לשיולי ביה, אמר להו: תיתי לי דקיימי כל דאמר רבנן. א"ל: הא מי
מקיימת לעולם אל יספר אדם בטובתו של חבירו, שמתוך טובתו בא לידי גנותו
אמר להו: לא שמיעא לי, ואי הוה שמיעא לי קיימתה.

This text suggests a far more exacting approach than that of the
admonition in Psalms 34:13–14:

> Who is the man who desires life, who loves days to see goodness?
> Guard your tongue from evil and your lips from speaking deceit-
> fully.

מִי־הָאִישׁ הֶחָפֵץ חַיִּים אֹהֵב יָמִים לִרְאוֹת טוֹב: נְצֹר לְשׁוֹנְךָ מֵרָע וּשְׂפָתֶיךָ מִדַּבֵּר
מִרְמָה:

Rav Dimi cautions, one should not speak words of *praise* concerning another person, perchance the listener would respond with
words of derision.

Lashon harah is thus not necessarily pejorative or false. This teaching offers a remarkable ethical standard: Do not say anything about anyone at any time!

There is one clear exception. In response to a legitimate professional inquiry or a request for a character reference, we have an obligation to speak the truth based on our knowledge and judgment. Such a response, whether positive or negative, is not considered *lashon harah*. Speak the truth, and scrupulously avoid any extraneous comments.

The Rabbis suggest another exception: Regarding an individual who is known to foster conflict within a family, community, or any group, one is permitted to speak the truth, though it may not be complimentary. The pragmatic judgment concerning the well-being of family and community at times demands a candid response. The Rabbis were not naive idealists; they understood the complexities of the human experience and the necessity for responsible speech and action.

The "Evil" Inclination / יצר הרע

וַיַּרְא אֱ־לֹהִים אֶת־כָּל־אֲשֶׁר עָשָׂה וְהִנֵּה־טוֹב
מְאֹד: (בראשית א:לא)

And G-d saw all that He had made, and found it
very good. (Bereishit 1:31)

Rabbi Nachman bar Shemuel bar Nachman said in the name of
Rav Shemuel bar Nachman: "And found it good" (*ve-hinneh tov*),
the expression in the verse without the adverb "very" – this refers
to the good inclination; "And found it very good" – this refers to
the evil inclination. But is the evil inclination indeed "very good"?
Yet, were it not for the evil inclination, a man would not build a
house nor marry a wife nor have children nor do business. Similarly, Solomon says "[I have also noted that all labor and skillful
enterprise] come from men's envy of each other." (Ecclesiastes 4:4)
(Midrash Bereishit Rabbah 9:7)

מדרש בראשית רבה ט:ז

רבי נחמן בר שמואל בר נחמן בשם רב שמואל בר נחמן אמר "הנה טוב" זה
יצר טוב. "והנה טוב מאד" זה יצר רע, וכי יצר הרע טוב מאד? אתמהא, אלא
שאלולי יצר הרע לא בנה אדם בית ולא נשא אשה, ולא הוליד ולא נשא ונתן,
וכן שלמה אומר כי היא קנאת איש מרעהו. (קהלת ד:ד)

This midrash presents an original moral statement. In fact, it affirms and legitimizes a healthy ego which motivates and prompts
us to have a family, position, and wealth.

There is a fundamental difference between the *yetzer harah*,
"evil inclination" in rabbinic teaching, and the "id" in psychoan-
alytic theory. The *yetzer harah* is a subconscious and clear drive
to pursue that which is in our own best interest without regard

to right or wrong. The *yetzer harah* is called "very good" in this midrash because it is the catalyst for the human endeavor, for ego. It appears that the midrash accepts a dimension of evil which has potentially positive consequences.

Why build a house, when building a house takes so much effort? Why marry, when marriage means less freedom, more limitations, and more responsibility? Why have children, when having children means years of support, anxiety, even conflict?

The *yetzer harah* is a synthesis of ego and id, driving or motivating towards the good – i.e: home, marriage, children, etc. – though not necessarily towards what is holy or wholesome. Nonetheless, the results may be significant and potentially very positive.

Life would appear to be much less demanding and certainly less perilous for one who does not build a house, marry, have children or seek a profession. What would catapult a person into a life of complex responsibility and unpredictable results if not a healthy dose of self-centered desires? There is a need, suggests the midrash, for self interest in order for the individual to accept major responsibilities. Humans need "selfish," self-centered objectives in order to engage in what seems difficult. Enlightened self interest can be good. Thus it takes the *yetzer harah*, this bit of "evil," or ego, to motivate us to engage in acts which are the catalyst of human endeavors. The Torah therefore guides us toward choices which are both moral and potentially satisfying to the ego (though they may also be dangerous and destructive).

Another midrash gives a precise description of the human being:

Rabbi Levi said: There are six things that serve a person. Three are under one's control, and three are not. The eye, the ear, and the nose are not under one's control – one sees what one does not wish to see, one hears what one does not wish to hear, and one smells what one does not wish to smell. The mouth, the arm, and the foot are under a person's control.

(Midrash Bereishit Rabbah 63:7)

מדרש בראשית רבה סג:ז
אמר ר' לוי ששה דברים משמשין את האדם שלשה ברשותו ושלשה אינן
ברשותו, העין והאוזן וחוטם שלא ברשותו, חמי מה דלא בעי, שמע מה דלא
בעי, מריח מה דלא בעי, הפה והיד והרגל ברשותו.

This midrash refers to six parts of the human body. Eyes, ears, and
nose all function involuntarily, i.e., without the will and judgment
of the individual. Yet our hands and feet are at our "command."
We use them when and how we choose. The human is thus
viewed as a complex being capable of choice, yet also limited. We
are called upon by the Torah to accept ethical responsibility for
both our voluntary and our involuntary attributes, such that our
actions lead to *tikkun olam* / repair of the world – i.e., improving
the human condition as a result of our choices and actions.

The Heretic / הַמִּין

וַיַּרְא אֱ-לֹהִים אֶת־כָּל־אֲשֶׁר עָשָׂה וְהִנֵּה־
טוֹב מְאֹד וַיְהִי־עֶרֶב וַיְהִי־בֹקֶר יוֹם הַשִּׁשִּׁי:
(בראשית א:לא)

And G-d saw all that He had made, and found it
very good, and there was evening and there was
morning, the sixth day. (Bereishit 1:31)

It happened that a heretic came to Rabbi Akiva and said, "Who
created the universe?" He replied, "The Holy One, blessed is
He." He [the heretic] said, "give me a clear proof." He replied,
"come back to me tomorrow." The next day, he [the heretic] came
to him and he [Rabbi Akiva] said, "what are you wearing?" He [the
heretic] replied, "a garment."

"Who made it?" [Asked Rabbi Akiva.] "The weaver." [Re-
sponded the heretic.] "I don't believe you. Give me a clear proof."
[And the heretic responded,] "What evidence can I show you and
don't you know that the weaver made it?" Rabbi Akiva replied,
"And you, don't you know that the Holy One, blessed is He created the universe?"

The heretic left, but the students asked, "what is the clear
proof?" He replied, "My sons, just as the house attests to the
builder, the garment attests to the weaver, and the door attests to
the carpenter, so the universe attests to the Holy One, blessed is
He, that He created it."   (Midrash Temurah, end of chapter 3)

מדרש תמורה סוף פרק ג
מעשה שבא מין ואמר לרבי עקיבא: העולם הזה מי בראו? אמר לו הקב"ה.
אמר לו הראני דבר ברור, אמר לו למחר תבוא אלי. למחר בא אצלו אמר לו מה
אתה לובש אמר לו בגד, אמר לו מי עשאו, אמר לו האורג, אמר לו איני מאמינך

25

הראיני דבר ברור, אמר לו ומה אראה לך ואין אתה יודע שהאורג עשאו, אמר לו
ואתה אינך יודע שהקב"ה ברא את עולמו. נפטר אותו המין, אמרו לו תלמידיו
מה הדבר ברור, אמר בני כשם שהבית מודיע על הבנאי והבגד מודיע על האורג
והדלת על הנגר כך העולם מודיע על הקב"ה שהוא בראו.

This story is remarkable for its timeless relevance and its profound approach to the inquiries of a "heretic" or any person of little or no faith. Rather than dismissing the heretic for his obvious
heresy, Rabbi Akiva engages him in a dialogue. First, he asks the
heretic to return the next day. By doing so Rabbi Akiva demonstrates that the issue under discussion deserves serious thought.
When the discussion resumes, the rabbi articulates the logic of
his faith. His approach is one of calm, reason, and respect, in
which we detect no intolerance.

In fact, we still have heretics, and they are still part of the
community! Indeed they belong to synagogues and participate in
Jewish communal affairs, though in faith and practice they may
be far removed from traditional thought or observance.

America has produced a unique phenomenon: non-observant,
non-believing Jews who are full and significant participants in
and contributors to the Jewish community. They give of their
time, talent, and resources, yet remain "outsiders." They are
non-observant and non-believing, yet identify fully and significantly as Jews. Perhaps they are not "heretics" as in Talmudic
times, yet Rabbi Akiva's response is instructive. The question for
the community remains, how does one respond to the challenges
of a heretic? Rabbi Akiva demonstrated clearly that the response
must not be one of dismissal; rather, the response must involve
a willingness to enter into serious dialogue, with respect and understanding.

In our time, we need to engage "heretics" beyond only the
philanthropic venues of Jewish communal needs. We need to
engage them in a manner responsive to their intellectual curi-
osity and capacity. Today's heretic deserves to be respected and
challenged to explore the rich and demanding venue of Jewish
intellectual and philosophic tradition. Approach the heretic with
sophistication and knowledge. Once engaged in the worlds of To-

rah and secular knowledge, the heretic may well come to respect Torah and its rich heritage. The heretic may then seek answers as a serious, knowledgeable, and committed Jew. Never dismiss the heretic. Rabbi Akiva teaches, דע מה שתשיב לאפיקורוס/ "Know what to answer the heretic" (Pirkei Avot 3:19) must be the challenge and agenda of the Jewish establishment and individual.

Faith / אמונה

וַיַּרְא אֱ־לֹהִים אֶת־כָּל־אֲשֶׁר עָשָׂה וְהִנֵּה־טוֹב מְאֹד
וַיְהִי־עֶרֶב וַיְהִי־בֹקֶר יוֹם הַשִּׁשִּׁי: (בראשית א:לא)

And G-d saw all that He had made, and found it
very good, and there was evening and there was
morning, the sixth day. (Bereishit 1:31)

At the conclusion of the previous midrash, Rabbi Akiva's students ask him, "In the final analysis, what is certain about creation?" In response, he introduces the concept: "My children, as the house attests to the builder, and the garment attests to the weaver, and the door attests to the carpenter, so the universe testifies to the fact that the Holy One, blessed is He, created the universe."

We hear no discussion on the part of the students. In contrast to the behavior of the heretic, there are no more questions, no challenges, no rejections. For those who believe in the existence of G-d, there is no need to probe beyond Akiva's teaching.

Faith in G-d is exactly that – faith / *emunah*. Though the atheist can never explain creation *ex nihilo*, the creation of "something out of nothing" (יש מאין), no one has ever responded successfully to the question of how matter first came into being without reference to a Creator. An accident? A series of accidents? The concept of a creator is inevitable in any logical quest for an understanding of the "beginning."

What is the wisdom and truth this midrash comes to teach? *Emunah*, faith, is ultimately not subject to empiricism. Faith is belief / trust / confidence in the divine Being, though never precluding or forbidding a quest for a better understanding of a clear faith, as is (for example) demonstrated in the Rambam's (Maimonides) "Guide of the Perplexed."

Even the Insects / זבובין ופרעושים

וַיַּרְא אֱ-לֹהִים אֶת־כָּל־אֲשֶׁר עָשָׂה וְהִנֵּה־טוֹב
מְאֹד: (בראשית א:לא)

And G-d saw all that He had made, and found it
very good. (Bereishit 1:31)

Our Rabbis say: What is the meaning of "The greatest advantage
in all the land is His" (Ecclesiastes 5:8) [It means that] even things
that you see as superfluous – such as flies, fleas, and mosquitoes
– were part of the creation of the world, as it says, "And G-d saw
all that He had made, and found it very good" (Bereishit 1:31).
(Midrash Shemot Rabbah 10:1)

מדרש שמות רבה י:א
רבותינו אמרין מה "ויתרון ארץ בכל היא" (קהלת ה:ח) אפילו דברים שאתה רואה
אותן כאלו הם מיותרין בעולם כגון זבובים ופרעושים ויתושין הן היו בכלל
ברייתו של עולם שנאמר "וירא אֱ-לֹהים את כל אשר עשה והנה טוב מאד."
(בראש'ת א:לא)

This midrash insists that all of G-d's creations – even the lowly
and despised fleas and mosquitos – have some purpose. All of creation is potentially within the genre of tov m'od, "very good." The
"goodness," or the "blessing" of G-d's creation, depends upon the
one created "in G-d's image" – i.e., the human being – with the
ability to think, learn, know, choose, and act. With ever increasing knowledge of the universe and its inherent powers, humans
are in a unique position to determine the goodness and blessing
of the rest of G-d's creations.

All is potentially tov m'od ("very good"), yet equally potentially

29

rah m'od ("very bad"). The human power both to heal and to destroy has become ever more sophisticated, far-reaching, and radical in its consequences. The ancient wisdom of the Midrash understood that human potentialities are vast and perhaps limitless.

Would there be no distinctions of "good" and "evil" in the natural world if there were no humans? Does the natural world have a moral choice? Does a hurricane occur because the climatic conditions "decided" to destroy? If there is no choice for evil, can there be a choice for good? The possibility of *tov m'od* allows for the possibility of *rah m'od* – but only for humans.

These complex issues continue to perplex us. Perhaps they confront us with the limitations of even the most knowledgeable and sophisticated of human society.

The Purpose of Creation / יוֹם הַשִּׁשִּׁי

וַיְהִי־עֶרֶב וַיְהִי־בֹקֶר יוֹם הַשִּׁשִּׁי: (בראשית א:לא)

*And there was evening and there was morning,
the sixth day. (Bereishit 1:31)*

Rabbi Simon ben Marta said: Until now, we reckon time according to the count of the world, but from now on, we reckon time according to a different count. (Midrash Bereishit Rabbah 9:14)

מדרש בראשית רבה ט:יד

אמר רבי סימון בר מרתא עד כאן מונין למנינו של עולם, מיכן ואילך מונין למנין אחר.

Rabbi Simon ben Marta said: This is what the verse is teaching us: "the sixth day [*ha-shishi*]" – with the definite article (the "ה"). "Until now" – from the first day of creation until the sixth day, "we reckon time– days." "According to the count of the world" – from the day it was created. "From now on" – from this sixth day, which is the day humankind was created, "we reckon time" – i.e. years, "according to a different count" – from the day humankind was created, and not from the first day. And this is why the verse says, "the sixth day" – with the definite article – the last for the old count and the first for the new count, for we reckon years from the sixth day. (Yefeh To'ar ibid.)

יפה תואר שם

אמר רבי סימון בר מרתא זאת בא ללמדנו הכתוב: "השישי – ב"ה" – עד כאן" מיום ראשון של ימי בראשית עד יום השישי הזה – מונין – הימים למנינו של העולם מיום יצרתו, מיכן ואילך מיום ששי זה, שהוא יום יצירת האדם – מונין – את מנין השנים – למנין אחר – מיום יצירת האדם, וגמר הבריאה, ולא מיום

31

ראשון, וזהו שאמר הכתוב: השישי ב"ה" האחרון למנין הישן והראשון למנין
החדש, שאנו מונין ממנו השנים.

The specificity of the הידיעה "ה" – "the definite article" (i.e., *yom
ha-shishi*, the sixth day) – is cause for the Midrash to view this period of creation as something distinct from the earlier periods of
creation. Here the creation of the "human" is cause for a different
view of the process of creation. It is the end of the "old count,"
which this Midrash states clearly in its commentary.

Torah puts the human being at the pinnacle of G-d's design.
The entire purpose of creation – its raison d'etre – is the creation
of the human being. The universe has been created so that the
human species may learn its potentiality and strive to fulfill it, thus
making possible *tikkun olam:* i.e., the establishment of a world in
which G-d is clearly manifest through a society of justice, truth
and peace in which all people enjoy G-d's infinite blessings.

The Torah is the blueprint through which this ultimate good is
to be accomplished. The purpose of *mitzvot* is to guide this process. Each *mitzvah* is designed to enhance the human experience,
to bring greater harmony and sensitivity within the human family
and thus bring people closer to one another and to G-d. This
process will ultimately demonstrate that the "human" is indeed
created *b'tzelem elokim*, "in the image of G-d." As human beings
establish and sustain a world in which, universal lasting peace and
equal opportunity for all becomes a reality, we manifest our divine, yet human, qualities and potentiality.

The Meaning of Rest / שבת

וַיְכַל ה' בַּיּוֹם הַשְּׁבִיעִי מְלַאכְתּוֹ אֲשֶׁר עָשָׂה,
וַיִּשְׁבֹּת בַּיּוֹם הַשְּׁבִיעִי מִכָּל־מְלַאכְתּוֹ אֲשֶׁר
עָשָׂה: (בראשית ב:ב)

By the seventh day G-d completed His work
which He had done, and He abstained on the
seventh day from all His work which He had
done. (Bereishit 2:2)

The verse (Bereishit 2:2) states: "And G-d finished on the 7th
day His work of creation." One might conclude "G-d finished"
the creative process on the "7th day," thus G-d "worked" on the
(Shabbat) 7th day. The great 12th century scholar Rabbi Shlomo
Yitzchaki ("Rashi") comments on this conundrum. Based on a
Midrash, he writes:

מה היה העולם חסר? "מנוחה", באת שבת באת מנוחה, כלתה ונגמרה
המלאכה (רש"י בראשית ב:ב)

What is it that the world lacked after the "six days of creation,"
all was done, the universe was brought into being, the human
being was created, now what else was necessary? Says "Rashi,"
מנוחה, "Rest." Not only the absence of labor, שבת – Shabbat is a
state of peacefully experiencing life in its physical, spiritual, social, and intellectual dimensions. This is what was created on the
7th day – Shabbat. G-d finished on the 7th "day" and created
"rest," not merely an absence of labor, but a positive and unique
quality of rest. Shabbat was given so that the human being may
enjoy a quality of life which transcends the daily vicissitudes of
the human experience.

33

"רבי חייא בר אבא: לא נתנה השבת אלא לתענוג" (פסיקתא רבתי פיסקא כג)

"Shabbat was given only so that a person may enjoy life" teaches this rabbinic text. Not only do the positive commandments' observance enhance the quality of our lives, but the prohibitions of Shabbat come to enhance the quality of life, for we are removed from the daily pursuit of the mundane. All Shabbat prohibitions are designed to enable a person to enjoy "the present" without the ever-present compulsion to acquire, to alter, to pursue. Shabbat allows, and in fact encourages, human pleasures in all their manifestations; physical, emotional, and intellectual, so long as there are no changes in the reality of the physical environment as a result of our actions.

One may argue that the exception to this rule of "not altering the present" is the intimate encounter of husband and wife which, in fact, is viewed by the tradition as a *mitzvah*. Tradition views the sanctity of this experience G-d like in its holiness, thus quintessentially in perfect harmony with the essence of Shabbat.

Body and Soul /
עפר מן האדמה – נשמת חיים

וַיִּיצֶר ה' אֱ-לֹהִים אֶת־הָאָדָם עָפָר מִן־הָאֲדָמָה
וַיִּפַּח בְּאַפָּיו נִשְׁמַת חַיִּים: (בראשית ב:ז)

The Lord G-d formed man from the dust of the
earth. He blew into his nostrils the breath of life,
and man became a living being. (Bereishit 2:7)

All that you can see was part of the genesis of the heavens and
earth as it says, "In the beginning, G-d created heaven and earth."
(Bereishit 1:1) On the second day He created part of 'that which
is above,' as it says, "G-d said, 'Let there be an expanse, etc.'"
(Bereishit 1:6) On the third day, He created part of 'that which is
below,' as it says, "G-d said, 'Let the earth sprout vegetation, etc.'"
(Bereishit 1:11) On the fourth day He created part of 'that which
is above,' as it says, "G-d said, 'let there be lights, etc.'" (Bereishit
1:14). On the fifth day, He created part of 'that which is below,' as
it says, "G-d said, 'Let the water bring forth swarms, etc.'" (Bereishit 1:20). On the sixth day, He came to create Adam. He said: "If
I create him from 'that which is above,' that which is above will
now have a majority over that which is below by one creation, and
there will be no peace in the world; but if I create him from 'that
which is below,' that which is below will now have a majority over
that which is above by one creation, and there will be no peace in
the world. Rather, I will create him from both 'that which is above'
and 'that which is below' for the sake of peace.   (Midrash
Bereishit Rabbah 12:8)

מדרש בראשית רבה יב:ח

כל מה שאתה רואה תולדות שמים וארץ הן שנאמר "בראשית ברא א-לוהים
את השמים ואת הארץ" (בראשית א:א), בשני ברא מן העליונים שנאמר "ויאמר

א־לוהים יהי רקיע" (שם א:ו), בשלישי ברא מן התחתונים," ויאמר א־לוהים
תדשא הארץ" (שם א:יא), ברביעי ברא מן העליונים, "ויאמר א־לוהים יהי
מאורות" (שם א:יד), בחמישי ברא מן התחתונים,"ויאמר א־לוהים ישרצו המים"
(שם א:כ), בששי בא לבראות את אדם. אמר אם אני בורא אותו מן העליונים
עכשיו העליונים רבים על התחתונים בריה אחת ואין שלום בעולם, ואם אני
בורא אותו מן התחתונים עכשיו התחתונים רבים על העליונים בריה אחת
ואין שלום בעולם, אלא הרי אני בורא אותו מן העליונים ומן התחתונים
בשביל שלום.

The Midrash anticipates the classic debate concerning the purely
spiritual and the purely material dimensions of the human experience. The metaphor used by the Midrash is "that which is above"
and "that which is below." G-d creates "Heaven," that which is
above, and "Earth," that which is below. Creation is thus simul-
taneously both "heavenly" and "earthly," spiritual and physical.

If Adam, the human, was created only as a physical entity –
עפר מן האדמה – "dust from the earth" – the world would be more
physical than spiritual, more earth-focused than Heaven-focused.
But G-d created the human out of the dust of the earth and then
gave the human נשמת חיים – "a living soul." Both the human and
the universe are thus a synthesis of the spiritual *and* the physical.

Physical pleasure is viewed as evil in some other religions –
witness the vows of celibacy, poverty and self-denial of monks
and priests. In Judaism, it is the denial of the holy synthesis of
physical/spiritual which is considered sinful. For example, the
Nazarite is to bring a sin offering after his/her period of self-denial, thus acknowledging that while permissible in certain situations, self-denial is not what G-d wants of us.

Both the physical and the spiritual have their source in G-d.
There is no dichotomy in Judaism between soul and flesh, mind
and body. Both are potentially capable of demonstrating the inherent presence of the Divine, and will do so if they reflect the
Divine desire that the result be *tov*, that it be inherently good.
Both pleasure and struggle are the human experience and are
holy if they manifest G-d's desire that it be *tov*. Life may be enjoyed if by G-d's judgment it is *tov*. (*Tov* in this sense suggests the
"moral good.") Asceticism may be evil if it does not reflect *tov*.

The balance is always *tov*. In fact, at the very end of the creation process the Torah states:

"And G-d saw all that He had made and found it very good."
(Bereishit 1:31)

(בראשית א:לא)

וַיַּרְא ה' אֶת כָּל אֲשֶׁר עָשָׂה וְהִנֵּה טוֹב מְאֹד.

From the very beginning, the תורה emphasizes the importance of טוב, the good in life.

The Human Struggle / טוֹב וָרָע

הֲלוֹא אִם־תֵּיטִיב שְׂאֵת וְאִם לֹא תֵיטִיב לַפֶּתַח
חַטָּאת רֹבֵץ וְאֵלֶיךָ תְּשׁוּקָתוֹ וְאַתָּה תִּמְשָׁל־בּוֹ:
(בראשית ד:ז)

Surely, if you do right, there is uplift. But if you
do not do right, sin couches at the door; Its
urge is toward you, Yet you can be its master."
(Bereishit 4:7)

Thus said the Holy One, blessed is He to Israel: "My children, I
created the evil inclination within you, and I created Torah for you
as its antidote. If you engage in it (ie. Torah study), the [evil incli-
nation] will not have control over you, as it says, "Surely if you do
right, there is uplift" (Bereishit 4:7), but if you do not engage in
Torah study, you will be given into its hands, as it says, "[but if you
do not do right,] sin crouches at the door" (ibid.).

(Sifrei, Ekev Piska 45)

ספרי, עקב פסקא מה
כך אמר להם הקב"ה לישראל בני, בראתי לכם יצר הרע, בראתי לכם תורה
תבלין. כל זמן שאתם עוסקים בה, אינו שולט בכם, שנאמר "הלוא אם תיטיב
שאת" (בראשית ד:ז), ואם אין אתם עוסקים בתורה הרי אתם נמסרים בידו,
שנאמר "ואם לא תיטיב לפתח אתה רובץ" (שם).

Inherent in the human being is the struggle between good and
evil. All people are created with both the *yetzer hatov* / inclination to do good, and the *yetzer harah* / inclination to do evil. The
purpose of Torah is to teach the truth and enable us to make the
correct choice.

A *tsaddik* / righteous person is one who strives to do good and on occasion fails; the *rashah*/evil person strives to do evil and on occasion does good. All human beings engage in a struggle, and the quality and meaning of our lives is determined by the objective of our struggle.

Cain and Abel / קין והבל

וַיֹּאמֶר קַיִן אֶל־הֶבֶל אָחִיו וַיְהִי בִּהְיוֹתָם בַּשָּׂדֶה
וַיָּקָם קַיִן אֶל־הֶבֶל אָחִיו וַיַּהַרְגֵהוּ: (בראשית ד:ח)

And Cain said to his brother Abel, and it came to
pass when they were in the field, Cain set upon
his brother Abel and killed him. (Bereishit 4:8)

"Cain said to his brother Abel, and . . . when they were in the
field" (Bereishit 4:8) – What were they discussing? They said,
"Come, let us divide the world." One took all land, and the other
took all moveable goods. This one said, "The land on which you
are standing belongs to me," and that one said, "that which you
are wearing belongs to me." This one said, "take them off!" and
that one said, "fly off!" Through this dispute, "Cain set upon his
brother Abel and killed him" (ibid.). Rabbi Yehoshua of Sikhnin
said in the name of Rabbi Levi: They both took land and they both
took moveable goods. So what was the reason for their dispute?
This one said, "The Temple will be built within my boundaries,"
and that one said, "the Temple will be built within my boundaries," as it is said, "and when they were in the field" (ibid.) – "field"
refers to the Temple.   (Midrash Bereishit Rabbah 22:7)

מדרש בראשית רבה כב:ז

"ויאמר קין אל הבל אחיו ויהי בהיותם וגו'" (בראשית ד:ח), על מה היו מדיינים,
אמרו בואו ונחלוק את העולם אחד נטל הקרקעות ואחד נטל את המטלטלין.
דין אמר ארעא דאת קאים עליה דידי, ודין אמר מה דאת לביש דידי, דין אמר
חלוץ, ודין אמר פרח, מתוך כך "ויקם קין אל הבל אחיו ויהרגהו" (שם). רבי
יהושע דסכנין בשם רבי לוי אמר שניהם נטלו את הקרקעות, ושניהן נטלו את
המטלטלין, ועל מה היו מדיינין, אלא זה אומר בתחומי בהמ"ק בית המקדש
נבנה, וזה אומר בתחומי בהמ"ק נבנה, שנא' ויהי "בהיותם בשדה" (שם), ואין
שדה אלא בהמ"ק . . .

40

The battle for "turf" is given in this midrash as the underlying cause of the tragic story of Cain and Abel: a battle for material possessions, land, gold, things. Human greed – from the genesis of human experience to contemporary avarice – leads invariably to envy, conflict and even death.

The second reason cited in the midrash for this conflict is "religious war." Each brother wants the privilege of having King Solomon's holy Temple built on his own turf. For millennia, lives have been sacrificed in the name of "religious" zeal and exclusivity. Crusades and inquisitions have haunted the human religious experience in every age and society. When spirituality allows for the *respect* of the other view without the need to *accept* or reject the other view, humankind will finally put the ancient conflict of Cain and Abel to rest.

Guilt and Confession

וַיֹּאמֶר ה' אֶל־קַיִן אֵי הֶבֶל אָחִיךָ וַיֹּאמֶר לֹא
יָדַעְתִּי הֲשֹׁמֵר אָחִי אָנֹכִי: (בראשית ד:ט)

The Lord said to Cain, "Where is your brother
Abel?" And he said, "I do not know. Am I my
brother's keeper?" (Bereishit 4:9)

Thus you learn that whoever accepts responsibility for their actions, the Holy One, blessed is He saves them and admits them to the afterlife, whereas anyone who does not accept responsibility for their actions, the Holy One, blessed is He curses him, for we find with Cain that the moment that he killed Abel, the Holy One, blessed is He said to him, 'Where is your brother Abel?' . . . (Shitah Chadasha Birkat Yaakov, cited in Torah Shelemah Vol. 2 p. 323)

שיטה חדשה ברכת יעקב, מובא בתורה שלמה, בראשית ד:י (עמ' שכג')
הא למדת שכל מי שהוא מודה במעשיו הקב"ה מצילו ומביאו לחיי העולם
הבא, וכל מי שאינו מודה במעשיו הקב"ה מקללו, שכן מצינו בקין בשעה
שהרג את הבל אמר לו הקב"ה "אי הבל אחיך "(בראשית ד:ט) ...

Vidui (confession) is the articulation of *chet* (sin). The acknowledgement of guilt is fundamental to spiritual and psychological redemption. The verbal expression of guilt marks the beginning of the cleansing process of repentance. This is not to suggest that the *vidui* (confession) alone is sufficient. The Rabbis say:

A person who has sinned [through robbery] and has confessed but has not returned [what they stole] – to what may this be compared? To a person who is grasping an [impure] creature in his hand, because even if he immerses [in a mikveh] repeatedly

42

seeking to be cleansed, his immersion is not effective. (Babylonian Talmud, Taanit 16a)

תענית טז.

אדם שיש בידו עבירה ומתודה ואינו חוזר בו, למה הוא דומה? לאדם שתופס שרץ בידו, שאפילו טובל כמה פעמים לא עלתה לו טבילה.

The expression of regret is meant to stimulate the individual to alter behavior, thus enabling the *chozer b'tshuvah* (i.e., the one who seeks to return to a righteous life) to begin a life of mitzvot. One cannot radically change sinful behavior without first acknowledging and expressing guilt. Guilt may be understood as analogous to fever in the body. The cause of guilt must be exposed as the cause of fever must be determined. To mask the fever would be to allow the underlying illness to continue its assault upon the body. *Vidui* is thus the first step in the process of healing.

The discipline of psychoanalysis is intended to enable the individual to articulate his or her inner thoughts and emotions – to acknowledge subconscious desire, anger, and frustration. Through *vidui*, Judaism affirms the human capacity not only to acknowledge but also to change destructive patterns of thought, emotion, and behavior. We are not doomed to an unending, ruinous pattern of life. Addiction to repugnant behavior is not unalterable.

During the High Holy Days we declare: ותשובה ותפילה וצדקה מעבירין את רועה הגזרה/Behavioral change, prayers, actions seeking forgiveness, and acts of righteousness – all these demonstrate that new, healthier patterns of behavior are possible, which then may alter our own destiny.

The Potential of a Single Person

וַיֹּאמֶר מֶה עָשִׂיתָ, קוֹל דְּמֵי אָחִיךָ צֹעֲקִים אֵלַי
מִן הָאֲדָמָה: (בראשית ד:י)

Then He said, "What have you done? Hark, your
brother's blood cries out to Me from the ground."
(Bereishit 4:10)

How would they instill fear (in the witnesses) for witnesses in capital cases? They would bring them in and instill fear in them as follows: "Perhaps you will say something based upon supposition or upon a rumor, or something heard indirectly from someone else or from a trustworthy person. Perhaps you are unaware that in the end we will intensively cross-examine you. Be aware that capital judgments are unlike monetary judgments – in monetary judgments, a person can pay money and atone for himself.

In capital judgments, he bears the responsibility for the defendant's blood and the blood of his potential descendants. For thus we find with Cain, who killed his brother, and it says 'the blood (*demei* – plural) of your brother is crying out to me.' (Bereishit 4:10) It does not say *dam* (singular) but *demei* (plural) – of your brother – His blood, and the blood of his potential descendants." (Mishna Sanhedrin 4:5)

משנה סנהדרין ד:ה

כיצד מאיימין (את העדים) על עדי נפשות?, היו מכניסין אותן ומאיימין עליהן:
שמא תאמרו מאומד ומשמועה, עד מפי עד, ומפי אדם נאמן שמענו. שמא אי
אתם יודעין שסופנו לבדוק אתכם בדרישה ובחקירה. הוו יודעין שלא כדיני
ממונות דיני נפשות. דיני ממונות – אדם נותן ממון ומתכפר לו, דיני נפשות –
דמו ודם זרעיותיו תלוין בו עד סוף העולם, שכן מצינו בקין שהרג את אחיו,
שנאמר (בראשית ד) "דמי אחיך צעקים", אינו אומר דם אחיך אלא דמי אחיך –
דמו ודם זרעיותיו.

44

The implications of the destruction of a single person are equally applicable to the saving of a single person. If we assert that to kill one person is to destroy an entire world, then we must also assert that to save the life of one person – to help one individual in a substantive manner – must be to save an entire world:

> "Whoever saves one life in Israel is as if he has saved the entire world." (Mishna Sanhedrin 4:5)

משנה סנהדרין ד:ה

וכל המקיים נפש אחת מישראל . . . כאילו קים עולם מלא . . .

To help an individual realize his/her human potential means to enable development in the present and the future. Inherent in each human being lies the seeds of spiritual, political, esthetic, and creative potentialities of generations to come. We can never foresee how one small act may in some catalytic fashion affect the destiny of *K'lal Yisrael*, and even of humanity. One need but take a cursory view of history to appreciate the powerful impact individuals have had upon society and civilization.

Speaking Ill of Another / לשון הרע

וַיֹּאמֶר קַיִן אֶל־ה׳ גָּדוֹל עֲוֹנִי מִנְּשׂוֹא:
(בראשית ד:יג)

"Cain said to the Lord, My punishment is too
great to bear!" (Bereishit 4:13)

There are four things for which payment is collected from a person in this world, and the principle carries forward into the next
world: Worshipping idols, inappropriate sexual relations, spilling
blood, and speaking ill of a person is equivalent to all of them.
(Jerusalem Talmud Peah 1:1)

ירושלמי פאה פרק א הלכה א
ארבעה דברים שהן נפרעין מן האדם בעולם הזה והקרן קיימת לו לעולם הבא
ואלו הן עבודה זרה גילוי עריות שפיכות דמים ולשון הרע כנגד כולן.

The destructive power of *lashon harah* (speaking ill of another) is
viewed by the Sages as more devastating than that of murder due
to its insidious nature. *Lashon harah* spreads, potentially destroy-
ing in geometric proportion not only the individual who may
be the direct focus, but also the wider circle of family, friends,
business associates, community, and even an entire people. The
Midrash comments below, concerning Moshe, when he says אכן
נודע הדבר / "Indeed the matter is known" (Shemot 2:14) (after the
incident in which he killed an Egyptian):

Moshe thought to himself, "What was Israel's sin that they, of all
of the nations, were enslaved?" When he heard the Israelite say,
"Do you mean to kill me as you killed the Egyptian?" (Shemot
2:14) he said, "They speak ill of others, how will they be worthy
of redemption?" Therefore he said, "Then the matter is known" –

46

meaning, now I know why they are enslaved. (Midrash Shemot Rabbah 1:30)

מדרש שמות רבה א:ל
היה משה מהרהר בלבו ואומר מה חטאו ישראל שנשתעבדו מכל האומות, כיון
ששמע דבריו שאמר, "הלהרגני אתה אמר כאשר הרגת את המצרי" (שמות ב:יד),
אמר לשון הרע יש ביניהן היאך יהיו ראויין לגאולה לכך אמר "אכן נודע הדבר"
עתה ידעתי באיזה דבר הם משתעבדים. (שם)

According to this provocative midrash, Moshe finds the insidious quality of *lashon harah* (speaking ill of another) so threatening that he attributes the community of Israel's enslavement to this sin.

Rabbi Alexandri announced, "Who seeks life?" Everyone came and crowded around him. They said to him, "Give us life!" He replied, "'Who is the man who is eager for life? . . . Guard your tongue from evil . . . (Psalms 34:13–14)." (Babylonian Talmud, Avodah Zarah 19b)

עבודה זרה יט:
מכריז רבי אלכסנדרי: מאן בעי חיי? כנוף ואתו כולי עלמא לגביה, אמרי ליה:
הב לן חיי, אמר להו: "מי האיש החפץ חיים וגו' נצור לשונך מרע וגו' סור מרע
ועשה טוב וגו' (תהלים לד)."

Why is *lashon harah* so harshly condemned in Jewish tradition? Words have wings. They move indiscriminately, without regard to person, validity, or consequence. Once spoken, words are not limited by time or space. Thus the comment of Rabbi Alexandri, "Who seeks life? Guard your tongue from evil and your lips from speaking guile." (Psalms 34:13–14)

Moral Development

וַיֹּאמֶר לוֹ ה' לָכֵן כָּל־הֹרֵג קַיִן שִׁבְעָתַיִם יֻקָּם
וַיָּשֶׂם ה' לְקַיִן אוֹת לְבִלְתִּי הַכּוֹת־אֹתוֹ כָּל־
מֹצְאוֹ: (בראשית ד:טו)

And the Lord said to him, "Therefore, whoever
kills Cain, vengeance will be wrought upon him
sevenfold," and the Lord placed a mark on Cain
that no one who find him slay him. (Bereishit 4:15)

Rabbi Nechemiah said: Cain's judgment was not like the usual
judgment for murderers. Cain committed murder, but he had no
one from whom to learn [not to kill]. From then on, "anyone who
kills Cain" [Bereishit 4:15] will be killed.

(Midrash Bereishit Rabbah 22:12)

מדרש בראשית רבה כב:יב
ר' נחמיה אמר לא כדינן של רוצחנין דינו של קין, קין הרג ולא היה לו ממי
ללמוד, מכאן ואילך כל הורג קין [בראשית ד:טו] יהרג . . .

We view the individual within the context of his heritage and
environment. In this midrash, Cain is not held as guilty as one
would expect, because he had no opportunity to learn of the sin of
murder. When we judge we must consider the individual's intellectual, spiritual, and experiential background. Moral judgment is
not innate, teaches the midrash – it must be acquired.

In fact, our sages teach that we are born with the *yetzer
harah*/evil inclination and only acquire the *yetzer hatov*/good
inclination, at puberty (bar/bat mitzvah):

The *yetzer hara* [evil inclination]. What is meant by this? Our
Sages said that for thirteen years, from the time that a child comes

48

from his *mother's womb*, the yetzer hara is greater than the *yetzer hatov* [good inclination]... But after thirteen years the *yetzer hatov* is born in him. (Avot D'Rabbi Natan, Ch. 16)

אבות דר' נתן פרק טז
יצר הרע כיצד אמרו שלש עשרה שנה גדול יצר הרע מיצר טוב ממעי אמו של
אדם היה גדל ובא עמו . . . לאחר י"ג שנה נולד יצר טוב

We are born to act instinctually without choice to eat, sleep, etc., as the body demands without conscious decision or moral judgment. At about the age of 12 or 13 we are given the mental capacity to understand, to act above instinct, and to make moral choices. To develop that moral consciousness, one must have the opportunity to know/learn what is right and what is wrong.

Thus our sages teach that children born of Jewish parents and raised by non-Jews (in times of war or through adoption), are not held accountable for their failure to fulfill Torah and mitzvot, since they had no one to teach them.

This view of responsibility can be applied to all parents and children. Children cannot be condemned for failure to maintain loyalty to their Jewish heritage if they are raised without knowledge of that heritage. In homes today where religion is considered irrelevant, or where amorality is the norm, can young people be held responsible for their lack of religious loyalty or moral judgment?

Consolation

וַיֵּדַע אָדָם עוֹד אֶת־אִשְׁתּוֹ וַתֵּלֶד בֵּן וַתִּקְרָא
אֶת־שְׁמוֹ שֵׁת כִּי שָׁת־לִי אֱ־לֹהִים זֶרַע אַחֵר
תַּחַת הֶבֶל כִּי הֲרָגוֹ קָיִן: (בראשית ד:כה)

*And Adam knew his wife again, and she bore
a son and named him Seth, meaning, G-d has
provided me with another offspring in place of
Abel, for Cain had killed him.* (Bereishit 4:25)

When Rabbi Yochanan ben Zakai's son died, his students came to
console him. Rabbi Eliezer entered and sat before him and said,
"My master, if you desire it, I would like to say something." He
replied, "Say it." So he said, "The first human being had a son
who died and he accepted consolation. And from what source do
we know that he accepted consolation? From that which it says,
"Adam knew his wife again . . ." (Bereishit 4:25). So too you should
accept consolation." Rabbi Yochanan replied, "Is it not sufficient
that I am pained over my own predicament that you found it necessary to remind me of the first human being's pain?"

(Avot D'Rabbi Natan, 14)

אבות דרבי נתן יד
כשמת בנו של רבן יוחנן בן זכאי נכנסו תלמידיו לנחמו. נכנס רבי אליעזר וישב
לפניו וא"ל רבי רצונך אומר דבר אחד לפניך א"ל אמור. א"ל אדם הראשון היה
לו בן ומת וקבל עליו תנחומין. ומניין שקבל עליו תנחומין שנא' (בראשית ד:כה)
"וידע אדם עוד את אשתו" אף אתה קבל תנחומין א"ל לא די לי שאני מצטער
בעצמי אלא שהזכרת לי צערו של אדה"ר.

How often do we attempt to console mourners by telling them of
some other person's tragedy? Pain is not diminished when hearing of the pain of others. When we recite המקום ינחם אתכם בתוך שאר

50

אבלי ציון וירושלים – "May G-d comfort you among the mourners of Zion and Jerusalem," we state the fact that there exists a larger community of mourners, and that mourning is inherent in the historic Jewish experience. Confronting this reality creates the environment for the process of healing to begin. Nonetheless, it is improper and unhelpful for a visitor to relate one's own tragedy and the specific tragedies endured by other people. The purpose of visiting the mourner is to allow the mourner to articulate sorrow and pain. We then empathize with the mourner, thus aid the healing.

This statement המקום ינחם אתכם וכו' / "May G-d comfort you . . ." attests to the power of faith in ה' when seeking communal or personal consolation.

The Uniqueness of the Individual

זֶה סֵפֶר תּוֹלְדֹת אָדָם בְּיוֹם בְּרֹא אֱ־לֹהִים אָדָם
בִּדְמוּת אֱ־לֹהִים עָשָׂה אֹתוֹ: (בראשית ה:א)

This is the book of the generations of Adam –
When G-d created man, He made him in the
likeness of G-d. (Bereishit 5:1)

Rabbi Nechemiah says: From what source do we know that a single person carries the same weight [ie. is equivalent to] the entire work of creation? From that which it says, "This is the book of the generations of Adam," (Bereishit 5:1) and it says, "These are the generations of the heavens and earth when they were created." (Bereishit 2:4) Just as there [ie. when discussing the creation of the heavens and earth] the words for creating and forming are used, and these same words for creating and forming are used here [ie. when discussing the creation of the first person]. [We learn that a single person is equivalent to the entire work of creation]

(Avot D'Rabbi Natan, 31)

אבות דרבי נתן לא
רבי נחמיה אומר מנין שאדם אחד שקול כנגד כל מעשה בראשית שנאמר
(בראשית ה:א) "זה ספר תולדות אדם" ולהלן הוא אומר (בראשית ב:ד) "אלה
תולדות השמים והארץ בהבראם" מה להלן בריאה ועשיה אף כאן בריאה
ועשיה. . . .

Rabbi Nechemiah seeks to equate the creation of the human being with all the works of creation. He employs the rather peculiar term "weight" in his analogy, to express the transcending significance of each individual: i.e., each individual "weighs" as much as all of creation.

In addition, Rabbi Nechemiah recognizes the complexity of each person: Creation was multi-faceted, creation took time, creation had "light and darkness," creation was completed with "Shabbat." The story of creation accepts the limitation inherent in Shabbat; i.e., rest itself is a part of Creation. The individual who seeks to be creative must also be willing to accept limitations without frustration. To rest is to be "G-d-like," so long as it is associated with the creative process. The observance of Shabbat in part compels us to pause and reflect upon our activities, opportunities, challenges, and limitations.

The Blessings of Each Generation

זָכָר וּנְקֵבָה בְּרָאָם וַיְבָרֶךְ אֹתָם וַיִּקְרָא אֶת־
שְׁמָם אָדָם בְּיוֹם הִבָּרְאָם: (בראשית ה:ב)

Male and Female He created them. And when
they were created, He blessed them and called
them Man. (Bereishit 5:2)

And from where did the forefathers learn to bless each one in his
generation? From the Holy One, blessed is He, for when [G-d]
created the first human being, [G-d] blessed each of them, as it
says, "Male and Female . . . and He blessed them" (Bereishit 5:2).
(Midrash Tanhuma VeZot HaBerachah 1:1)

מדרש תנחומא וזאת הברכה א:א
ומנין למדו האבות לברך כל אחד ואחד לדורו מן הקב"ה שבשעה שברא אדם
הראשון ברכו שנאמר "זכר ונקבה וגו' ויברך אותם." (בראשית ה:ב)

This midrash teaches that each generation needs to be blessed for
its unique concerns and aspirations.

The Talmud states further:

Each generation and its interpreters, each generation and its sages,
each generation and its communal leaders. (Babylonian Talmud,
Avodah Zara 5a)

עבודה זרה ה.
דור דור ודורשיו דור דור וחכמיו דור דור ופרנסיו.

The Talmudic sages understood the dynamics of generational
change: Each generation has its scholars, sages, and philanthro-

pists, who must respond to the unique challenges and opportunities of their age.

In the halachic system, the most contemporary scholar is the most relevant. Our age of interplanetary flight, computer technology and organ transplants challenges the very fabric of halachic relevance. Certainly, in the field of medicine, there already exists a sophisticated body of rabbinic legal literature which addresses classic halachic sensitivities and standards. Scholars familiar with scientific advances and rabbinic law are developing a systematic discipline which will pave the way for an on-going dialogue between Torah and science.

"End of life," abortion, organ transplants, etc. are among the medical ethical challenges which are being addressed by rabbinic scholars recognized for their knowledge and sensitivity. Many other contemporary innovations result in moral and ethical perplexities which ought to be the concern of Judaism's legal and ethical tradition. In sum therefore, Judaism and its halachic (i.e. legal) view responds to all of life's vicissitudes.

Remember

הַנְּפִלִים הָיוּ בָאָרֶץ בַּיָּמִים הָהֵם וְגַם אַחֲרֵי־
כֵן אֲשֶׁר יָבֹאוּ בְּנֵי הָאֱ־לֹהִים אֶל־בְּנוֹת הָאָדָם
וְיָלְדוּ לָהֶם : . . . (בראשית ו:ד)

It was then, and later too, that the "niphilim"
appeared on earth — when "divine beings"
cohabited with the daughters of men who bore
them offspring . . . (Bereishit 6:4)

Yehudah bar Rabbi Ami said: The latter ones did not learn from
the former ones: The generation of the flood did not learn the
lesson from the generation of Enosh, and the generation of the
dispersal [who had built the Tower of Babel] did not learn from
the generation of the flood, [and this is derived from the seemingly extraneous phrase of] "and later too."

(Midrash Bereishit Rabbah 26:7)

מדרש בראשית רבה כו:ז
יהודה בר רבי אמי אמר אחראי לא ילפון מן קדמאי: דור המבול לא לקחו מוסר
מדור אנוש, ודור הפלגה מדור המבול, "וגם אחרי כן". (בראשית ו:ד)

The verse speaks of "Nephilim" and" Divine Beings," yet the midrash speaks of the people of the "Generation of the flood" and
the "Generation of Enosh," etc. One generation of people did
not learn from the previous generation. Thus both "Nephilim"
and "Divine Beings" are really metaphors for people. People who
were part of an immoral society or perhaps an amoral society.

History provides the best lessons for humanity, yet it has often
been said that history teaches us only that it teaches us nothing.
When you seek the essence of Jewish tradition you discover that

the word *zachor* (remember) is central to the life cycle of the Jew. All of the festivals have historical roots. Even those without historical source have been linked by the Rabbis to historical events; for example, Rosh Hashannah is commemorated as the "birthday of the world," and Yom Kippur is remembered as the day Moshe came down from Sinai the second time with the second set of tablets (having broken the first set upon seeing the Golden Calf: Ta'anit 30b).

Shabbat, the pivotal celebration of time in the Jewish calendar, is remembered, "for on it He rested from all His work which G-d had created . . ." (Bereishit 1:3). Pesach is of course a remembrance of the Shemot from Egypt, a celebration of that catalytic moment of emancipation:

"Seven days you shall eat unleavened bread." (Shemot 12:15)

שמות יב:טו

שִׁבְעַת יָמִים מַצּוֹת תֹּאכֵלוּ.

"You shall observe the [Feast of] Unleavened Bread, for on this very day I brought your ranks out of the land of Egypt."
(Shemot 12:17)

שמות יב:יז

וּשְׁמַרְתֶּם אֶת־הַמַּצּוֹת כִּי בְּעֶצֶם הַיּוֹם הַזֶּה הוֹצֵאתִי אֶת־צִבְאוֹתֵיכֶם מֵאֶרֶץ מִצְרָיִם.

G-d would not give His people the tablets of the Covenant until they were a free people. Only after the exodus from Egyptian enslavement could there be a Sinai experience. It did however necessitate a hiatus of some time, from the emancipation to the giving and receiving of the Ten Commandments at Sinai. Moreover, it was 40 years from the emancipation from Egyptian slavery to the establishment of a sovereign state.

In fact, all those who left Egypt over the age of 20, never entered the Land of Canaan. Endless acts of rebellion from the Golden Calf incident to the mutinous rebellion of Korach, with many more in between, demonstrate that the slave mentality of Egypt did not readily adjust or respond to a life of choice and consequence. Thus the wanderings in the Wilderness of Sinai for 40 years.

In our time, most of the nations emancipated from their European masters after World War II experienced much turmoil until a peaceful harmonious society was established. Freedom is far more complicated than slavery. Choice, inherent in freedom, demands understanding, values, and acceptance of responsibility of one's actions, both of the individual and the society. Only a free people are capable of entering into and experiencing revelation. Thus we recall the receiving of Torah on Shavuot, seven weeks after the first day of Pesach (Vayikra 23:15). Here, freedom and law are linked: Free people must accept the rule of law in order to develop a civilized society. Our freedom from slavery allowed us the opportunity to accept the Ten Commandments at Sinai. We are always required to remember slavery, freedom, and Sinai.

Anticipating Trouble

וַיִּנָּחֶם ה' כִּי־עָשָׂה אֶת־הָאָדָם בָּאָרֶץ וַיִּתְעַצֵּב
אֶל־לִבּוֹ: (בראשית ו:ו)

And the Lord regretted that He had made man on
earth, and his heart was saddened. (Bereishit 6:6)

A certain heretic (epikoros) asked Rabbi Joshua ben Korchah, "Do
you not say that the Holy One, blessed is He sees all that will
occur?" He replied, "Yes." You say that the Holy One, blessed
is He sees that which will be born (ie. knows the future), and he
replied "Yes." "But is it not written '. . . and the Lord was sad.'?"
Rabbi [Joshua ben Korchah said] "Have you ever had a baby boy?"
He replied, "Yes." He said, "And what did you do?" He replied, "I
was happy, and made everyone else happy as well." He said, "And
did you not know that his destiny is to die [as all humans do]?"
He replied, "In the time of rejoicing there is rejoicing, and in
the time of mourning there is mourning." He said, "This is what
happened with the Holy One, blessed is He." (Midrash Bereishit
Rabbah 27:4)

מדרש בראשית רבה כז:ד
אפיקורוס אחד שאל את רבי יהושע בן קרחה אמר לו אין אתם אומרים שהקב"ה
רואה את הנולד, אמר לו הן, והא כתיב "ויתעצב אל לבו" (בראשית ו:ו). אמר לו
נולד לך בן זכר מימיך אמר לו הן, אמר לו מה עשית אמר לו שמחתי ושימחתי
את הכל, אמר לו ולא היית יודע שסופו למות, א"ל בשעת חדוותא חדוותא
בשעת אבלא אבלא, א"ל כך מעשה לפני הקב"ה.

It is written in the book of Ben Sira . . . "Do not be distressed over
tomorrow's trouble, 'for you do not know what the day will bring'
(Mishlei 27:1)". Tomorrow may come and you will be no more,

59

and so you would have worried about a world which is not yours.
(Babylonian Talmud, Yevamot 63b)

יבמות סג:

וכתוב בספר בן סירא . . . אל תצר צרת מחר "כי לא תדע מה יולד יום" (משלי
כז:א) שמא מחר בא ואיננו, נמצא מצטער על העולם שאין שלו.

It is enough to deal with each trouble when it happens!
(Babylonian Talmud, Berachot 9b)

ברכות ט:

דיה צרה בשעתה.

To illogically anticipate catastrophe is to be paralyzed. Our task
is to engage in normal and healthy pursuits, and to be prudent
without attempting to anticipate every possible negative consequence of present action. We are told in the Talmud, for example,
that the Israelite husbands and wives enslaved in Egypt refused to
engage in marital relations since by Egyptian decree their male
babies would be cast into the Nile. According to a midrash, after Pharaoh's decree, Amram separates from his wife Yocheved.
Their daughter Miriam chastises him, saying "Your decree is
more severe than that of Pharaoh. He decreed that all male babies shall be destroyed; you have separated from my mother, thus
no children at all shall be born." In response to this admonition,
Amram resumes his relationship with his wife, leading to the
birth of Moshe. (Babylonian Talmud Sotah 12)

The midrash on Bereishit cited above does not assume that
such a "happy ending" is inevitable. Rather, it simply concludes
that "each experience unto itself is to be dealt with" (i.e., do not
anticipate or be overly anxious concerning possible trauma in the
future).

Acquiring Merit

וְנֹחַ מָצָא חֵן בְּעֵינֵי ה': (בראשית ו:ח)

But Noach found favor with the Lord. (Bereishit 6:8)

Said Rabbi Simon: We have found that the Holy One, blessed is He does kindness for the later generations on account of the merit of the earlier generations. And from where do we know that the Holy One, blessed is He does so for the earlier generations on account of the merit of the later generations? "But Noach found favor with the Lord" (Bereishit 6:8) By what merit? By the merit of his descendants. (Midrash Bereishit Rabbah 29:5)

מדרש בראשית רבה כט:ה

אמר ר' סימון מצינו שהקב"ה עושה חסד עם האחרונים בזכות הראשונים,
ומנין שהקב"ה עושה עם הראשונים בזכות האחרונים, "ונח מצא חן בעיני ה'"
(בראשית ו:ח), באיזו זכות? בזכות תולדותיו.

This midrash introduces the novel concept of the "merit of our descendants." We are familiar with the merit of our ancestors: Our prayers are replete with references to them. Every *Amidah*, thrice daily (and more often on Shabbat and Holy Days) we refer to Avraham, Yitzchak, and Yaakov. Whenever we recite prayers for the sick we include the names of the Patriarchs and Matriarchs. Yet in this midrash we are told that Noach acquired merit by virtue of his descendants (among whom were, of course, the Patriarchs and Matriarchs).

The merit we acquire by virtue of our ancestors is a gift, conferred upon us serendipitously. We are not able to influence our ancestors, but we do have the opportunity to influence our descendents. The merit we enjoy by virtue of our descendants is at least in part the result of the values, commitments, and sacrifices we demonstrate and foster in our lifetime.

Noach, having maintained his values despite living within a corrupt society, demonstrated the human ability to transcend evil and corruption. Perhaps, as some midrashim suggest, Noach was "good" only relative to his evil society; regardless, he did maintain sufficient ethical standards to serve as a moral link to the future.

Our society challenges us to be modern-day Noachs – not to build an ark and sail away, but rather to maintain and strengthen our ethical commitments.

Balancing Praise and Criticism

אֵלֶּה תּוֹלְדֹת נֹחַ נֹחַ אִישׁ צַדִּיק תָּמִים
הָיָה בְּדֹרֹתָיו אֶת־הָאֱ־לֹהִים הִתְהַלֶּךְ־נֹחַ:
(בראשית ו:ט)

This is the line of Noach: Noach was a righteous
man; he was blameless in his age; Noach walked
with G-d. (Bereishit 6:9)

Another interpretation regarding the principle that we do not
praise a person in his presence. Rabbi Elazar ben Azariah said:
We find that one does give some praise in a person's presence, for
we find concerning Noach, "for you alone I have found righteous
before Me in this generation" (Bereishit 7:1). And when not in
his presence, He says "This is the line of Noach – Noach was a
righteous man; he was blameless in his age" (Bereishit 6:9).

(Sifrei, Bamidbar 102)

ספרי במדבר ק"ב

ד"א שאין אומרים שבחו של אדם בפניו. ר' אלעזר בן עזריה אומר מצינו שאומר
מקצת שבחו של אדם בפניו שכן מצינו בנח "כי אותך ראיתי צדיק לפני בדור
הזה" (בראשית ז:א) ושלא בפניו הוא אומר "אלה תולדות נח נח איש צדיק תמים
היה בדורותיו" (שם ו:ט).

We tend to flatter people in their presence and criticize them
in their absence. This midrash suggests the opposite: Praise the
person when speaking to others, and criticize the person when
you are alone.

Praise requires no courage (unless the subject is obviously un-
deserving). To criticize wisely, however, demands conviction, determination and the ability to convey the criticism constructively.

63

It is important to evaluate the capacities of the person you wish to criticize: We read in Mishlei (9:7), "Do not criticize a fool for he will hate you; criticize a wise person and he will love you."

Yet above all these admonitions, rises the deep concern expressed by the 20th century giant Rabbi Israel Meir HaCohen, the "Chofetz Chaim." He devoted his life to exhorting us *not to speak about anyone at any time* (with the exception of character or professional references within very exacting standards and limitations) – neither praise nor criticism. Speak only to the individual who, in your opinion, has behaved in a manner you find offensive or illegal, from a Jewish or secular viewpoint.

Imitating G-d's Righteousness

אֵלֶּה תּוֹלְדֹת נֹחַ נֹחַ אִישׁ צַדִּיק תָּמִים
הָיָה בְּדֹרֹתָיו אֶת־הָאֱ-לֹהִים הִתְהַלֶּךְ־נֹחַ:
(בראשית ו:ט)

*This is the line of Noach: Noach was a righteous
man; he was blameless in his age; Noach walked
with G-d. (Bereishit 6:9)*

Why was he named "righteous man?" Since he fed the creatures
of the Holy One, blessed is He, and by doing so he became like
his Creator, as it is written, "For the Lord is righteous; He loves
righteous deeds" (Psalms 11:7).   (Midrash Tanhuma Noach, 4)

מדרש תנחומא נח פרק ד
למה נקרא שמו צדיק, הואיל וזן את בריותיו של הקב"ה נעשה כבוראו, כענין
שנאמר "כי צדיק ה' צדקות אהב" (תהלים יא:ז).

The person who provides for and feeds G-d's creatures becomes
part of G-d's creative process and is considered to be a *tsaddik*,
a righteous person. Because G-d is righteous, so too G-d loves
those who are righteous.

One must imitate G-d's qualities of righteousness in a proac-
tive, not a passive, manner. Righteousness is not to be understood
as sanctimony. What are the qualities required to be considered
a *tsaddik*? The Talmudic definitions of righteousness are remarkably pragmatic:

And Rabbi Chama son of Rabbi Chanina said: Why is it written
"Follow after the Lord your G-d" (Devarim 13:5)? Is it possible
for a person to follow the Divine presence? Does it not already

state "For the Lord your G-d is a consuming fire" (Devarim 4:24)? Rather, [it means] follow [i.e. emulate] his ways. Just as He clothes the naked, as it is written, "And the Lord G-d made skins for Adam and his wife, and clothed them" (Bereishit 3:21), so you should clothe the naked. The Holy One, blessed is He visited the sick, as it is written, "The Lord appeared to him by the terebinths of Mamre" (Bereishit 18:1), so you should visit the sick. The Holy One, blessed is He comforted mourners, as it is written, "After the death of Avraham, G-d blessed his son Yitzchak" (Bereishit 25:11), so you should comfort mourners. The Holy One, blessed is He buried the dead, as it is written, "He buried him in the valley" (Devarim 34:6), so you should bury the dead. "Skin" (Bereishit 3:21) – Rav and Shmuel, one said: something made from leather; and the other said: something that the skin enjoys. Rabbi Simlai expounded: The Torah begins with acts of kindness and ends with acts of kindness, as it is written, "And the Lord G-d made skins for Adam and his wife, and clothed them" (Bereishit 3:21), and it ends with acts of kindness, as it is written, "He buried him in the valley" (Devarim 34:6). (Babylonian Talmud, Sotah 14a)

סוטה יד.

ואמר רבי חמא ברבי חנינא, מאי דכתיב: (דברים יג:ה) אחרי ה' א-להיכם תלכו? וכי אפשר לו לאדם להלך אחר שכינה? והלא כבר נאמר: (דברים ד:כד) כי ה' אלהיך אש אוכלה הוא אלא להלך אחר מדותיו של הקב"ה, מה הוא מלביש ערומים, דכתיב: (בראשית ג:כא) ויעש ה' א-לוהים לאדם ולאשתו כתנות עור וילבישם, אף אתה הלבש ערומים הקב"ה ביקר חולים, דכתיב: (בראשית יח:א) וירא אליו ה' באלוני ממרא, אף אתה בקר חולים הקב"ה ניחם אבלים, דכתיב: (בראשית כה:יא) ויהי אחרי מות אברהם ויברך א-לוהים את יצחק בנו, אף אתה נחם אבלים הקב"ה קבר מתים, דכתיב: (דברים לד:ו) ויקבר אותו בגיא, אף אתה קבור מתים. כתנות עור – רב ושמואל, חד אמר: דבר הבא מן העור, וחד אמר: דבר שהעור נהנה ממנו. דרש ר' שמלאי: תורה – תחלתה גמילות חסדים וסופה גמילות חסדים תחילתה גמילות חסדים, דכתיב: (בראשית ג:כא) ויעש ה' א-לוהים לאדם ולאשתו כתנות עור וילבישם וסופה גמילות חסדים, דכתיב: ויקבר אותו בגיא. (דברים לד:ו)

The Torah teaches that "after the Lord your G-d you shall walk" (Devarim 13:5). Is it possible to walk after the Divine Presence?

What the text requires of us, according to this midrash, is to "walk" emulating G-d's attributes. As He is compassionate, so must we be. As He visits the sick, so should we. In essence, the task of the individual is to make G-d's presence manifest in human society and experience.

Plundering

וַיֹּאמֶר אֱלֹהִים לְנֹחַ קֵץ כָּל־בָּשָׂר בָּא לְפָנַי כִּי־
מָלְאָה הָאָרֶץ חָמָס מִפְּנֵיהֶם וְהִנְנִי מַשְׁחִיתָם
אֶת־הָאָרֶץ: (בראשית ו:יג)

G-d said to Noach, I have decided to put an end
to all flesh, for the earth is filled with lawlessness
because of them: I am about to destroy them with
the earth. (Bereishit 6:13)

G-d said to Noach, "I have decided to put an end to all
flesh. . . ."(Bereishit 6:13) Rabbi Yochanan said: Come and see
the power of robbery (chamas), for the generation of the flood
violated everything, but their judgment was not sealed until they
began (literally, "extended their hands into") robbing, as it says,
". . . for the earth is filled with lawlessness (chamas) because of
them: I am about to destroy them with the earth" (Bereishit 6:13).
(Babylonian Talmud, Sanhedrin 108a)

סנהדרין קח.

ויאמר ה' לנח "קץ כל בשר בא לפני" (בראשית ו:יג). אמר רבי יוחנן: בא וראה
כמה גדול כחה של חמס, שהרי דור המבול עברו על הכל ולא נחתם עליהם
גזר דינם עד שפשטו ידיהם בגזל, שנאמר "כי מלאה הארץ חמס מפניהם והנני
משחיתם את הארץ" (שם).

Chamas (plundering/robbing) is understood by the Rabbis to be
the ultimate breakdown of society. In the book of Job we read: עַל
לֹא־חָמָס בְּכַפַּי וּתְפִלָּתִי זַכָּה /"Though I did no injustice [lit. plundering]
and my prayer was pure" (Job 16:17). The mere absence of *chamas*
makes Job's prayer worthy.

Rabbi Joshua the Priest son of Rabbi Nechemiah, said: Is there
such a thing as an ugly prayer? Rather, anyone whose hands are
filthy with robbery who calls to the Holy One, blessed is He (in
prayer), the Holy One, blessed is He does not respond to him.
Why? Because his prayer is done in sin. As it says, "G-d said to
Noach, 'I have decided to put an end to all flesh for the earth
is filled with lawlessness [robbery] because of them'" (Bereishit
6:13). But Job, whose toil did not include robbery, his prayer was
pure, therefore it says, "Though I did no injustice [lit., there is
no injustice in my palm] because there is no injustice in my palm
and in my toil, my prayer is pure" (Job 16:17). (Midrash Shemot
Rabbah 22:3)

מדרש שמות רבה כב:ג

א"ר יהושע הכהן ב"ר נחמיה וכי יש תפלה עבורה אלא כל מי שידיו מלוכלכות
בגזל הוא קורא להקדוש ב"ה ואינו עונה אותו למה שתתפלתו בעבירה שנאמר
(בראשית ו:יג) "ויאמר ה' לנח קץ כל בשר וגו'", אבל איוב שלא היה בעמלו גזל
היתה תפלתו זכה לכך אומר "על לא חמס בכפי לפי שאין עול בכפי ובעמלי
תפלתי זכה" (איוב טז:יז)

In this sense, *gezel*/robbery is considered to be an assault upon
the fabric of society. Moreover, the Midrash distinguishes between חמס וגזל /*chamas and gezel*:

What is considered *chamas* (robbery) and what is considered *gezel*
(robbery)? Rabbi Chanina said: *chamas* when it is not even worth
a penny (*perutah*); and *gezel* when it is worth something (at least a
perutah). (Midrash Bereishit Rabbah 31:5)

מדרש בראשית רבה לא:ה

איזהו חמס ואיזה היא גזל, א"ר חנינא חמס אינו שוה פרוטה, וגזל ששוה פרוטה.

[What is the difference between *chamas* and *gezel*?] *Gezel* – he takes
from its owners by force; *chamas* he snatches it from its owners.
(Midrash Or Afelah manuscript, cited in Torah Shelemah, p. 400
n. 159)

מדרש אור האפלה: תורה שלמה דף ת הערה קנט
שהגזל לוקח אותו מבעליו בחזקה והחמס חוטף אותו מבעליו.

There is a distinction between an overt act of violence – *gezel* which results in theft and a relatively benign act – *chotef* – grabbing someone's possession. *Gezel* – "theft," stealing something which has monetary value, and *chotef*, stealing something which has only intrinsic value, i.e. a family heirloom, while having no monetary value, has a transcending value to its owner. Both *gezel* – the theft of a valuable item through an act of violence and *chamas* – a non-violent act of taking something of no monetary value, are acts which destroy the fabric of a society, here considered the cause of the flood.

Finding Merit in the Other

וַיֹּאמֶר ה' לְנֹחַ בֹּא־אַתָּה וְכָל־בֵּיתְךָ אֶל־
הַתֵּבָה כִּי־אֹתְךָ רָאִיתִי צַדִּיק לְפָנַי בַּדּוֹר הַזֶּה:
(בראשית ז:א)

Then the Lord said to Noach, "Go into the ark,
with all your household, for you alone have I
found righteous before me in this generation."
(Bereishit 7:1)

Rabbi Joshua said: Why did Noach see it fit not to pray on behalf
of his generation? He thought to himself, "perhaps I will not be
saved," as it is written, "for you alone have I found righteous before Me in this generation" (Bereishit 7:1) – relative to the generation etc. . . . . . Rabbi Elazar said: Even so, he should have prayed
on behalf of the world because the Holy One, blessed is He is
pleased with a person who speaks a good [word] about his sons.

(Zohar, Omissions – Bereishit, 1:254b)

זוהר חדש א' בהשמטות רנד:
א"ר יהושע מה ראה נח שלא ביקש רחמים על דורו? אמר בלבו אולי לא אמלט
דכתיב "כי אותך ראיתי צדיק לפני בדור הזה" (בראשית ז:א) כלומר לפי הדור,
וכו' . . . א"ר אלעזר אפילו הכי הוה ליה למבעי רחמי על עלמא בגין דניחא ליה
להקב"ה מאן דיימר טבא על בנוי.

Rabbi Yehoshua questions Noach's silence in the face of G-d's
intention to destroy the world. Even if a world is found to be to-
tally corrupt does it not deserve to be saved? Perhaps a righteous
person ought to consider making a plea out of *chesed*/loving-
kindness. This is what bothers Rabbi Yehoshua: Why did Noach
not at least *try?* Compare this to Avraham's behavior when told

71

of the impending destruction of S'dom: Avraham is persistent as he argues with G-d to save S'dom. Noach passively acquiesces to G-d's judgment: No question is uttered, nor any prayer.

We need to find a reason, perhaps even a dubious reason, why the world, the community, or the individual is worthy of being saved. The concept of מלמד זכות / finding merit in the "other," is a fundamental ethical imperative in *musar*, Jewish ethical literature. The standard is to judge the other meritoriously unless you have convincing evidence to the contrary.

Two Views of Noach's Faith

וַיָּבֹא נֹחַ וּבָנָיו וְאִשְׁתּוֹ וּנְשֵׁי־בָנָיו אִתּוֹ אֶל־
הַתֵּבָה מִפְּנֵי מֵי הַמַּבּוּל: (בראשית ז:ז)

Noach with his sons, his wife, and his sons' wives,
went into the ark because of the waters of the
Flood. (Bereishit 7:7)

Said Rabbi Yochanan: Noach was deficient in faith, and had the
waters not reached his ankles, he would not have entered the Ark.
(Midrash Bereishit Rabbah 32:6)

מדרש בראשית רבה לב:ו

א"ר יוחנן נח מחוסר אמנה היה, אלולי שהגיעו המים עד קרסוליו לא נכנס
לתיבה.

If we see Noach as a "relative" *tsaddik*, then he may be viewed
as he is in this Midrash, as a man of limited faith who would
not enter the ark until pushed (literally, by the water). However,
if we view Noach as an authentic *tsaddik* in spite of his corrupt
society, then we could say that perhaps he demonstrated faith in
the possibility of his world's redemption until the last moment,
until he had "zero options." Perhaps Noach was reluctant to get
on the ark because he did not want to give up on his world until
the very last minute.

It is fascinating that our sages (of blessed memory) viewed Noach as having such limited faith. It is true that there is no mention
in the text that he ever called upon his contemporaries to mend
their ways, yet the Talmud (Sanhedrin 108a) suggests that he did
so. According to this tradition, Noach was required to build the
ark in full view so that he might be asked its purpose, thus giving

him the opening to admonish his peers to change their ways and thereby avert the flood.

Are we not similarly obligated to speak up concerning contemporary political-social issues? Do we speak up and confront our peers, and our political and religious leaders, or do we build our own little "arks" to take refuge, thus casting aside concern for all others and all else?

Yes, Noach did survive – but he inherited a vast wasteland; and we dare not forget that Noach "the survivor" had an humiliating end. The lesson: It does not suffice to seek survival in isolation. One must seek to foster a just society in order that *all* may survive.

Respect for the Material World

וְאַךְ אֶת־דִּמְכֶם לְנַפְשֹׁתֵיכֶם אֶדְרֹשׁ מִיַּד כָּל־
חַיָּה אֶדְרְשֶׁנּוּ וּמִיַּד הָאָדָם מִיַּד אִישׁ אָחִיו
אֶדְרֹשׁ אֶת־נֶפֶשׁ הָאָדָם: (בראשית ט:ה)

But for your own life-blood I will require a
reckoning: I will require it of every beast; of man,
too, will I require a reckoning for human life, of
every man for that of his fellow man! (Bereishit 9:5)

Just as a person is liable for damage caused to another, so too is a
person liable for causing damage to himself. If he spat at or dirtied
his own face in front of another person, pulled out his own hair,
tore his own clothes, broke his own vessels, or scattered his money
out of anger – he is exempt under human law, but liable under
Divine law, as it says, "but for your own life-blood I will require a
reckoning" (Bereishit 9:5).

(Tosefta Bava Kamma 9:31, translation following manuscripts)

תוספתא מסכת בבא קמא ט:לא
וכשם שחייב על נזקי חבירו כן הוא חייב על נזקי עצמו הוא עצמו שרק וטש
בפניו נגד חבירו מתלש בשערו מקרע את כסותו משבר את כליו מפזר את
מעותיו בחמתו פטור מדיני אדם ודינו מסור לשמים שנאמר "אך את דמכם
אדרש וכו'" (בראשית ט:ה).

Who is the Tanna who taught the following saying: A person is
not permitted to harm himself? If you say it is the Tanna in the
following [tradition]: "'But for your own life-blood I will require
a reckoning' (Bereishit 9:5) – Rabbi Elazar says: [if] by your own
hands I will require a reckoning" – but perhaps killing [suicide] is
different [than merely injuring oneself].

(Babylonian Talmud, Bava Kama 91b)

75

בבא קמא צא:

מאן תנא דשמעת ליה דאמר: אין אדם רשאי לחבל בעצמו? אילימא האי תנא
הוא, דתניא: (בראשית ט') "ואך את דמכם לנפשותיכם אדרש" (בראשית ט:ה) –
ר' אלעזר אומר: מיד נפשותיכם אדרש את דמכם ודלמא קטלא שאני.

Respect for self, property and person, is as sacred a moral obligation as is respect for the person and property of others. Each
person is sacred and each useful object has purpose, thus the
Torah demands respect regardless of ownership. *Bal tashchit* – to
waste anything useful – is considered a transgression of Torah
law. Another interesting observation of our sages is:

One who tears [clothing] excessively over a death is punished [by
lashing] because of the prohibition against destructiveness.
(Babylonian Talmud, Bava Kama 91b)

בבא קמא צא:

המקרע על המת יותר מדאי לוקה משום בל תשחית.

Even as an expression of mourning, when Halachah demands the
tearing of clothing as a symbol of loss, our sages condemn excessive destruction of property as immoral.

Conservation of natural resources was also a concern of the
Talmudic scholars:

For Rav Yosef said: In this instance Rabbi [Judah the Patriarch]
taught: A person should not pour out the water from his cistern if
others need it. (Babylonian Talmud, Yevamot 11b)

יבמות יא:

דאמר רב יוסף כאן שנה רבי: לא ישפוך אדם מי בורו ואחרים צריכים להם.

Here we are told that the great (and wealthy) Rabbi Yehudah
HaNasi would never let water spill from his cistern because others might be in need of it. Rabbi Yehudah could easily afford to
purchase additional water, yet every drop was precious to him
– not only because water was precious, but also simply because of

this moral sense that it is wrong to waste anything of value. This teaching is critical today, when many Americans regularly discard what could otherwise feed and clothe the underprivileged in our land.

Lashon Harah / Gossip

שֹׁפֵךְ דַּם הָאָדָם בָּאָדָם דָּמוֹ יִשָּׁפֵךְ כִּי בְּצֶלֶם
אֱ-לֹהִים עָשָׂה אֶת־הָאָדָם: (בראשית ט:ו)

Whoever sheds the blood of man, by man shall
his blood be shed; For in His image did G-d make
man. (Bereishit 9:6)

Rabbi Joshua says: Gossip [or, speaking ill of someone] is not only
comparable to murder. In fact, gossip is compared to idolatry,
murder, and sexual misconduct. It is similar to murder as it is written, "Whoever sheds the blood of man, by man shall his blood be
shed" [Bereishit 9:6]. So too here, since he gossips [manuscripts
read: "since he reports on him to the government"], it is as if he
spilled his blood. (Midrash Mishlei 6:12)

מדרש משלי ו:יב
ר' יהושע אומר אינו דומה לשון הרע אלא לשופך דמים מפני שלשון הרע
כעבודה זרה, ושפיכות דמים, וגילוי עריות, כשופך דמים דכתיב "שופך דם
האדם באדם דמו ישפך" אף כאן הואיל ומלשין כאילו שופך את דמו.

Gossip – even about the truth – is considered in Judaism to be on
a level of immorality equal to the three sins which are considered
of sufficient magnitude to justify martyrdom when one is coerced
to transgress them.

The Talmud teaches:

Rabbi Alexandri announced, "Who seeks life?" Everyone came
and crowded around him. They said to him, "Give us life!" He
replied, "Who is the man who is eager for life? . . . Guard your
tongue from evil . . ." (Psalms 34:13–14). (Babylonian Talmud,
Avodah Zarah 19b)

עבודה זרה יט:

מכריז רבי אלכסנדרי: מאן בעי חיי? מאן בעי חיי? כנוף ואתו כולי עלמא לגביה,
אמרי ליה: הב לן חיי, אמר להו: "מי האיש החפץ חיים וגו' נצור לשונך מרע"
(תהלים לד:יג-יד).

"Death and life are in the power of the tongue" (Mishlei 18:21) –
Do not say "since I have been given permission to speak, I will say
whatever I wish." For the Torah has already warned you: "Guard
your tongue from evil and your lips from deceitful speech" (Psalms
34:14). (Midrash Tanchuma, Metzora 4)

מדרש תנחומא מצורע פרק ד

"מות וחיים ביד לשון" (משלי יח:כא) – אל תאמר הואיל ונתנה לי רשות לדבר
הרי אני מדבר כל מה שאני מבקש, הרי כבר הזהירה התורה אותך "נצור לשונך
מרע ושפתיך מדבר מרמה" (תהלים לד:יד).

Anyone who speaks gossip and anyone who receives gossip and
anyone who gives false testimony about someone else – are worthy
of being thrown to the dogs. (Babylonian Talmud, Pesachim 118a)

פסחים קיח.

כל המספר לשון הרע, וכל המקבל לשון הרע, וכל המעיד עדות שקר בחבירו
– ראוי להשליכו לכלבים.

Our sages invoke the most severe condemnation of both the ac-
tive and passive participants in *lashon harah* / gossip. There are
numerous other references in which our sages attribute various
calamities in Jewish history to *lashon harah*. The lesson is obvious:
Never speak ill of anyone. The Chofetz Chaim (Rabbi Israel Meir
HaCohen z"l) even extends this lesson to include speaking ill of
oneself. Neither truth nor motive justify *lashon harah*. There is
an exception: In very guarded circumstances, a parent or teacher
may reveal a pejorative fact about an individual in order to protect a child or student.[1]

---

1. There are other circumstances in which such protection may be in
   order. The Jerusalem Talmud (Peah 1:1) states that it is permissible
   to speak the truth about בעלי המחלוקת – people who habitually stir up
   conflict. Concerning such individuals, one may caution the community

Our sages tell us that when G-d repeated Sarah's remark concerning Avraham's old age, G-d chose not to tell the entire truth for the sake of *shalom bayit* (peace in the home). Thus at times even truth must be compromised in order not to repeat *lashon harah*. Perhaps the best suggestion is that found in Ethics of the Fathers 1:17 regarding the virtue of silence:

I have found nothing better for the human being than silence.

אבות א:יז
לא מצאתי לגוף טוב משתיקה.

---

in order to neutralize the effect of their activities. This standard also applies in the realm of professional references, where objective information (both positive and negative) regarding a person's skills as well as their integrity are vital. Likewise, such forthrightness would be pragmatic in social references such as in "match-making." With supreme care and the highest ethical standards, one may speak the objective truth about someone in these or similar situations.

The Body as a Vessel

שָׁפֵךְ דַּם הָאָדָם בָּאָדָם דָּמוֹ יִשָּׁפֵךְ כִּי בְּצֶלֶם
אֱ־לֹהִים עָשָׂה אֶת־הָאָדָם: (בראשית ט:ו)

Whoever sheds the blood of man, By man shall
his blood be shed; For in His image did G-d make
man. (Bereishit 9:6)

"A man of kindness gives to himself" (Mishlei 11:17) – this refers to
Hillel the elder, for when parting from his students, he continued
walking with them. His students said to him, "Master, where are
you going?" He said to them, "to fulfill a commandment (mitzvah)." They said to him, "what mitzvah is this?" He said to them,
"to bathe in the bath house." They said to him, "Is this really a
mitzvah?" He said to them, "Yes! If the one who is in charge of
the images of the king – which they place in theaters and circuses
– scours and washes them, and [as a result] is provided with food,
and is even elevated among the dignitaries of the kingdom, I, who
was created in the image and likeness [of G-d] – as it is written,
'For in His image did G-d make man' (Bereishit 9:6) – how much
more so."

(Midrash Vayikra Rabbah 34:3)

מדרש ויקרא רבה לד:ג

"גומל נפשו איש חסד" (משלי יא:יז) – זה הלל הזקן שבשעה שהיה נפטר
מתלמידיו היה מהלך והולך עמם. אמרו לו תלמידיו ר' להיכן אתה הולך? אמר
להם לעשות מצוה. אמרו לו וכי מה מצוה זו? אמר להן לרחוץ בבית המרחץ.
אמרו לו וכי זו מצוה הוא? אמר להם הן. מה אם איקונין של מלכים שמעמידים
אותו בבתי טרטיאות ובבתי קרקסיאות מי שנתמנה עליהם הוא מורקן ושוטפן
והן מעלין לו מזונות ולא עוד אלא שהוא מתגדל עם גדולי מלכות אני שנבראתי
בצלם ובדמות דכתיב (בראשית ט:ו) "כי בצלם א־לוהים עשה את האדם" על
אחת כמה וכמה.

81

To maintain one's physical purity by bathing is viewed as a mitz-vah. The human, created *b'tsellem Elokim* / "in the image of G-d," is intrinsically holy. The physical body which "contains" the *tsellem* (the "image") must be maintained in a manner befitting a *tsellem Elokim*. The synthesis of physical and spiritual holiness is here established. The human appetites are equally holy, though emanating from physical needs, providing these appetites are nourished in keeping with the moral and ethical perspective established in Torah.

It is ethical to care for oneself. A verse in Mishlei states it succinctly: "A man of kindness gives to himself" (11:17).

Levels of Righteousness

וַיָּחֶל נֹחַ אִישׁ הָאֲדָמָה וַיִּטַּע כָּרֶם: (בראשית ט:כ)

Noach, the tiller of the soil, was the first to plant
a vineyard. (Bereishit 9:20)

Rabbi Berekhiah said: Moshe is more beloved than Noach. Noach – after being called a "righteous man" (Bereishit 6:9), was
called "a man of the earth" (Bereishit 9:20). Moshe – after being
called "an Egyptian man" (Shemot 2:19), was called "man of G-d"
(Devarim 33:1).   (Midrash Bereishit Rabbah 36:3)

מדרש בראשית רבה לו:ג

אמר רבי ברכיה משה חביב מנח, נח משנקרא "איש צדיק" (בראשית ו:ט) נקרא
"איש אדמה" (שם ט:כ), אבל משה משנקרא "איש מצרי" (שמות ב:יט) נקרא "איש
הא-לוהים" (דברים לג:א).

Noach is first referred to in the Torah as a *tsaddik*, a righteous man,
and later as a "man of the earth." Moshe, in contrast, is first referred to as a "man of Egypt" and later as a "man of G-d." The midrash suggests that not every righteous person is of similar quality.

The Talmud expands on this point:

Is there a righteous person who is "good" and a righteous person
who is "not good"? Indeed one who is good toward heaven (the
Almighty) and good toward people is a righteous person who is
good. One who is good toward heaven and not good toward people is a righteous person who is not good. (Babylonian Talmud,
Kiddushin 40a)

קידושין מ.

וכי יש צדיק טוב, ויש צדיק שאינו טוב? אלא, טוב לשמים ולבריות - זהו צדיק
טוב, טוב לשמים ורע לבריות - זהו צדיק שאינו טוב.

A person may indeed be righteous and fulfill all of G-d's commandments on a "technical" level, and yet remain detached or indifferent to humanity; not violating any of the negative commandments yet remaining isolated from society. That is what the Talmud would view as a *tsaddik she'ayno tov* / "a *tsaddik* who is not good." Thus we can well understand the distinction made between Noach who is first called a *tsaddik* and then a "man of the earth," because he was not very involved with his generation. This would be in keeping with the teaching that Noach was only a *tsaddik* (a righteous person) in his generation (i.e., compared to the others of his society), whereas Moshe – who left the security of Egyptian nobility when he saw an Egyptian killing a Hebrew – is called a *tsaddik* because he elevated himself through his involvement with the people. Thus we learn the distinction between a *tsaddik tov* and a *tsaddik she'ayno tov*, a "good" righteous person and a righteous person who is "not good."

Get the Facts

וַיֵּרֶד ה' לִרְאֹת אֶת־הָעִיר וְאֶת־הַמִּגְדָּל אֲשֶׁר
בָּנוּ בְּנֵי הָאָדָם: (בראשית יא:ה)

The Lord came down to look *at the city and the
tower that man had built.* (Bereishit 11:5)

"The Lord came down to look" (Bereishit 11:5). All is revealed
before the Holy One, blessed is He, yet it is written here "The
Lord came down to look"? Rather, [the purpose of this verse is]
to teach humanity good manners so they do not render a [hasty]
verdict and do not speak about something which they have not
seen.   (Midrash Tanhuma, Noach 28)

מדרש תנחומא נח פרק כח
"וירד ה' לראות" (בראשית יא:ה), הכל גלוי לפני הקב"ה, וכתיב כאן "וירד ה'
לראות", אלא ללמד דרך ארץ לבריות שלא לגמור את הדין ושלא לומר דבר
מה שלא רואין.

"The Lord came down to look" (Bereishit 11:5). This comment
was not necessary, but comes to teach judges not to judge the defendant guilty until they see and understand. [Based upon] Midrash Rabbi Tanhuma. (Rashi to Bereishit 11:5)

רש"י בראשית יא:ה
לא הוצרך לכך, אלא בא ללמד לדיינים שלא ירשיעו הנידון עד שיראו ויבינו.

Judgment of people or situations demands direct, not "hearsay,"
knowledge. Rashi addresses the judges, admonishing them not
to reach a decision until they have "seen and understood". The
Midrash speaks to everyone concerning *derech eretz* (i.e., courtesy,
good manners, politeness, respect): Do not say anything about

a situation unless you know the facts established in an objective manner. If the Torah describes G-d as having "gone down to see" in order to demonstrate that G-d's judgment is based upon direct knowledge, how much more so must *we* base our judgment upon direct knowledge.

Consultation

הָבָה נֵרְדָה וְנָבְלָה שָׁם שְׂפָתָם אֲשֶׁר לֹא יִשְׁמְעוּ
אִישׁ שְׂפַת רֵעֵהוּ: (בראשית יא:ז)

Let us, then, go down and confound their speech
there, so that they shall not understand one
another's speech. (Bereishit 11:7)

"Let us go down" (Bereishit 11:7). He consulted the [Divine]
court out of His extreme modesty. (Rashi to Bereishit 11:7)

רש"י בראשית יא:ז
"הבה נרדה" (בראשית יא:ז) - בבית דינו נמלך מענוותנותו יתירה:

It is not written "Let Me go down," but "Let Us go down." G-d
– so to speak – does not do anything until He consults with His
attendants. (Midrash Hagadol, Noach)

מדרש הגדול נח
"ארדה" אין כתוב אלא "נרדה" (בראשית יא:ז) - כביכול אין הקב"ה עושה דבר
עד שנמלך עם פמליא שלו.

Both Rashi and the Midrash focus upon the phrase הבה נרדה *(ha-vah nerdah)* / "Come let *Us* go down," to teach the importance of consultation before reaching judgment. In Pirkei Avot [Ethics] we are likewise taught: אל תהי דן יחידי (אבות ד:י)/"Do not judge by yourself" (Ethics 4:10). The sages wish for us to be prudent and discerning in making judgments. Similar to the previous teaching regarding "getting the facts," here we are taught the value of consulting with others before making judgments: i.e., if G-d can be depicted metaphorically as seeking counsel, how much more so must *we* do so?

87

To Bless One Another

וְאֶעֶשְׂךָ לְגוֹי גָּדוֹל וַאֲבָרֶכְךָ וַאֲגַדְּלָה שְׁמֶךָ וֶהְיֵה
בְּרָכָה: (בראשית יב:ב)

And I will make of you a great nation, And I will
bless you; I will make your name great, and you
shall be a blessing. (Bereishit 12:2)

"And you shall be a blessing" (Bereishit 12:2) – The blessings are
handed over to your control. Until now, they had been in my control – I blessed Adam, Noach, and you – but from now on you will
bless whomever you wish.   (Rashi to Bereishit 12:2)

רש"י בראשית פרק יב:ב
"והיה ברכה" (בראשית יב:ב) – הברכות נתונות בידך, עד עכשיו היו בידי, ברכתי
את אדם ואת נח ואותך. מעתה אתה תברך את אשר תחפוץ.

This midrash establishes the norm in Judaism that each person is
endowed with the ability to bless another. The following passage
also confirms the power of *bracha*/blessing given to Avraham,
and in a sense to all humans:

Once Avraham entered [the world], the Holy One, blessed is He
said, "It is not appropriate that I must bless My creatures. Instead,
I will pass over My blessings to Avraham and to his descendants
and whoever they give a blessing to, I will seal the blessing through
them as it says, 'And you shall be a blessing'" (Bereishit 12:2).
                    (Midrash Tanchuma, VeZot HaBerachah, 1)

מדרש תנחומא וזאת הברכה פרק א
כיון שבא אברהם, אמר הקב"ה אינו דרך כבוד לפני שאהיה זקוק לברך

88

את בריותי, אלא הריני מוסר את הברכות לאברהם ולזרעו, וכל מי שקובעין בו
ברכה, אני חותם על ידיהם, שנאמר "והיה ברכה" (בראשית יב:ב).

It is G-d's special gift to humankind that we have the power to
bestow blessings upon one another. The power to bless is not
reserved only for the Kohen or sage or famed holy person. The
power to bless is inherent in every human being. "Let not the
blessing of any person be taken lightly in your eyes" (Babylonian
Talmud Megilah 16a). G-d respects and considers the blessings
we bestow upon one another as prayers for their wellbeing. Blessings are efficacious when uttered with sincerity and piety, regardless of the status of the one bestowing the blessing.

To Be an Ivri

וַיַּעֲבֹר אַבְרָם בָּאָרֶץ עַד מְקוֹם שְׁכֶם עַד אֵלוֹן
מוֹרֶה וְהַכְּנַעֲנִי אָז בָּאָרֶץ: (בראשית יב:ו)

Abram passed through the land as far as the
site of Shechem, at the terebinth of Moreh. The
Canaanites were then in the land. (Bereishit 12:6)

"The Canaanites were then in the land" (Bereishit 12:6). What
does this (seemingly unnecessary phrase) come to teach? That
even though the Canaanites were in the land, he did not learn
from [i.e. emulate] their deeds.   (Pesikta Zutarti – Lekh Lekha)

פסקתא זוטרתי לך לך

"והכנעני אז בארץ" (בראשית יב:ו) מה ת"ל אלא שאע"פ שהיה הכנעני בארץ לא
למד ממעשיהם.

Avraham's greatest power (even when he was still Avram) was his
ability to remain true to his faith, values, and principles in spite of
the pagan and immoral world around him. This midrash gives us
the key ingredient for survival in any society: Do not learn from
its corrupt values, philosophies, and actions. Be the *Ivri*/"Hebrew" meaning, be on the *other side* of issues and choices.[1] Do
not fear isolation or rejection. When the pagan prophet Bilaam
says הֶן־עָם לְבָדָד יִשְׁכֹּן וּבַגּוֹיִם לֹא יִתְחַשָּׁב/"Behold it is a nation that will
dwell in solitude and will not be reckoned among the nations"
(Bamidbar 23:9), he is referring to our ability – or perhaps our
destiny – to be "a nation separate/alone" for others to behold

---

1.   The Hebrew word *Ivri* stems from the verb *La'avor*, meaning "to cross
     over to another side." Therefore, to be an *Ivri* is to have moral courage
     to stand on your principles, even if this means that you stand alone.

and emulate. This position does not suggest that we live apart from others, but rather that we live *distinctly* while in the midst of others and thus serve as a "light unto the nations."

> Rabbi Judah says: The entire world was on one side, and he was on the other side. (Midrash Bereishit Rabbah 42:8)

מדרש בראשית רבה פרשה מב סימן ח

רבי יהודה אומר כל העולם כולו מעבר אחד והוא מעבר אחר.

Commenting on a later verse (Bereishit 14:13), Rabbi Yehuda suggests that even before any dramatic encounter with the Almighty, Avram was an opponent of the established pagan society. This brief yet profound statement by Rabbi Yehuda defines one dimension of the responsibility of an individual Jew: Oppose evil, even when you are a lonely minority voice. Always be the *Ivri*, on the "other side," in opposition to the majority in a misguided, evil society. The moral truth will ultimately prevail. Avram was the role model for such moral courage.

We impact society not by converting others (although that is always a voluntary possibility), but by convincing others of the wisdom of our faith by precept and example. We endeavor to influence society towards *tikkun olam*/ repair of the world – to make all of society ethical and moral by virtue of how we behave in our families and communities and ultimately the manner in which we use the power of sovereignty, with its military, its courts, and its social and political vehicles, thus the need for a sovereign Jewish state, i.e. Israel.

The prophet Isaiah boldly articulated our mandated task and historic destiny:

> I the Lord have called you in righteousness and will hold your hand and will keep you and give you for a covenant of the people, for a light of the nations. (Isaiah 42:7)

ישעיהו מב:ז

אֲנִי ה' קְרָאתִיךָ בְצֶדֶק וְאַחְזֵק בְּיָדֶךָ וְאֶצָּרְךָ וְאֶתֶּנְךָ לִבְרִית עָם לְאוֹר גּוֹיִם:

And again he proclaims:

I will also give you for a light to the nations, that My salvation may
be to the end of the earth. (Isaiah 49:6)

ישעיהו מט:ו

וּנְתַתִּיךָ לְאוֹר גּוֹיִם לִהְיוֹת יְשׁוּעָתִי עַד־קְצֵה הָאָרֶץ:

The Proper Social Environment

וַיֵּרָא ה' אֶל־אַבְרָם וַיֹּאמֶר לְזַרְעֲךָ אֶתֵּן אֶת־
הָאָרֶץ הַזֹּאת וַיִּבֶן שָׁם מִזְבֵּחַ לַה' הַנִּרְאֶה אֵלָיו:
(בראשית יב:ז)

The Lord appeared to Abram and said, "I will
assign this land to your offspring." And he built
an altar there to the Lord who had appeared to
him. (Bereishit 12:7)

Rabbi Levi said: When Avraham went out in Aram Naharaim and
in Aram Nachor, he saw the people eating, drinking and sinning.
He said, "May it be that I not have a share in this land." When
he reached the Ladder of Tyre, he saw the people weeding when
it was time for weeding and hoeing when it was time for hoeing,
and he said, "May I have a share in this land!" The Holy One,
blessed is He said to him, "I will assign this land to your offspring"
(Bereishit 12:7).   (Midrash Bereishit Rabbah 39:7)

מדרש בראשית רבה לט:ז

אמר רבי לוי בשעה שהיה אברהם מהלך בארם נהרים ובארם נחור, ראה אותן
אוכלים ושותים ופוחזים, אמר הלואי לא יהא לי חלק בארץ הזאת וכיון שהגיע
לסולמה של צור ראה אותן עסוקין בניכוש בשעת הניכוש, בעידור בשעת
העידור, אמר הלואי יהא חלקי בארץ הזאת, אמר לו הקב"ה "לזרעך אתן את
הארץ הזאת" (בראשית יב:ז).

Avraham sought a society which, though pagan, had wholesome
social and economic norms. While Avraham was able to with-
stand and indeed transcend his pagan environment and culture,
he sought a society which at least on some level had basic human

93

values. Regardless of one's moral stamina, one should avoid a community in which the social order is polluted.

In our day, free and lawful western societies demonstrate a spirit of amoral standards in many categories of human conduct. It seems that our guaranteed rights have led to an amoral attitude toward what Judaism considers fundamental standards of human behavior.

The legal system in the United States, protects us and allows us to choose among a wide range of human conduct that is considered acceptable. Ethics have become "subjective," dependent upon the "situation." Thus the situation, rather than an objective truth, often becomes the criterion for human conduct.

Judaism, however, has always manifested an uncompromising view of morality. Wherever Jews have lived, the social, political, and cultural environments presented a direct challenge to our moral values. The ultimate question for Jews in the 21st century is: Can we maintain an uncompromised standard of Torah morality in a free society which has an amoral code of behavior? We survived in many oppressive societies by remaining in "the opposition" or the "counter-culture." Will we be able to take that stance in a free society? The answer will determine the destiny of Jews who live in a free society.

The Woman as a Source of Blessing

וַיַּעְתֵּק מִשָּׁם הָהָרָה מִקֶּדֶם לְבֵית־אֵל וַיֵּט אָהֳלֹה
בֵּית־אֵל מִיָּם וְהָעַי מִקֶּדֶם וַיִּבֶן־שָׁם מִזְבֵּחַ לַה'
וַיִּקְרָא בְּשֵׁם ה': (בראשית יב:ח)

From there he moved on to the hill country east
of Bethel and pitched his tent, with Bethel on the
west and Ai on the east; and he built an altar
to the Lord and invoked the Lord by name."
(Bereishit 12:8)

"And pitched his tent" (Bereishit 12:8). The text is written *ohalah*
– her tent. This teaches that he pitched Sarah's tent first and only
then pitched his own tent.   (Midrash Bereishit Rabbah 39:15)

מדרש בראשית רבה לט:טו

"ויט אהלה" (בראשית יב:ח) אהלה כתיב מלמד שנטע אהל שרה תחלה ואח"כ
נטע אהלו.

According to the midrash, Avraham is concerned first, with pro-
curing a tent for Sarah, and only then one for himself. Why two
tents, and why Sarah's first?

The simple answer is that Sarah had servants, and her personal
needs were met in her tent. From a modern perspective, Avraham might be considered a "gentleman," or one might say that he
was being "egalitarian." There is more to Avraham's motivation,
however.

The Rabbis teach us that a home is blessed because of the presence of a righteous woman whose wisdom, values and strength
permeate the home. This midrash demonstrates that Avraham
understood the crucial role of Sarah in his household, and that
her presence needed to be manifest first. Our sages also teach us

that ביתו זו אשתו/"a man's home is his wife" (Babylonian Talmud Yoma 2a) which demonstrates her centrality in the family and the influence that she exerts on the home.

Moreover, this idea is further expressed in the Rabbinic interpretation of Bereishit 12:16:

> "And because of her, it went well with Abram; he acquired sheep, oxen, asses, male and female slaves, she-asses and camels."
>
> (Bereishit 12:16)

(בראשית יב:טז)

וּלְאַבְרָם הֵיטִיב בַּעֲבוּרָהּ וַיְהִי־לוֹ צֹאן־וּבָקָר וַחֲמֹרִים וַעֲבָדִים וּשְׁפָחֹת וַאֲתֹנֹת וּגְמַלִּים:

And Rabbi Chelbo said: A man should always be careful to honor his wife, for blessing is only found in a man's home on account of his wife, as it says, "And because of her, it went well with Avram" (Bereishit 12:16). Similarly, Rav said to the people of Mechoza, "honor your wives so that you become wealthy." (Babylonian Talmud, Bava Metzia 59a)

בבא מציעא נט.

ואמר רבי חלבו לעולם יהא אדם זהיר בכבוד אשתו, שאין ברכה מצויה בתוך ביתו של אדם אלא בשביל אשתו, שנאמר "ולאברם הטיב בעבורה" (בראשית יב:טז). והיינו דאמר להו רבא לבני מחוזא: אוקירו לנשייכו כי היכי דתתעתרו.

"Her husband puts confidence in her" (Mishlei 31:11) – this refers to Sarah our matriarch, for Avraham became wealthy on her account, as it says, "And because of her, it went well with Avram" (Bereishit 12:16). (Midrash Mishlei 31:11)

מדרש משלי לא:יא

"בטח בה לב בעלה" (משלי לא:יא). זו שרה אמנו, שהעשיר אברהם בשבילה, שנאמר "ולאברם היטיב בעבורה" (בראשית יב:טז).

Our sages consider the woman to be the key source of *bracha*/blessing in the home. The idea of *akeret habayit*/the "mistress of the home," is a basic Jewish value. On Friday evening before the recitation of *kiddush*, "A Woman of Valor" (Mishlei 31) is recited in order to bring attention to the honored status of the woman in the Jewish family and the centrality of the woman's role in bringing blessings into the home. There are many Rabbinic sources, from throughout history, which evidence a profound respect and admiration for wives, as well as for women in general. The notion of women being inferior because of a lack of ritual obligation finds no support in this midrash. While women were traditionally denied or excused from a public ritual role (e.g. *minyan*), this lack of public status did not imply a lack of respect or admiration for women.

Levels of Faith

קוּם הִתְהַלֵּךְ בָּאָרֶץ לְאָרְכָּהּ וּלְרָחְבָּהּ כִּי לְךָ
אֶתְּנֶנָּה: (בראשית יג:יז)

Rise, walk about the land, through its length and
its breadth, for I give it to you. (Bereishit 13:17)

The Holy One, blessed is He said to [Moshe], "Alas for those
who are gone and not forgotten. For I revealed myself several
times to Avraham, Yitzchak, and Yaakov as *El Shadai* and they did
not criticize My ways or say to Me, 'What is Your name?' I told
Avraham, 'Rise, walk about the land, through its length and its
breadth, for I give it to you,' (Bereishit 13:17) and [even though]
when he wanted a place to bury Sarah he did not find one until he
purchased it with four hundred silver shekels, he did not criticize
My ways."   (Babylonian Talmud, Sanhedrin 111a)

סנהדרין קיא.

אמר לו הקדוש ברוך הוא: חבל על דאבדין ולא משתכחין הרי כמה פעמים
נגליתי על אברהם יצחק ויעקב בא-ל ש-די, ולא הרהרו על מדותי, ולא אמרו לי
מה שמך. אמרתי לאברהם (בראשית יג:יז) "קום התהלך בארץ לארכה ולרחבה כי
לך אתננה", בקש מקום לקבור את שרה – ולא מצא, עד שקנה בארבע מאות
שקל כסף, ולא הרהר על מדותי.

This midrash describes G-d's disappointment with Moshe when
he asks G-d "What is your name?" (Shemot 3:13) The *emunah*/faith of Moshe was apparently judged to be less profound
than that of Avraham. G-d praises Avraham in this Midrash for
having to buy a burial place for Sarah though he was promised
the land by G-d. Avraham did not demand from G-d evidence of
the fulfillment of the promise.

Yet one may argue that Avraham, like Moshe, had doubts. For example, G-d promised Avraham a son from his wife Sarah: "And I will bless her and give you a son also of her" (Bereishit 17:16). We then read: "Then Avraham fell upon his face and laughed, and said in his heart, 'Shall a child be born to him that is a hundred years old? And shall Sarah who is ninety years old give birth?'" (Bereishit 17:17). Is this an expression of delighted surprise, or of doubt? If it is doubt, then how is it that Avraham is held up as the model of a faithful, unquestioning individual?

Avraham's faith is ultimately judged by his *actions*, not by his thoughts. When G-d first appears to Avram early in his journey of faith (Bereishit 12:1), G-d tells him to leave his native land, his birthplace, his family, and his home, to go to a land yet to be shown to him. There is an immediate response of obedience: "And Avram went" (Bereishit 12:4). That is a concrete manifestation of faith. Avraham's internal response of doubt to the promise of a son may be understood as a human "reflex", rather than as an expression of serious theological doubt.

Given unique circumstances, one may have doubt in the midst of true faith, even as Avraham did. Avraham remained G-d's trusted servant despite this experience of doubt. A profound lesson: Even those of faith may in moments of crisis be troubled with doubt. The transcending question is: Can one in the midst of trauma-induced doubt, ultimately recover one's faith as did Avraham?

Faith is abstract, action is concrete. We often express faith with words, yet fail to demonstrate this faith in our actions. Do not tell Me you love Me, says G-d: Show that love in a tangible way. Avraham may indeed have doubted, yet he demonstrated faith in his actions.

One may ask, why does G-d need to prove Avraham's faith with the instance of Sarah's burial? Was not the more radical instance of the *Akedah*/binding of Yitzchak (in which Avraham is required by G-d to sacrifice his son Yitzchak, G-d's promise of the future) sufficient?

Perhaps the Torah is concerned with the faith of the average person who may not rise to Avraham's level of faith of being prepared to sacrifice one's child. The story of the purchase of Sarah's grave is a "trial" more within the scope of the average human being. Perhaps the lesson is that we should not endeavor to teach moral/ethical values from instances which are beyond the reach of the average human being. Torah and its values are for everyone, not only for the courageous and extraordinary. Torah speaks to everyone, with his/her unique ability, talent, potential, and level of faith.

Returning to the midrash regarding Moshe: While G-d seems disappointed with Moshe and in fact criticizes him, nonetheless the relationship remains profound. How vital is this lesson of a relationship of faith which allows for serious criticism? To criticize a loved one or cherished friend need not be a negative experience. Out of loyalty comes a desire to enable the other to grow and develop spiritually, emotionally and intellectually. Silence, rather than sensitive criticism, is then an act of betrayal.

Choosing Where to Live

וַיִּקְחוּ אֶת־לוֹט וְאֶת־רְכֻשׁוֹ בֶּן־אֲחִי אַבְרָם
וַיֵּלֵכוּ וְהוּא יֹשֵׁב בִּסְדֹם: (בראשית יד:יב)

*They also took Lot; the son of Abram's brother,
and his possessions, and departed; for he had
settled in Sodom. (Bereishit 14:12)*

What caused this (Lot and his property being taken captive) to happen? His [Lot's] settling in S'dom.   (Rashi to Bereishit 14:12)

רש"י בראשית יד:יב
מי גרם לו זאת, [כל הצרות] ישיבתו בסדום:

As always, Rashi never allows a seemingly superfluous phrase or verse to pass without comment. Here, he is troubled by the Torah's need to tell us of Lot's travels to S'dom. Rashi explains that it was Lot's choice to settle in this city of nefarious behavior that led to his tragic destiny and the tragic destiny of his children.

The Midrash comments on the nature of society in S'dom:

The people of S'dom, because they hated one another, the Holy One, blessed is He removed [lit. "destroyed"] them from this world and from the next world. (Avot D'Rabbi Natan 12:6)

אבות דרבי נתן יב:ו
אנשי סדום מתוך שהיו שונאים זה את זה אבדן הקב"ה מן העולם הזה ומן
העולם הבא.

This classic rabbinic text dramatizes the incompatibility of the Divine and "man's inhumanity to man." The Divine cannot abide human injustice – which raises the painful question of the

Holocaust, perhaps history's most incomprehensible act of human cruelty. To suggest any answer would be presumptuous.

Rashi wants us to understand that just as G-d cannot abide an evil society, neither should we. What caused Lot's ultimate difficulties was the fact that he chose to settle in S'dom. A person seeking to lead an ethical and spiritual life should not choose to dwell in a society of obvious depravity. Where we live, in part, determines the quality of our moral, ethical, and cultural life. Few have the capacity to transcend the dynamic influences of a society lacking in positive moral values. Lot chose to live in S'dom, and that choice led to the tragedies which followed.

The book of Mishlei teaches: "He that walks with wise men shall be wise, but a companion of fools shall suffer harm" (Mishlei 13:20). Social environment affects our moral and ethical life. No doubt it is possible to transcend one's milieu, yet it takes extraordinary moral fortitude.

Thus we learn, choose with great care where you live. What are the institutions in the community which will allow you to grow spiritually, intellectually, morally? What is the social climate of the community? Are there peers and elders who will challenge you to grow?

Would a cultured person live in a community without access to a library, schools, theater, etc?

A Jew cannot live in a community without synagogues, child and adult schools, charitable institutions, and the components of a rich religious, cultural, and democratic environment. Choose to live in S'dom of any genre and your quality of life is inevitably impoverished.

The Deeds of the Parents

וַיְבָרֲכֵהוּ וַיֹּאמַר בָּרוּךְ אַבְרָם לְאֵל עֶלְיוֹן קֹנֵה
שָׁמַיִם וָאָרֶץ: (בראשית יד:יט)

He blessed him, saying, "Blessed be Abram of
G-d most high, Creator of heaven and earth."
(Bereishit 14:19)

Rabbi Chiya said: Children whose fathers caused them to be
blessed through their deeds – this refers to Avraham, as it is said,
"Blessed be Abram of G-d most high." (Bereishit 14:19)

(Midrash Shemot Rabbah 16:27)

מדרש שמות רבה טו:כז

אמר ר' חייא: בנים שאבותם ברכו אותן במעשיהם זה אברהם שנאמר "ברוך
אברם לאל עליון." (בראשית יד:יט)

Avram is referred to as "Blessed be Avram of G-d," which this
midrash links to the notion that children are blessed through the
deeds of their parents. A valuable parenting challenge: Parents
bless their children through precept and example.

Perhaps the most instructive "parent education" text is the
daily recitation of the *Sh'ma* (Devarim 6:6): "And these matters
that I command you this day shall be upon your heart. You shall
teach them thoroughly to your children and you shall speak of
them when you sit in your house, when you walk on the way,
when you lie down and when you arise." The child's instruction
thus begins with the ordinary, functional matters of everyday life:
i.e., sitting, walking, lying down and getting up. Only then does
the ritual instruction begin: "Bind them as a sign upon your arm
and as frontlets between your eyes, and write them on the door-
posts of your house and upon your gates." (Devarim 6:8–9)

Children learn from their parents' response to daily, mundane events which may seem trivial, but which in fact provide the most significant foundation upon which a child's Jewish ethical judgment is developed.

A Higher Standard

וַיֹּאמֶר אַבְרָם אֶל־מֶלֶךְ סְדֹם הֲרִמֹתִי יָדִי אֶל־ה'
אֵל עֶלְיוֹן קֹנֵה שָׁמַיִם וָאָרֶץ: (בראשית יד:כב)

And Abram said to the king of Sodom, "I Swear
to the Lord, G-d most high, Creator of heaven
and earth:" (Bereishit 14:22)

At that moment Avraham sanctified the name of the Holy One,
blessed is He (by refusing the booty) so that the king of S'dom
would not think that Avraham had gone to war with the four kings
for [reasons of] money, but rather that he had gone to war only
in order to save Lot and his property, because he [Lot] was his
nephew.   (Midrash Aggadah, Bereishit 14:22)

מדרש אגדה בראשית יד:כב
אותה שעה קידש אברהם שמו של הקב"ה שלא יחשוב מלך סדום שעל ידי
ממון עשה אברהם מלחמה עם ארבעה מלכים ולא עשה מלחמה אלא להציל
את לוט ואת רכושו לפי שהיה בן אחיו.

Why a person does what he does, may be as important as *what*
he does. The Torah is quick to attribute motive to Avraham's actions: i.e., it was to save Lot, not to acquire wealth. This teaching
provides a clear response to the slanderous, stereotypical notion
that Jews act for "purse" rather than purpose.

The moral/ethical behavior of the Jew must exceed the technical, legal requirements of society. An act may be legal, yet if it
does not meet the higher standard of conduct required by Torah
standards, it is unacceptable.

"Luck"

וַיּוֹצֵא אֹתוֹ הַחוּצָה וַיֹּאמֶר הַבֶּט־נָא הַשָּׁמַיְמָה
וּסְפֹר הַכּוֹכָבִים אִם־תּוּכַל לִסְפֹּר אֹתָם וַיֹּאמֶר
לוֹ כֹּה יִהְיֶה זַרְעֶךָ: (בראשית טו:ה)

He took him outside and said, "Look toward
heaven and count the stars, if you are able to
count them." And He added, "So shall your
offspring be." (Bereishit 15:5)

Rav Yehudah said in the name of Rav: From where do we know
that Israel [i.e. the Jewish people] is not controlled by *Mazal* [i.e.
constellations]? As it is written, "He took him outside . . ." (Bereishit 15:5). Avraham said to the Holy One, blessed is He, "Master
of the Universe, 'my steward will be my heir'" (Bereishit 16:3).
G-d replied, "No, 'none but your very own issue [shall be your
heir]'" (Bereishit 16:4). He said to Him, "Master of the universe,
I consulted my astrology, and I am not able to have a son." He
replied, "Leave aside your astrology, for Israel is not controlled by
the constellations." [i.e. Astrology – *Mazal*]

(Babylonian Talmud Shabbat 156a)

שבת קנו.

אמר רב יהודה אמר רב: מניין שאין מזל לישראל שנאמר (בראשית טו:ה) "ויוצא
אתו החוצה". אמר אברהם לפני הקדוש ברוך הוא: רבונו של עולם (בראשית
טו:ג) "בן ביתי יורש אתי". אמר לו: לאו, (בראשית טו:ד) "כי אם אשר יצא ממעיך".
אמר לפניו: רבונו של עולם, נסתכלתי באיצטגנינות שלי ואיני ראוי להוליד בן.
אמר ליה: צא מאיצטגנינות שלך, שאין מזל לישראל.

It is remarkable how much emphasis we place upon *mazal* in
everyday interactions – saying *mazal tov* upon every happy occa-

106

sion, as well as the expression "you should only have *mazal*." We apparently have a strong folk attachment to the notion of *mazal*.

The Talmud understands *mazal* as referring to the supposed power of the zodiac. Today we tend to translate *mazal* as "luck." Yet if *mazal* is luck, then life is void of meaning. Do we really mean to suggest that choice, behavior, and faith are irrelevant in determining one's destiny?

Perhaps a contrasting perspective of *mazal* might give us a more responsible understanding of life:

> A person who is controlled by *Mazal* is assisted. Whereas an animal, which is not controlled by *Mazal*, is not assisted.
>
> (Babylonian Talmud Shabbat 53b)

שבת נג:

אדם דאית ליה מזלא מסייע ליה, בהמה דלית לה מזלא לא מסייע ליה.

To understand *Mazal* we turn to the text:

> A human, who is controlled by *Mazal* – [meaning] they have the knowledge to be able to protect themselves.
>
> (Rashi to Babylonian Talmud, Bava Kama 2b)

רש"י בבא קמא ב:

אדם דאית ליה מזלא – שיש לו דעת לשמור את גופו.

In this context, Rashi offers another understanding of the popular view of *mazal* as "luck" or *mazalot*/signs of the zodiac. On the contrary, Rashi suggests that *mazal* is *da'at* (knowledge), the catalytic factor in human destiny. While one may argue that we are all born "hard-wired" with certain basic qualities – our genetically endowed intelligence, talents, etc. – nonetheless we determine how those gifts will be used. We have the freedom to choose how to respond to situations, to use that power/wisdom/talent for good or for evil. We have the freedom to squander these gifts on experiences and deeds – insignificant and ultimately meaningless – or to engage society to "fix the world"/*Tikkun Olam*.

Rashi refuses to accept the concept that human and beast are ruled by some blind astrological fate. When the Talmud differentiates between human and animal, it suggests that *mazal* is the critical factor. Rashi's interpretation of *mazal* as choice emancipates us from the burden of ancient superstitions which still seem to prevail. With this brief teaching, Rashi returns us to the absolute moral / ethical / religious paradigm: The human being is responsible for all choices, decisions and actions. Choice is the operative and ultimate human capacity: In the words of Rashi "*Mazal* – that is choice."

"Behold I set before you this day a blessing and a curse: A blessing if you obey the commandments of the Lord your G-d which I command you this day; and a curse if you do not obey the commandments of the Lord your G-d" (Devarim 11:26).

The Torah explicitly states this fundamental principle: You must choose to be human, to be Jewish, to be moral. While you do have antecedents – genes, social, economic, environmental, and religious – nonetheless, many individuals throughout history have transcended their origin, due to the choices they made, which had profound effects upon them and, indeed, upon history.

Tsedakah

וְהֶאֱמִן בַּה' וַיַּחְשְׁבֶהָ לּוֹ צְדָקָה: (בראשית טו:ו)

And because he put his trust in the Lord, He
reckoned it to his merit. (Bereishit 15:6)

Rabbi Akiva's students asked him, "Which is greater, repentance
(*teshuvah*) or charity (*tsedakah*)?" He said to them, "Repentance,
for one may sometimes give charity to someone who is not worthy, but repentance depends only on oneself." They said to him,
"Master, but do we not already find that charity (or righteousness)
is greater than repentance? Regarding Avraham it says, '[And because he put his trust in the Lord,] He reckoned it righteousness
(*tsedakah*)' (Bereishit 15:6). And elsewhere it says, 'It will therefore be righteousness (*tsedakah*) when we observe faithfully ...'
(Devarim 6:25). And furthermore, David came and interpreted,
'Your righteousness (*tsidkatekha*) is like the high mountains'
(Psalms 36:7)." (Midrash Mishlei 6:6)

מדרש משלי ו:ו
שאלו תלמידיו את ר' עקיבא אי זו היא גדולה, תשובה או צדקה, אמר להם
תשובה, שהצדקה פעמים נותנה למי שאינו כדאי, אבל התשובה מעצמו הוא
עושה אותה, אמרו לו רבי והלא כבר מצינו שהצדקה גדולה מן התשובה,
באברהם הוא אומר "ויחשבה לו צדקה" (בראשית טו:ו), ובמקום אחר הוא אומר
"וצדקה תהיה לנו כי נשמור לעשות" (דברים ו: כה), ולא עוד אלא שבא דוד
ופירש "צדקתך כהררי אל" (תהלים לו:ז).

Great is righteousness (*tsedakah*), for through it Avraham our forefather was praised, as it is said, "And because he put his trust in the
Lord, He reckoned it *tsedakah*" (Bereishit 15:6) and it says, "For

I have singled him (Avraham) out . . . for doing what is just and right (*tsedakah*) . . ." (Bereishit 18:19).

(Midrash Mishlei 14:34)

מדרש משלי יד:לד

גדולה צדקה שבה נשתבח אברהם אבינו, שנאמר "והאמין בה' ויחשבה לו צדקה" (בראשית טו:ו) , ואומר "כי ידעתיו וגו' לעשות צדקה וגו'" (שם בראשית יח:יט).

The act of *tsedakah* (righteousness) which requires one to give of oneself – one's possessions, time, and/or talents – is viewed as an act of transcending value. Rabbi Akiva seems to deprecate the value of *tsedakah* if it is given to one who is "not worthy," suggesting that *tsedakah* itself is then less worthy. *Teshuvah*, however, being something which can only be judged by G-d, is intrinsically either valid or false.

It is interesting to note that Rabbi Yehudah disagrees with Rabbi Akiva. In the passage concerning Avraham, the text gives witness to the fact that G-d considered Avraham's *tsedakah* authentic; thus Rabbi Yehudah argues that *tsedakah* transcends in value all other acts, even *teshuvah*, regardless of the recipient.

Moreover, the second text from the Midrash on Mishlei states: "Great is *tsedakah*, for through it Avraham was praised (by G-d)." This act of kindness or righteousness was acknowledged by G-d to be a demonstration of Avraham's faith. The objective act, manifesting an understanding of G-d's expectations, earned Avraham the praise of G-d. Judaism requires faith-driven engagement.

Once again, the sages place the value of *tsedakah* (the act) on a level transcending that of *teshuvah* (the thought). The pragmatic, immediate consequence of *tsedakah* is judged to be superior to the uncertain consequences of *teshuvah*. Who can judge *teshuvah* other than G-d? *Tsedakah*, on the other hand, has immediate and obvious consequences, to its beneficiary and benefactor.

Our sages want us to appreciate even the miniscule act or amount of *tsedakah*, since in the aggregate it will become a significant amount and will positively influence others and ultimately society as a whole. Other illustrations of this perspective may be found in the following texts:

What is the meaning of the verse "He donned *tsedakah* like a coat of armor" (Isaiah 59:17)? To say that just as in a coat of mail, every scale adds up to a great coat of armor, so too in charity, every single *perutah* adds up to a great sum.

(Babylonian Talmud Bava Batra 9b)

בבא בתרא ט:

מאי דכתיב "וילבש צדקה כשריון" (ישעיה נט:יז)? לומר לך, מה שריון זה, כל קליפה וקליפה מצטרפת לשריון גדול, אף צדקה – כל פרוטה ופרוטה מצטרפת לחשבון גדול.

The mitzvah of *tsedakah* is equal to all of the mitzvot. (Babylonian Talmud Bava Batra 9a)

בבא בתרא ט.
שקולה צדקה כנגד כל המצות.

A rather remarkable text is one which boldly rejects the relevance of *motive* in the act of *tsedakah*:

One who says, "this coin is for charity so that my son may live and so that I may merit life in the world to come" – this is a truly righteous person. (Babylonian Talmud Rosh Hashanah 4a)

ראש השנה ד.
האומר סלע זו לצדקה בשביל שיחיו בני, ובשביל שאזכה בה לחיי העולם הבא – הרי זה צדיק גמור.

The sages here seem unconcerned with motive, which raises the complex question of the mitzvah:

צדק צדק תרדוף / "Justice justice you shall pursue" (Devarim 16:20). Yet we can detect that the sages are seeking a more effective tool to help the needy, as they suggest:

Greater is the one who gives a loan more than the one who gives charity, and the one "who places in the pocket" (Rashi [Pesachim 53b]: "gives the scholar goods to sell or gives him business") is greatest of all. (Babylonian Talmud Shabbat 63a)

שבת סג.

גדול המלוה יותר מן העושה צדקה, ומטיל בכיס יותר מכולן.

Greater is the act of lending someone funds or tools or facilities, for by this act we become involved with the needy and demonstrate a continuous interest and involvement. This teaching is similar to Maimonides' approach to *tsedakah*, of helping the needy to become independent of the need for *tsedakah*.

There is an enigmatic teaching concerning *tsedakah*:

> "Happy are those who protect justice, who act with righteousness (*tsedakah*) at all times" (Psalms 106:3). And is it possible to give charity (*tsedakah*) at all times? Our Rabbis in Yavneh – and some say it was Rabbi Eliezer – interpreted: This refers to the one who feeds his sons and daughters when they are young. (Babylonian Talmud Ketubot 50a)

כתובות ג.

"אשרי שומרי משפט עושה צדקה בכל עת" (תהלים קו:ג) – וכי אפשר לעשות צדקה בכל עת? דרשו רבותינו שביבנה, ואמרי לה רבי אליעזר: זה הזן בניו ובנותיו כשהן קטנים.

Are the sages here suggesting that feeding one's children is an act of *tsedakah*? Or is the implication that one ought to give to those who do not "appreciate" or those who do not express gratitude (exemplified by young children)? That may be the meaning intended. *Tsedakah* is an act of righteousness – an act which is obligatory within a society of righteous people who live by laws of righteousness. We dare not consider *tsedakah* to be altruistic kindness. Rather, it is a fundamental obligation for every member of the community. Thus the analogy to feeding one's children, an obligation understood and accepted even by the most miserly, is used to teach that we are all obligated to share our means with those in need.

No one is exempt from the mitzvah of *tsedakah*. As the sages say: אפילו עני המתפרנס מן הצדקה יעשה צדקה / "Even the poor person who is supported by charity should give charity" (Babylonian Talmud Gittin 7b). The obligation to share is incumbent upon us all. In addition, there is always someone who may be helped by a kind word or a sympathetic ear. To be impervious to a needy person is inexcusable.

At the same time, there is the harsh admonition concerning those who give charity to the point of impoverishment:

In Usha they decreed: One who wishes to give [charity] liberally [literally "squander his money"], should not give more than one-fifth [of his money]. So it was also taught: One who wishes to give [charity] liberally should not give more than one-fifth [of his money] lest he come to require [the assistance of] others. (Babylonian Talmud Ketubot 50a)

כתובות נ.

באושא התקינו המבזבז אל יבזבז יותר מחומש. תניא נמי הכי: המבזבז אל יבזבז יותר מחומש שמא יצטרך לבריות.

While each of us has the obligation to share with those in need, we must consider our personal needs as well. Thus the sages ruled that one may not give more than one fifth of one's wealth to *tsedakah*, so as not to risk becoming in need of *tsedakah* ourselves.

The Value of Shalom

וְאַתָּה תָּבוֹא אֶל־אֲבֹתֶיךָ בְּשָׁלוֹם תִּקָּבֵר בְּשֵׂיבָה
טוֹבָה: (בראשית טו:טו)

As for you, You shall go to your fathers in peace,
You shall be buried at a ripe old age. (Bereishit 15:15)

Peace is dear, for the reward for all the deeds and merits performed
by Avraham was peace, as it says, "You shall go to your fathers in
peace" (Bereishit 15:15).   (Midrash Bamidbar Rabbah 11:7)

מדרש במדבר רבה יא:ז
חביב הוא השלום שכל מעשים וזכיות שעשה אברהם אבינו לא נתן שכרו אלא
שלום שנא' "ואתה תבא אל אבותיך בשלום" (בראשית טו:טו).

The intrinsic value of *shalom* is of such absolute significance that
G-d considers it to be the greatest blessing to bestow upon Avraham. Many statements of our sages reflect this concept, yet one
may also suggest that *shalom* requires truth:

Any peace that is not accompanied by rebuke is not [true] peace.
(Midrash Bereishit Rabbah 54:3)

מדרש בראשית רבה נד:ג
כל שלום שאין עמו תוכחה אינו שלום.

The sages require a willingness on the part of the friend or relative
(i.e., parent, spouse, sibling) to admonish when appropriate while
striving for peace. One could argue, that it is permissible to seek
peace at the expense of truth, providing no one incurs a tangible
loss. When G-d tells Sarah that she is to give birth and Sarah responds with a judgment that both she and her husband Avraham

are too old, G-d reports to Avraham only that Sarah said that *she* was too old to bear a child. The value of *shalom bayit*/ peace in the household, is a transcending value, at times even at the expense of truth. The Talmud states:

> Great is peace, for even the Holy One, blessed is He modified [the truth in a minor way] for the sake [of peace]. For at first it is written [when Sarah thinks to herself], "and my husband is so old" (Bereishit 18:12) and subsequently it is written [when G-d reports what Sarah thought to Avraham], "'and I am old'" (Bereishit 18:13). (Babylonian Talmud Yevamot 65a)

יבמות סה.

גדול השלום, שאף הקדוש ברוך הוא שינה בו, דמעיקרא כתיב: "ואדוני זקן", ולבסוף כתיב: "ואני זקנתי" (בראשית יח:יב) (שם יח:יג).

One may turn to the sages for a radical statement of the fundamental and transcending value of *shalom*:

> Rabbi Shimon ben Gamliel said: Great is peace, for the Holy One, blessed is He wrote things in the Torah that never happened only for the sake of peace. They are: When Yaakov died – "When Yosef's brothers saw that their father was dead . . ." (Bereishit 50:15) – what did they do? They went to Bilhah and said to her, "Go enter into Yosef's presence and say to him, 'Before his death, your father left this instruction'" (Bereishit 50:16 and see 17) – yet Yaakov had never left any of this instruction; rather, [the brothers] made this up on their own. Rabban Shimon ben Gamliel said: See how much ink is spilled, how many quills are broken, how many pieces of leather processed, and how many school-children are lashed in order to teach in the Torah something that never happened. See how great is the power of peace! (Midrash Tanhuma, Tsav 10)

מדרש תנחומא צו פרק י

אמר ר' שמעון בן גמליאל גדול הוא השלום שכתב הקב"ה דברים בתורה שלא היו, אלא בשביל השלום, אלו הן, שכשמת יעקב "ויראו אחי יוסף כי מת אביהם וגו'" (בראשית נ:טו), מה עשו הלכו אצל בלהה ואמרו לה "הכנסי אצל יוסף ואמרי לו, אביך צוה לפני מותו לאמר" (שם שם בראשית נ:טז), ומעולם לא צוה

יעקב מכל הדברים האלו כלום, אלא מעצמן אמרו דבר זה, אמר רבן שמעון
בן גמליאל ראה כמה דיו משתפך, וכמה קולמוסין משתברין, (וכמה ינוקין
מתרצעין), וכמה עורות (אבודין) עבודין, וכמה ינוקין מתרצעין, ללמד דבר
שלא היה בתורה, ראה כמה גדול כח השלום.

Our sages are willing to introduce the radical idea that the Torah
reports a conversation between Yaakov and his sons (excluding, of
course, Yosef) *which in fact never occurred*, in order to assure that
peace prevail between Yosef and his brothers after the death of
Yaakov.

It is remarkable that the sages would go so far to support their
commitment to the value of peace. Unlike the story of Avraham
and Sarah mentioned above – from which the sages infer that for
the sake of *shalom bayit* (peace in the home) one may fail to tell
the truth. However, in this instance, the sages suggest that G-d
allows an entire statement to be fabricated and recorded in the
Torah in order to ensure peace among brothers.

At the same time, they caution us: כל שלום שאין עמו תוכחה אינו
שלום / Any peace that is not accompanied by rebuke is not [true]
peace. Words of admonition may be necessary to obtain peace;
one cannot escape problems by subverting truth. However, our
sages teach that there is a distinction to be made between truth
that serves to bring peace and truth that wounds and destroys
individuals and families. The bold, uncaring reality of truth may
bring pain, and must therefore be applied carefully, if at all.

Our sages also insist that we remember the admonition of the
Torah concerning an enemy in times of war:

Rabbi Yosi HaGelili said: Great is peace, for even in a time of war
we only begin by offering peace. This is what is written, "When
you approach a town to attack it [you shall offer it terms of peace]"
(Devarim 20:10). (Midrash Vayikra Rabbah 9:9)

מדרש ויקרא רבה ט:ט
אמר ר' יוסי הגלילי: גדול השלום שאפילו בשעת מלחמה אין פותחין אלא
בשלום הה"ד "כי תקרב אל עיר וגו'" (דברים כ:י).

Not only should we seek peace by avoiding conflict, argumenta-
tion etc., but we should also pursue peace actively:

> A person should always adhere to . . . bringing peace, as it is writ-
> ten, "seek peace and pursue it" (Psalms 34:15). And Rabbi Abahu
> said: [we learn this principle] from a linguistic analogy between
> "pursuing" and "pursuing" – it is written here "seek peace and
> pursue it" (Psalms 34:15) and it is written there "he who pursues
> doing good and kind deeds attains life, success, and honor" (Mish-
> lei 21:21). (Babylonian Talmud, Yevamot 109a-b)

יבמות קט.-קט:

לעולם ידבק אדם .... בהבאת שלום דכתיב: "בקש שלום ורדפהו" (תהלים
לד:טו). ואמר רבי אבהו: אתיא רדיפה רדיפה, כתיב הכא: "בקש שלום ורדפהו"
(תהלים לד:טו), וכתיב התם: "רודף צדקה וחסד ימצא חיים צדקה וכבוד" (משלי
כא:כא).

> Rabbi [Judah the Patriarch] says: Great is peace, for even if Israel is
> worshipping idols but maintain peace among themselves, G-d says
> – so to speak – "I cannot harm them," as it is written, "Ephraim is
> addicted to images – let him be" (Hosea 4:17). However, if their
> heart is divided, what is written? "If his heart is divided, he feels
> his guilt" (Hosea 10:2). Thus we learn that peace is great and con-
> flict is despised.
>   (Midrash Bereishit Rabbah [Theodor-Albeck edition] 38:6)

מדרש בראשית רבה לח:ו

רבי אומר גדול שלום שאפילו ישראל עובדים עבודה זרה ושלום ביניהן אמר
הקב"ה כביכול איני שולט בהם שנ' "חבור עצבים אפרים הנח לו" (הושע ד:יז),
אבל אם חלוק לבם מה כת' "חלק לבם עתה יאשמו" (שם הושע י:ב) הא למדת
שגדול השלום ושנואה המחלוקת.

It seems beyond comprehension that our sages would suggest,
even as a statement of hyperbole, that G-d would rather tolerate
a community of idol-worshippers who were at peace with one
another, than a community of "pious" people who cannot get

along. The sages obviously consider *shalom* to be the quintessential value for every sphere of endeavor and for every relationship.

> Rabbi Yehoshua ben Levi said: Great is peace, for peace to the land is like leaven to dough. (Tractate Derekh Eretz Zuta, Perek haShalom)

מסכת דרך ארץ זוטא - פרק השלום
אמר רבי יהושע בן לוי הוא גדול השלום שהשלום לארץ כשאור לעיסה.

If a community – or a family – is to thrive and prosper spiritually, it must consider *Shalom* to be its compass.

Faith and Childrearing

וַיְהִי אַבְרָם בֶּן־תִּשְׁעִים שָׁנָה וְתֵשַׁע שָׁנִים וַיֵּרָא
ה' אֶל־אַבְרָם וַיֹּאמֶר אֵלָיו אֲנִי־אֵ־ל שַׁ־דַּי
הִתְהַלֵּךְ לְפָנַי וֶהְיֵה תָמִים: (בראשית יז:א)

When Abram was ninety-nine years old, the
Lord appeared to Abram and said to him, "I am
El Shaddai. Walk in My ways and be blameless."
(Bereishit 17:1)

It is written concerning Noach, "Noach walked with G-d," (Bere-ishit 6:9) whereas regarding Avraham it is written, "Walk before Me." (Bereishit 17:1) The one who reads [this] thinks that Noach is greater than Avraham, but it is not so. Rabbi Yochanan and Resh Lakish [each commented.] Rabbi Yochanan said: A parable – to what is this similar? To a king who had two sons, an older (liter-ally, "greater") one and a younger (literally, "smaller") one. The younger one would hold on to him so that he would not fall; the older one would walk ahead of him. Similarly, it is written about Noach, "Noach walked with G-d" – so that he not sink in [the negative behavior of] the generation of the flood. But to Avra-ham, who was singular in the world and who was righteous, the Holy One, blessed is He said: "walk before Me and be blameless." Resh Lakish said: A parable – to what is this similar? To a king who had a dear friend who was sinking in the mud and the king grabbed his hand and lifted him out of the mud. Similarly, Noach was sinking in the mud and the Holy One, blessed is He, saw him and gave him a hand and lifted him from the mud. And to what is Avraham similar? To a king who was walking in the darkness. His dear friend came and saw him and gave him light. The king said to him, "as long as you are providing light for me, walk before me."

119

Similarly, in the days of Avraham, the entire world was wicked and he was righteous. The Holy One, blessed is He said to him, "Since you are illuminating in the east, 'walk before Me.'"

(Midrash Tanchuma Lekh Lekha 26)

מדרש תנחומא לך לך פרק כו

כתיב בנח "את הא-להים התהלך נח" (בראשית ו:ט), וכתיב באברהם "התהלך לפני" (בראשית יז:א), מי שהוא קורא סבור שהיה נח גדול מאברהם, ואינו כן, ר' יוחנן וריש לקיש, ר' יוחנן אמר משל למה הדבר דומה, למלך שהיו לו שני בנים, אחד גדול ואחד קטן, הקטן היה אוחז בו כדי שלא יפול, והגדול היה הולך לפניו, כך כתיב בנח "את הא-להים התהלך נח", שלא ישתקע בדור המבול, אבל אברהם שהיה יחידו של עולם והיה צדיק, א"ל הקב"ה "התהלך לפני והיה תמים". אמר ריש לקיש משל למה הדבר דומה, למלך שהיה לו אוהב, והיה משוקע בטיט, ואחז בידו והעלה אותו מן הטיט, כך נח היה משוקע בטיט, ראהו הקב"ה נתן לו יד והעלהו מן הטיט, ואברהם למה היה דומה, למלך שהיה מהלך בחשיכה, בא אוהבו וראה אותו והאיר לו, א"ל המלך עד שאתה מאיר לי, בא והלך לפני, כך [בימי] אברהם היו כל העולם רשעים והוא צדיק, א"ל הקב"ה עד שאתה מאיר במזרח התהלך לפני.

This midrash teaches that G-d "walked with Noach," i.e., that Noach needed a direct support system. Noach was in the "mud" of his immoral and uncivilized generation, and it was necessary for G-d to guard him, hold his hand as it were, and extricate him from the filth of his society. Hence the Torah says that G-d walked *with* Noach. Conversely, Avraham was a shining light to the world, and to him G-d said, "walk *in front of* Me."

By saying "walk in front of Me," G-d said to Avraham in effect: "No need to walk with Me as did Noach. You are capable of walking in front of Me;" i.e., you can walk on your own, your faith gives you the strength and indeed challenges you to manifest your faith in a more dynamic and profound way. "You will be a light unto the nations as you demonstrate your faith."

Noach accepted G-d's judgment to bring a flood upon the earth without a word of protest or a plea for G-d to reconsider, while Avraham protested and pleaded with G-d regarding the fate of S'dom. Avraham challenged G-d, and G-d wants to be challenged. In Judaism, G-d is viewed as waiting for humans to plead, challenge, and even argue. This is what Judaism expects of a person of faith, to have a serious, dynamic personal relationship with G-d. "Walk before Me," says G-d – not passively, but actively.

This concept also has implications for child-raising practices, if we consider ourselves to be walking alongside our children in a difficult world. The Talmud teaches that in addition to academic subjects, parents must include a pragmatic education in the rearing of children. Parents must teach their child a profession, Torah, Mitzvot, Ethics, general knowledge, and some say, how to swim. All of these are vital practical and functional skills which illustrate the emphasis of practical education required to be provided by the parent. "Swimming" may be understood in the broader sense of taking care of yourself under all conditions. "Profession" how to earn a living, teaching the skills needed (or providing the means by which skills may be acquired) to physically (i.e. financially) provide for a future family.

"Torah, Mitzvot, Ethics and general knowledge" to instruct the child how to communicate effectively and become contributing members of society. A child needs to be taught responsibility for both self and society. This is Judaism's approach to "child-rearing."

Covenants

זֹאת בְּרִיתִי אֲשֶׁר תִּשְׁמְרוּ בֵּינִי וּבֵינֵיכֶם וּבֵין
זַרְעֲךָ אַחֲרֶיךָ הִמּוֹל לָכֶם כָּל־זָכָר: (בראשית יז:י)

*Such shall be the covenant between Me and you
and your offspring to follow which you shall
keep; every male among you shall be circumcised.*

(Bereishit 17:10)

Great is circumcision, for it is one of the three covenants that the
Holy One, blessed is He established between Himself and His
creations. They are: the rainbow, circumcision, and the Sabbath.

(Midrash HaGadol, Bereishit 17:10)

מדרש הגדול. בראשית יז:י
גדולה מילה שהיא אחד משלש בריתות שנתן הקב"ה בינו ובין בריותיו ואלו הן:
הקשת והמילה והשבת.

We have three distinct covenants with G-d. One is universal: All
humans have been entered into the covenant with G-d that there
will never again be a flood upon the entire earth. That covenant,
made with Noach and his family who were the only survivors of
the flood, applies to all of humankind.[1]

The second covenant, ברית מילה/the covenant of circumcision,
was made with Avraham and his male descendants, and applies to
Jewish males exclusively. The third covenant is the covenant of
Shabbat. It is a covenant between G-d and the People of Israel.

It is interesting to note that a male child must live through

---

1. Of course, this does not preclude the tragic ability of individuals or
nations to unleash mass destruction upon humankind. That is the price
we pay for the freedom of choice inherent in being human.

a Shabbat before entering the covenant of circumcision, as the Midrash observes:

> For there is no seven-day period without a Sabbath, and there is not circumcision without [the boy having already lived through] a Sabbath. (Midrash Vayikra Rabbah 27:10; Midrash Tanchuma, Emor 17)

מדרש ויקרא רבה כז:י, מדרש תנחומא אמור פרק יז
שאין שבעה בלא שבת, ואין מילה בלא שבת.

Thus the ברית של שבת/"the covenant of Shabbat", which applies to both men and women, must first be experienced by the baby boy before he is entered into the brit milah. First the *brit* of K'lal Yisrael, within the totality of the Jewish community, manifested through the covenant of Shabbat, then the particular brit of the males. As the Torah suggests, Shabbat is the אות/"sign" of the covenant between G-d and the People of Israel:

> It (Shabbat) shall be a sign for all time between Me and the People of Israel. (Shemot 31:17)

שמות לא:יז
ביני ובין בני ישראל אות הוא לעלם.

Taking Leave

וַיְכַל לְדַבֵּר אִתּוֹ וַיַּעַל ה' מֵעַל אַבְרָהָם:
(בראשית יז:כב)

And when He was done speaking with him, G-d was gone from Avraham. (Bereishit 17:22)

It is taught: The one who departs from his friend – whether of greater or lesser importance – must ask permission from them. From whom do you learn this? From Avraham. Once Avraham was speaking with the Holy One, blessed is He and the angels who serve [G-d] came to speak with him. [Avraham] said to them, "Let me first take leave of the Divine Presence which is greater than you and then I will speak with you." Once he finished speaking with the Holy One, blessed is He, he said before Him, "Master of the Universe, I must [attend to another] matter." He replied, "depart in peace." This is what is written, "And G-d was gone from Avraham" (Bereishit 17:22).   (Midrash Bereishit Rabbah 47:6)

מדרש בראשית רבה מז:ו
תני הנפטר מחבירו בין גדול בין קטן צריך ליטול ממנו רשות, ממי את למד
מאברהם פעם אחת היה אברהם מדבר עם הקב"ה באו מלאכי השרת לדבר
עמו, אמר להן נפטר מן השכינה שהיא גדולה מכם תחלה אח"כ אני מדבר
עמכם, כיון שדבר עם הקב"ה כל צרכו, אמר לפניו רבון העולמים צריך אני
לדבר, א"ל הפטר בשלום, הה"ד "ויעל א-לוהים מעל אברהם" (בראשית יז:כב).

This midrash endeavors to teach "good manners." One does not simply end a conversation and walk away because one's business is done, or because someone else has appeared. This is a wonderful lesson in דרך ארץ (*derech eretz*), the manner in which an ethical person behaves.

Avraham turns to his angelic visitors (who have appeared as

humans), and advises them that he must first "take leave of the Shechinah" – i.e., the Divine Presence – and only then will he address them. Thus our sages teach that when we need to end or interrupt a conversation (or put someone "on hold"), we must ask permission and not do so abruptly.

The term *derech eretz* (lit. the way of the land) is used to suggest an ethical standard of behavior towards other people. *Derech eretz* is about respect: For example, you are not to call your parents by their first names, and you are not to sit in the chair customarily used by your parent or teacher or sitting at the head of the table. These are the methods through which respect for "special people" is ingrained in the thought process of a child.

Obviously, this sensitivity has been largely forgotten in our society, leading to a diminished quality of interpersonal relationships. The prevalent use of foul language in our society, for example, stems from a lack of respect.

There are numerous rabbinic texts which establish criteria for ethical behavior in interpersonal relationships. We may call it "good manners," but the Rabbis believed it to be a critical dimension of one's conduct as a committed Jew. Two illustrations from Talmud:

Do not enter your house suddenly, all the more so someone else's house. (Babylonian Talmud Pesachim 112a)

פסחים קיב.
אל תכנס לביתך פתאום, כל שכן לבית חבירך.

You may not enter your home suddenly, and all the more so the home of your friend; i.e., knock before you enter a room, and/or declare your presence verbally.

The Torah taught proper etiquette that a person should not speak to someone else unless he has [first] addressed him (literally, "called him"). (Babylonian Talmud Yoma 4b)

יומא ד:
לימדה תורה דרך ארץ, שלא יאמר אדם דבר לחבירו אלא אם כן קורהו.

When you wish to speak to someone, begin the conversation by addressing the individual by name – thus recognizing them with respect. A courteous hello, to a store clerk, demonstrates a Jew's *derech eretz* (respect). This is a religious obligation by Torah standards, not simply "good manners."

Emulating G-d

וַיֵּרָא אֵלָיו ה' בְּאֵלֹנֵי מַמְרֵא וְהוּא יֹשֵׁב פֶּתַח-
הָאֹהֶל כְּחֹם הַיּוֹם: (בראשית יח:א)

*The Lord appeared to him by the terebinths of
Mamre; he was sitting at the entrance of the tent
as the day grew hot.* (Bereishit 18:1)

And Rabbi Chama son of Rabbi Chanina said: Why is it written
"Follow after the Lord your G-d" (Devarim 13:5)? And is it possi-
ble for a person to follow the Divine Presence? Does it not already
state "For the Lord your G-d is a consuming fire" (Devarim 4:24)
? Rather, [it means] follow [i.e. emulate] the ways of the Holy
One, blessed is He: Just as He clothes the naked, as it is written,
"And the Lord G-d made skins for Adam and his wife, and clothed
them" (Bereishit 3:21), so you should clothe the naked. The Holy
One, blessed is He visited the sick, as it is written, "The Lord
appeared to him by the terebinths of Mamre" (Bereishit 18:1), so
you should visit the sick.   (Babylonian Talmud Sotah 14a)

סוטה יד.

ואמר רבי חמא ברבי חנינא, מאי דכתיב: (דברים יג:ה) "אחרי ה' א-להיכם
תלכו"? וכי אפשר לו לאדם להלך אחר שכינה? והלא כבר נאמר: (דברים ד:כד)
"כי ה' א-להיך אש אוכלה הוא" אלא להלך אחר מדותיו של הקב"ה, מה הוא
מלביש ערומים, דכתיב: (בראשית ג:כא) "ויעש ה' א-לוהים לאדם ולאשתו כתנות
עור וילבישם", אף אתה הלבש ערומים הקב"ה ביקר חולים וכו' דכתיב "וירא
אליו ה' באלוני ממרא" (בראשית יח:א), אף אתה בקר חולים.

We are G-d-like when we emulate G-d's attributes. The Talmud
teaches that G-d visited Avraham while he was recuperating from
his ברית מילה/circumcision, and the sages understand the text
אחרי ה' א-להיכם תלכו/"Hashem your G-d you should follow"

(Devarim 13:5) to be saying that walking in the path of G-d means to emulate G-d's deeds. "Imitatio Dei" – כמו הוא אף אתה – "to imitate G-d," is a foundation of our relationship with G-d and the foundation of our system of values. As we read the "thirteen attributes of G-d" (gracious, compassionate, etc.) we are challenged to emulate G-d in our own actions, בין אדם לחברו, with one another.

On the subject of בקור חולים / visiting the sick, we find a fascinating observation in the Talmud:

> Rabbi Acha bar Chaninah said: Whoever visits a sick person takes away one sixtieth of his pain. (Babylonian Talmud Nedarim 39b)

נדרים לט:

אמר רבי אחא בר חנינא: כל המבקר חולה נוטל אחד מששים בצערו.

Visiting someone who is ill "removes one sixtieth of the illness." The Talmud goes on to explore this intriguing notion at length, but here we can view the issue in a very practical manner: Illness diminishes one's sense of self-worth and self-esteem. The patient is often depressed, helpless, and overwhelmed even to the point of despair. A concerned, empathic visitor offers hope and faith, thereby restoring to the patient at least a bit (i.e., "one sixtieth") of their sense of self-worth. Modern medicine teaches that "attitude" affects the recuperative process.

Welcoming Guests

וַיֹּאמַר אֲדֹנָי אִם־נָא מָצָאתִי חֵן בְּעֵינֶיךָ אַל־נָא
תַעֲבֹר מֵעַל עַבְדֶּךָ: (בראשית יח:ג)

*He said, "My lords, if it please you, do not go on
past your servant." (Bereishit 18:3)*

Rav Yehudah said in the name of Rav: Greater is welcoming guests
than greeting the Divine Presence, as it is written, "And he said,
Lord, if it pleases you, do not depart . . ." (Bereishit 18:3). Rabbi
Elazar said: Come and see – G-d's ways are not like the ways of
flesh and blood. The way of flesh and blood is that someone of
lesser importance cannot say to someone of greater importance,
"wait until I come to you." But regarding the Holy One, blessed
is He, it is written, "And he said, Lord, if it pleases you [do not
depart]."   (Babylonian Talmud Shabbat 127a)

שבת קכז.

אמר רב יהודה אמר רב: גדולה הכנסת אורחין מהקבלת פני שכינה, דכתיב
"ויאמר אם נא מצאתי חן בעיניך אל נא תעבר וגו'" (בראשית יח:ג). אמר רבי
אלעזר: בא וראה, שלא כמדת הקדוש ברוך הוא מדת בשר ודם: מדת בשר
ודם אין קטן יכול לומר לגדול המתן עד שאבא אצלך, ואילו בהקדוש ברוך הוא
כתיב "ויאמר אם נא מצאתי וגו'."

The Talmud teaches that the welcoming of guests (here meant
as strangers who are wayfarers with no place to eat and sleep)
is a spiritual experience which transcends that of welcoming the
Shechinah, i.e., G-d's presence. Indeed, the text in the Talmud
states this comparison explicitly in its opening line.

While the sages sought to endow the mitzvah of הכנסת
אורחים/"hospitality" with the highest spiritual significance, they

also taught practical rules of behavior. For example, although it was an obligation of every member of the community to welcome guests, nonetheless the citizens of Jerusalem had a clear and well-known method by which they advised wayfarers, which family was or was not in a position to accept them. The Talmud states:

> There was another great custom in Jerusalem: A cloth was spread over the door. While the cloth was spread, guests would enter. When the cloth was removed, guests would not enter. (Babylonian Talmud Bava Batra 93b)

בבא בתרא צג:

עוד מנהג גדול היה בירושלים, מפה פרוסה על גבי הפתח כל זמן שמפה פרוסה – אורחין נכנסין, נסתלקה המפה – אין האורחין נכנסין.

Thus, neither homeowner nor wayfarer need be embarrassed. The imperative to take in guests was not diminished, but the homeowner had the moral right to declare that he was in no position to play host. Enlightened self interest is a principle established in rabbinic Judaism.[1]

Moreover, the sages established codes of behavior for guests to follow while at the table of their hosts. A fascinating example may be found in the Talmud:

> And guests are not permitted to take what has been given to them and give it to the host's son or daughter unless they have asked the host's permission. (Babylonian Talmud Chullin 94a)

חולין צד.

ואין האורחין רשאין ליתן ממה שלפניהם לבנו ולבתו של בעל הבית אלא אם כן נטלו רשות מבעל הבית.

---

1. אדם קרוב אצל עצמו, literally translated as "a person is ultimately closest to himself,"(Babylonian Talmud Yevamot 25b) is a profound principle of Judaism. The common idea that "one must sacrifice oneself for another person" is not evident in Jewish ethical philosophy. Each individual has the obligation to provide for oneself and those closest, before providing for others.

The guests may give of their food to the children of the host only with the permission of the host. The menu itself may become an issue as the host considers the expense of feeding guests. Another midrash teaches that one may begin with an elegant offering (i.e., chicken) in the first meal, and gradually shift to offering beans:

> A person who receives a guest feeds him fowl on the first day, meat on the second day, until he is feeding him beans.
> (Midrash Bamidbar Rabbah – Pinchas)

מדרש במדבר רבה סוף פרשת פנחם

אדם שיקבל אורח ביום ראשון מאכילו עופות בשני בשר עד שמאכילו קטניות.

This midrash may be suggesting either a weaning process (such that the guest does not come to expect lavish treatment at every meal), or a reduced economic obligation on the part of the host. Again, the host has the right to protect his financial well-being under the rubric אדם קרוב אצל עצמו/ "a person is closest to him/her self."

The moral obligation imposed upon the individual by the To-rah is based once again on the pragmatic principle of moral en-lightened self-interest. We have an obligation to feed the hungry, yet the Torah does not impose upon us the obligation to feed our guests beyond our means. Feed? – yes. Wine and dine? – only commensurate with our financial ability.

Another midrash offers a fascinating glimpse of a social gather-ing of scholars, and provides another lesson on hospitality:

> R. Eliezer, R. Joshua, and R. Zadok were reclining at a meal at Rabban Gamliel's son's wedding. Rabban Gamliel poured a cup of wine for R. Eliezer, who did not want to accept it. R. Joshua did accept it. R. Eliezer said to [R. Joshua], "How can this be, Joshua, that we are sitting, and Rabban Gamliel is standing and serving?" R. Joshua replied, "Leave him be, and let him serve. Avraham, the greatest man in the world, served the angels thinking that they were Arabs who worship idols, as it is written, 'Looking up, he saw.' (Bereishit 18:2) Can we not argue a fortiori – if Avraham, the

greatest man in the world served angels while thinking that they were Arabs who worship idols, should Rabban Gamliel the son of Rabbi [Judah the Patriarch] not serve us?" (Sifrei, Ekev 38)

ספרי עקב לח

וכבר היה ר' אליעזר ור' יהושע ור' צדוק מסובים בבית משתה בנו של רבן גמליאל מזג רבן גמליאל כום לרבי אליעזר ולא רצה לקבל קיבלו ר' יהושע אמר לו ר' אליעזר מה זה יהושע שאנו מסובים ורבן גמליאל עומד ומשמש אמר לו ר' יהושע הנח לו וישמש. אברהם גדול העולם שימש מלאכי השרת וכסבור שהם ערביים עובדי ע"ז שנאמר "וישא עיניו וירא" (בראשית יח:ב) והלא דברים ק"ו אברהם גדול העולם שימש למלאכי השרת וכסבור שהם ערביים עובדי ע"ז רבן גמליאל ברבי לא ישמשנו.

This midrash introduces an interesting lesson in *derech eretz* (respect). Rabban Gamliel reasons: If the patriarch Avraham rose to serve and feed a group of unknown, pagan travelers (not knowing they were angelic messengers), should I not pour a cup of wine for Rabbi Eliezer?

The lesson is clear and effective. Avraham was renowned for his personal attention to travelers, hence the lesson that the mitzvah of hospitality requires the personal involvement of the host. The task of making a guest feel welcome is not to be left to servants.

Acts of Loving Kindness

כִּי יְדַעְתִּיו לְמַעַן אֲשֶׁר יְצַוֶּה אֶת־בָּנָיו וְאֶת־
בֵּיתוֹ אַחֲרָיו וְשָׁמְרוּ דֶּרֶךְ ה' לַעֲשׂוֹת צְדָקָה
וּמִשְׁפָּט לְמַעַן הָבִיא ה' עַל־אַבְרָהָם אֵת אֲשֶׁר־
דִּבֶּר עָלָיו: (בראשית יח:יט)

For I have singled him out, that he may instruct
his children and his posterity to keep the way of
the Lord by doing what is just and right, in order
that the Lord may bring about for Avraham what
He had promised. (Bereishit 18:19)

"The way of the Lord" (Bereishit 18:19) – this refers to acts of
kindness, Tsedakah (ibid.) – this is to be understood literally as
charity, and "justice" (ibid.) – these are laws. Based on this source
they stated: Acts of kindness are greater than charity, and charity
is greater than law.   (Midrash HaGadol)

מדרש הגדול

"דרך ה'" (בראשית יח:יט) זו גמילת חסדים, "צדקה" (שם) כמשמעה, "ומשפט"
(שם) אלו הדינים מכאן אמרו גמילת חסדים גדולה מן הצדקה וצדקה גדולה
מן הדין.

This midrash teaches that while *tsedakah* (charity) is greater in
moral significance than the implementation of the law, גמילת
חסדים/"acts of loving-kindness" transcend them both. Thus an
act of loving-kindness which does not necessitate economic or
material sacrifice, but rather involves giving of oneself to assist
another (from whom you may derive no economic benefit), is of
the highest moral virtue and significance.

The midrash seeks to establish an ultimate standard for interpersonal relationships:

First, דין/ Law. A society must be guided by a legal system which protects its citizens and establishes rules by which those citizens may live without encroaching upon the rights, property, and freedom of the "other." This system of law is narrow, unyielding, and applies equally to all.

Then the Torah introduces the concept of *tsedakah*, which demands an involvement of the individual with the needs and aspirations of the "other." To give of one's possessions is of a higher level of morality than merely complying with the legal system, for it requires one to take that which is legitimately owned and give it to another without hope of return.

An act of loving-kindness, however, is an even more complicated gift, for it demands neither simple adherence to the law nor the straight-forward giving of one's possessions to another. *Gemilut chasadim* demands of us that we be truly *involved* in the life of another human being, the person ceasing to be "other." When I lend someone money (interest free), for example, I become involved. When I do an act of loving-kindness I become involved with the other's life and struggles. Thus our sages teach that *gemilut chasadim* transcends both adherence to the law and the direct act of *tsedakah*.

There are many statements by our sages which focus upon the significance of *gemilut chasadim*, for example:

> Acts of kindness are greater than charity in three ways: Charity is done [only] with one's money, whereas acts of kindness are done both with one's body and with one's money. Charity is done for the poor, whereas acts of kindness are done both for the poor and for the wealthy. Charity is done for the living, whereas acts of kindness are done both for the living and for the dead.
>
> (Babylonian Talmud Sukkah, 49b)

סוכה מט:

בשלשה דברים גדולה גמילות חסדים יותר מן הצדקה, צדקה בממונו, גמילות חסדים בין בגופו בין בממונו. צדקה לעניים, גמילות חסדים בין לעניים בין לעשירים. צדקה לחיים, גמילות חסדים בין לחיים בין למתים.

And then there is this fascinating remark in the midrash:

Great are acts of kindness, because if not for them, humanity would not have been created. (Midrash Bereishit Rabbah 8:8)

מדרש בראשית רבה ח:ח
גדולה גמילות חסדים שאלמלא היא לא היה האדם נברא.

It seems that our sages wanted us to understand that a world which relies solely on law (a stark, black-and-white structure) or solely on charity (where the have-nots are always dependent on the haves) will not long endure because it is harsh, cold and demeaning.

The *gemilut chasadim* classically associated with "interest free loans" or other acts of interpersonal giving and involvement is the essence of a caring, giving, and thus a truly just society. Moreover, *gemilut chasadim* transcends all levels of society: economic, age, gender, and intelligence. All of us, in essence, are on some level "in need." The wealthy individual may need a friend or teacher, the powerful person may need an objective counselor or guide; all are in need of that which ultimately cannot be purchased or measured in gold.

Judging Others

אֵרֲדָה־נָּא וְאֶרְאֶה הַכְּצַעֲקָתָהּ הַבָּאָה אֵלַי עָשׂוּ
כָּלָה וְאִם־לֹא אֵדָעָה: (בראשית יח:כא)

I will go down to see whether they have acted altogether according to the outcry that has reached Me; if not I will take note. (Bereishit 18:21)

From this [source] they said: Do not judge your fellow until you reach his place.   (Midrash HaBe'ur, and see Mishnah Avot 2:5)

מדרש הבאור, וגם אבות ב:ה
מכאן אמרו אל תדין את חברך עד שתגיע למקומו.

Here, our sages focus upon G-d's willingness to "come down" to judge the situation up close rather than from a heavenly distance. The venue of the events is the only environment from which a proper reading of the situation may be gained.

Rashi compares the situation to the generation which built the "tower":

To teach judges not to render a verdict in capital cases without seeing, as I explained in the section of the dispersion (Bereishit 11:5). Another interpretation: "I will descend" (Bereishit 18:21) – to comprehend their eventual actions.   (Rashi to Bereishit 18:21)

רש"י בראשית יח:כא
למד לדיינים שלא יפסקו דיני נפשות אלא בראיה, הכל כמו שפרשתי בפרשת
הפלגה. דבר אחר, "ארדה נא" (בראשית יח:כא) – לסוף מעשיהם:

The significance and sanctity with which our sages endowed the process of judgment is an indication of the centrality of justice in Jewish law and society. For example, the Rabbis say:

Anyone who appoints a judge over the community who is not fit
– it is as if he plants an *ashera* (a tree used for idolatrous practice)
within [the People of] Israel. (Babylonian Talmud Sanhedrin 7b)

סנהדרין ז:
כל המעמיד דיין על הציבור שאינו הגון – כאילו נוטע אשירה בישראל.

The Rabbis equate the appointment of an unqualified judge with
the planting of an idol (*ashera*) in the community. Justice and its
implementation were to the Rabbis a central aspect of the community, equal, it seems, to faith in G-d. Elsewhere it is written:

"In the days of the judges' judging" (Ruth 1:1) – woe to the generation which judged its judges, and woe to the generation whose
judges must be judged. (Midrash Ruth Rabbah 1:1)

מדרש רבה רות א:א
"ויהי בימי שפוט השופטים" (רות א:א) אוי לדור ששפטו את שופטיהם ואוי לדור
ששופטיו צריכין להשפט.

In other words, woe unto a generation with a corrupt judicial
system.

The sages were equally concerned with how we judge one another in our daily interactions:

And do not judge someone else until you are in his position.
(Mishnah Avot 2:5)

משנה אבות ב:ה
ואל תדין את חברך עד שתגיע למקומו.

We may not judge another person in our familial, professional, or
social interactions unless we have been in their situation and fared
better. Judging in this case refers not to strictly judicial matters,
but to the constant – at times seemingly automatic – judgments
which arise in our minds in response to the words and actions of
others. The Rabbis caution us: Do not, in haste or in anger or in
ignorance, judge the other person until you have been in a similar
situation and have fared better.

Yet another principle of rabbinic Judaism concerning "judging" seems to be a precursor to an American legal principle:

And Rabbi Yitzchak said: We only judge a person according to his actions at the time, as it says, "for G-d has heeded the cry of the boy where he is" (Bereishit 21:17).
(Babylonian Talmud Rosh Hashanah 16b)

ראש השנה טז:
ואמר רבי יצחק: אין דנין את האדם אלא לפי מעשיו של אותה שעה, שנאמר
"כי שמע א-לוהים אל קול הנער באשר הוא שם" (בראשית כא:יז).

Here it is insisted that an individual may not be judged except on evidence, testimony, or observation concerning an event in the exact time, circumstance, and place in which the action occurred.

The Rabbis were concerned with justice even in matters which had minimal implications. They insisted that it was not so much the amount of loss as the issue of justice; i.e., the law is to be implemented. Thus this comment:

A case involving [only] a *perutah* (penny) is equivalent to a case involving one hundred *maneh* (gold or silver coins of a certain weight). (Babylonian Talmud Sanhedrin 8a)

סנהדרין ח.
דין של פרוטה, כדין של מאה מנה.

The law of a *peruta* (a penny) is as significant as the law of one hundred. The Talmud states:

A Jew and a non Jew who come to be judged (in a legal dispute) – if you (the judge) can judge in favor of the non Jew according to Jewish law then do so, and say to him "this is our law." If however you can rule in his favor according to the law for the gentiles then do so and say to him "this is according to your law." Rabbi Akiva says, "Do not try to evade or circumvent the law because you must act in a manner to sanctify the name of Hashem." (Babylonian Talmud Bava Kamma 113a)

בבא קמא קיג.

ישראל וגוי שבאו לדין, אם אתה יכול לזכהו בדיני ישראל זכהו, ואומר לו כך
דיננו, בדיני גוים זכהו ואומר לו אין עליו בעקיפין מפני קידוש השם.

The classic treacherous stereotype of the Jew as depicted by
Shakespeare and his anti-semitic disciples is the very antithe-
sis of this historic talmudic admonition. The sensitivity of this
judgment of Rabbi Akiva manifests in clear terms the demands of
Jewish ethical and legal norms.

Interrupting

וַיֹּאמֶר ה' אִם־אֶמְצָא בִסְדֹם חֲמִשִּׁים צַדִּיקִם
בְּתוֹךְ הָעִיר וְנָשָׂאתִי לְכָל־הַמָּקוֹם בַּעֲבוּרָם:
(בראשית יח:כו)

*And the Lord answered, "If I find within the city
of Sodom, fifty innocent ones, I will forgive the
whole place for their sake."* (Bereishit 18:26)

"And does not interrupt someone else" . . . Similarly, in the case
of Avraham our Father, when he was praying on behalf of the
people of S'dom, the Holy One, blessed is He said to him, "If
I find within the city of S'dom fifty innocent ones, I will forgive
the whole place for their sake." It was known and revealed before
the Holy One, blessed is He that if there had been three or five
righteous people in S'dom, sin would not have caused it, but the
Holy One, blessed is He waited for Avraham to finish speaking,
and only then replied, as it says, "When the Lord had finished
speaking to Avraham, He departed" (Bereishit 18:33).

(Avot D'Rabbi Natan, 37)

אבות דרבי נתן לז

"ואינו נכנס לתוך דברי חבירו וכו'" – כיוצא בו באברהם אבינו כשהיה מתפלל
על אנשי סדום אמר לו הקב"ה אם אמצא בסדום חמשים צדיקים ונשאתי לכל
המקום בעבורם גלוי וידוע לפני מי שאמר והיה עולם שאילו היו מצויין בסדום ג'
או ה' צדיקים לא גרם בה עון אלא המתין הקב"ה את אברהם עד שסיים דבריו
ואח"כ השיבו שנאמר "וילך ה' כאשר כלה" (בראשית יח:לג).

What is the proper way to engage in dialogue with another person who might be your peer, even your subordinate? In this text,
we read of the dialogue between Avraham and G-d. The question
is asked rhetorically: Didn't G-d know, even before Avraham be-

gan speaking, that S'dom was bereft of any moral beings? Why did G-d wait until Avraham delivered his entire speech before announcing that S'dom had no righteous people and therefore was to be destroyed? According to this teaching, the message G-d wants to deliver, for all time, is: Do not interrupt another person while they are speaking. In other words, if G-d would not interrupt a human being, how much more so should *we* not interrupt one another?

Prophecy

וַיֹּאמֶר אֱלֹהִים אֶל־אַבְרָהָם אַל־יֵרַע בְּעֵינֶיךָ
עַל־הַנַּעַר וְעַל־אֲמָתֶךָ כֹּל אֲשֶׁר תֹּאמַר אֵלֶיךָ
שָׂרָה שְׁמַע בְּקֹלָהּ כִּי בְיִצְחָק יִקָּרֵא לְךָ זָרַע:
(בראשית כא:יב)

But G-d said to Avraham, "Do not be distressed
over the boy or your slave; whatever Sarah tells
you, do as she says, for it is through Yitzchak
that offspring shall be continued for you."
(Bereishit 21:12)

From here [ie. this verse] we learn that Avraham was of secondary
importance with respect to Sarah in prophecy.
(Midrash Shemot Rabbah 1:1)

מדרש שמות רבה א:א
מכאן אתה למד שהיה אברהם טפל לשרה בנביאות.

Our sages wish to bestow a special status upon Sarah. While
Avraham may have been in a continuous dialogue with G-d, thus
manifesting a high degree of *nevuah*/prophecy, nonetheless the
sages judge Sarah to have had a higher degree of prophecy than
Avraham.

It is interesting to note that the sages believed that prophecy
assumed other forms after the end of the formal period of the
Nevi'im/prophets:

From the day that the Temple was destroyed, prophecy was taken
from the prophets and given to the sages. But is the sage not inherently a prophet (and therefore also in possession of prophecy
before the Temple was destroyed)? Rather, this is the statement:

Even though it was taken from the prophets, it was not taken from the sages. Ameimar said: And a sage is better than a prophet. (Babylonian Talmud Bava Batra 12a)

בבא בתרא יב.

מיום שחרב בית המקדש, ניטלה נבואה מן הנביאים וניתנה לחכמים. אטו חכם לאו נביא הוא? הכי קאמר: אע"פ שניטלה מן הנביאים, מן החכמים לא ניטלה. אמר אמימר: וחכם עדיף מנביא.

Our sages wanted to assure that *K'lal Yisrael* / the Jewish people would continue to have guidance and a sense of connection with G-d. As we view Jewish history, we certainly note the central and critical role of the *gedolim* / sages in each generation and in each community. What is fascinating is the universal similarity of the leadership role of the "great ones" of each generation. Whether it be the *Ga'on*[1] or the *Tsaddik*[2] or the *Chacham*,[3] the community as well as the individual always turn to these extraordinary individuals for guidance and comfort.

---

1. *Ga'on* or genius – a title which in ancient times represented both great knowledge and a position of leadership. In more recent times, it is a title reserved for individuals of extraordinary Torah knowledge and piety.
2. *Tsaddik* – a term most often used to describe great Chasidic leaders, although it applies and is indeed used to describe anyone of extraordinary piety.
3. *Chacham* – the term means a person of great wisdom, and is also used in the Sefardic community to refer to a rabbinic leader who is much admired and whose judgment and counsel is of supreme importance.

Judging

וַיִּשְׁמַע אֱ־לֹהִים אֶת־קוֹל הַנַּעַר וַיִּקְרָא מַלְאַךְ
אֱ־לֹהִים | אֶל־הָגָר מִן־הַשָּׁמַיִם וַיֹּאמֶר לָהּ מַה־
לָּךְ הָגָר אַל־תִּירְאִי כִּי־שָׁמַע אֱ־לֹהִים אֶל־קוֹל
הַנַּעַר בַּאֲשֶׁר הוּא־שָׁם: (בראשית כא:יז)

G-d heard the cry of the boy, and an angel of
G-d called to Hagar from heaven and said to
her, "What troubles you, Hagar? Fear not, for
G-d has heeded the cry of the boy where he is."
(Bereishit 21:17)

And Rabbi Yitzchak said: We only judge a person according to his
actions at that moment, as it says, "for G-d has heeded the cry of
the boy where he is" (Bereishit 21:17).
(Babylonian Talmud Rosh Hashanah 16b)

ראש השנה טז:

ואמר רבי יצחק: אין דנין את האדם אלא לפי מעשיו של אותה שעה, שנאמר
"כי שמע א־לוהים אל קול הנער באשר הוא שם" (בראשית כא:יז).

While our sages here discuss the concept of judging a person in
the present moment, it is possible to understand their statement
within the broader context of the past as well as the future.

On the one hand, each individual is allowed the privilege and
opportunity to change, which might indeed be either for good or
for evil, and thus the past may not play a significant role in judgment. From this perspective, the present is all that matters – thus
the instruction of our sages to "judge the person as he is now."

However, when one confronts an individual as he carries out
a given act, be it good or evil, we may be compelled to ask: Who
is he? What has he done in the past? Can we really judge him

in a vacuum of the present, i.e., without knowing what his past actions have been? Perhaps our sages in this instance are trying to be *dan l'kaf zechut* – trying to "judge him generously" – and thus conclude with a kindly verdict. Perhaps, then, the lesson ought to be: When judging another, endeavor to find whatever data you may have available to render a judgment which is generous and forgiving.

A perfect illustration of this approach to judging others is found in the Midrash:

> Rabbi Simon said: The angels jumped in to argue against [Ishmael]. They said before Him, "Master of the universe: The man who in the future will kill Your children by thirst, for him You will fill up the well?" He said to them, "Now what is he, righteous or wicked?" They said to Him, "Righteous." He said to them, "I only judge a person [as he is] at the time."
>
> (Midrash Bereishit Rabbah 53:14)

מדרש בראשית רבה נג:יד
אמר רבי סימון קפצו מלאכי השרת לקטרגו, אמרו לפניו רבון העולמים אדם שהוא עתיד להמית את בניך בצמא אתה מעלה לו באר, אמר להם עכשיו מה הוא, צדיק או רשע, אמרו לו צדיק, אמר להם איני דן את האדם אלא בשעתו.

This midrash teaches us that G-d was not concerned with the future generations of Ishmael and what they might do to the People of Israel. G-d's concern was with judging Ishmael in the present only.

Oath-taking

וַיֹּאמֶר אַבְרָהָם אָנֹכִי אִשָּׁבֵעַ: (בראשית כא:כד)

And Avraham said, "I swear it." (Bereishit 21:24)

It should have said "And Avraham swore." Rather, [it was formulated this way] to teach you that as soon as a person accepts upon
himself to take an oath, it is as if he already took the oath, even if
he has not yet actually taken an oath. And from this [we learn] that
Israel's words are like an oath.   (Midrash ha-Beur)

מדרש הבאור

היה לו לומר וישבע אברהם אלא ללמדך שכיון שקיבל אדם על עצמו להשבע
נעשה כאילו נשבע, ואף על פי שלא נשבע, ומכאן שישראל דבריהם כשבועה.

From here you learn that anyone who accepts upon himself to
take an oath, it is as if he has taken the oath. (Midrash HaGadol)

מדרש הגדול

מכאן אתה למד שכל המקבל על עצמו להשבע מעלין עליו כאלו נשבע.

Both these Midrashim make the point that for a Jew, the very
commitment to taking an oath is considered as serious as the actual taking of the oath (i.e., it is כאילו/as if the oath were actually
taken). The legal implications of oath-taking are awesome, thus
even a statement of intent has moral implications. Words have
power, and we should always choose our words with care.

Truth-telling

וְהוֹכַח אַבְרָהָם אֶת אֲבִימֶלֶךְ עַל אֹדוֹת בְּאֵר
הַמַּיִם אֲשֶׁר גָּזְלוּ עַבְדֵי אֲבִימֶלֶךְ:
(בראשית כא:כה)

*Then Avraham reproached Abimelech for the
well of water which the servants of Abimelech
had seized. (Bereishit 21:25)*

"Then Avraham rebuked Abimelech" (Bereishit 21:25). Rebuke
leads to peace. Thus you find with Avraham as it says, "Then
Avraham rebuked Abimelech" (ibid.). And what does it [then] say?
"And the two of them made a pact" (Bereishit 21:27).

(Sifrei Devarim 2)

ספרי דברים ב

"והוכיח אברהם את אבימלך וכו'" (בראשית כא:כה). התוכחה מביאה לידי שלום
וכן אתה מוצא באברהם שנאמר "והוכיח אברהם את אבימלך על אודות וגו'"
(שם) ומהו אומר? "ויכרתו ברית שניהם" (שם כא:כז).

Peace can only be achieved when there is a willingness to confront one another with words of truth, though they be painful.
The Torah tells us והוכיח אברהם/"then Avraham reproached Avimelech," and we are taught that Avraham told Avimelech that the
theft committed by his servants was a hindrance to their relationship. Obviously, Avraham was not hindered in his confrontation,
though Avimelech was a king.

It was only when Avimelech acknowledged to Avraham his ignorance of the theft that a covenant could be concluded.

It is important to remember that "the whole truth" is not
always the formula to peace, as in the previous text where G-d

failed to tell Avraham the entire truth so as to maintain peace between Avraham and Sarah. Yet the confrontation referred to in this Sifrei is of a nature and quality wherein there is no justification to avoid the truth.

Shalom bayit / peace in the home is not always of a similar quality to peace in other areas, such as peace between friends, business or professional associates. In the former, one must be very sensitive as to what may or may not be said, as was the case with Sarah and Avraham. Yet in matters of confrontation between individuals in various walks of life, this midrash suggests that truth – blatant and specific – is sacred.

Hospitality

וַיִּטַּע אֵשֶׁל בִּבְאֵר שָׁבַע וַיִּקְרָא־שָׁם בְּשֵׁם ה'
אֵ־ל עוֹלָם: (בראשית כא:לג)

And he [Avraham] planted a tamarisk at Beer-
sheba, and invoked there the name of the Lord,
the Everlasting G-d. (Bereishit 21:33)

"And called there the name of the Lord, the Everlasting G-d."
(Bereishit 21:33) Resh Lakish said: Do not read [the verse] as
"and he called" [*vayikra*], but rather as "and he caused [others] to
call" [*vayakri*]. This teaches that Avraham our father caused the
name of the Holy One, blessed is He to be called by the mouth
of everyone who passed by. How so? After they ate and drank [of
Avraham's food], they stood up to bless [Avraham], but he said to
them, "have you eaten of what belongs to me? You have eaten of
what belongs to the Everlasting G-d. Be thankful to, and praise
and bless, the One who spoke [causing] the world to come into
being!"
                          (Babylonian Talmud Sotah 10b)

סוטה י:

"ויקרא שם בשם ה' א־ל עולם" (בראשית כא:לג) – אמר ריש לקיש: אל תיקרי
ויקרא אלא ויקריא, מלמד, שהקריא אברהם אבינו לשמו של הקב"ה בפה
כל עובר ושב, כיצד? לאחר שאכלו ושתו עמדו לברכו, אמר להם: וכי משלי
אכלתם? משל אלהי עולם אכלתם, הודו ושבחו וברכו למי שאמר והיה העולם.

Note the manner in which Avraham introduces the pagans to
the reality of G-d: First he feeds them – no questions asked, no
commitments secured – and only then does he engage them in
dialogue as to who deserves to be thanked for the meal. In this
way Avraham introduces his guests to the idea of monotheism,

149

of the One universal and eternal Being, source of all. Perhaps many of his guests enjoyed the meal and left Avraham's G-d with Avraham; yet his hospitality and kindness were legendary.

In our day we could say that a Jew who behaves in an exemplary ethical and moral fashion – towards both Jew and non-Jew – is a *Kiddush Hashem*, for those who behold him or her will say with admiration and respect "That's how a Jew behaves." It is in this tradition of Avraham that we may motivate others to emulate Avraham in his spiritual commitments.

I am Here

וַיְהִי אַחַר הַדְּבָרִים הָאֵלֶּה וְהָאֱלֹהִים נִסָּה
אֶת־אַבְרָהָם וַיֹּאמֶר אֵלָיו אַבְרָהָם וַיֹּאמֶר הִנֵּנִי:
(בראשית כב:א)

Some time afterward, G-d put Avraham to the
test. He said to him, "Avraham," and he answered,
"Here I am." (Bereishit 22:1)

"He said to him 'Avraham,' And he answered, 'Here I am (hinneni)'" (Bereishit 22:1). What is the meaning of the expression
hinneni? It is an expression of humility, and it is an expression of
righteousness, for the humility of righteous people is constant.
(Midrash Tanchuma, Vayera 22)

מדרש תנחומא וירא כב
"ויאמר אליו אברהם ויאמר הנני" (בראשית כב:א), מהו לשון הנני לשון ענוה לשון
חסידות שכך ענותנותו של חסידים בכל מקום.

This midrash explains what is meant by הִנֵּנִי: "I am here not only
in body but I am also prepared to respond to you with humility and kindness." When we are summoned by a teacher, friend,
relative, or any other person to whom we choose to respond or
to whom we should respond – either because of obligation or as
an act of tsedakah – we should respond as Avraham did to G-d,
with humility and kindness. The very quality of the response may
inherently serve as a source of comfort and reassurance. There
obviously is a profound qualitative difference between a response
out of obligation and that of love and caring. The midrash tells us
that Avraham responded with humility and kindness even before
he was aware of the complex and profound request G-d was to
put before him.

The Power of Persuasion

וַיֹּאמֶר קַח־נָא אֶת־בִּנְךָ אֶת־יְחִידְךָ אֲשֶׁר־
אָהַבְתָּ אֶת־יִצְחָק וְלֶךְ־לְךָ אֶל־אֶרֶץ הַמֹּרִיָּה
וְהַעֲלֵהוּ שָׁם לְעֹלָה עַל אַחַד הֶהָרִים אֲשֶׁר אֹמַר
אֵלֶיךָ: (בראשית כב:ב)

And He said, "Please take your son, your favorite
one, Yitzchak, whom you love, and go to the
land of Moriah, and offer him there as a burnt
offering on one of the heights that I will point out
to you." (Bereishit 22:2)

"Please take" (Bereishit 22:2) – take with words (by persuasion).
(Midrash Sekhel Tov)

מדרש שכל טוב
"קח נא" (בראשית כב:ב) – קח בדברים.

This midrash suggests that when G-d asked Avraham to take his
son, G-d meant not physically but with *words*. You will not succeed at convincing someone to join you on a difficult journey using physical force (though you might succeed in the short-term),
but by verbal persuasion you will achieve a lasting concurrence.

The Limits of Objectivity

וַיַּשְׁכֵּם אַבְרָהָם בַּבֹּקֶר וַיַּחֲבֹשׁ אֶת־חֲמֹרוֹ וַיִּקַּח
אֶת־שְׁנֵי נְעָרָיו אִתּוֹ וְאֵת יִצְחָק בְּנוֹ וַיְבַקַּע עֲצֵי
עֹלָה וַיָּקָם וַיֵּלֶךְ אֶל־הַמָּקוֹם אֲשֶׁר־אָמַר־לוֹ
הָאֱ־לֹהִים: (בראשית כב:ג)

Avraham arose early in the morning and saddled
his ass and took with him two of his servants and
his son Yitzchak. He split the wood for the burnt
offering, and set out for the place of which G-d
had told him. (Bereishit 22:3)

"Avraham arose early in the morning and saddled his ass" (Bereishit 22:3). Rabbi Shimon bar Yochai said: Both love and hatred
"corrupt the rule" [i.e. cause transgression] of proper conduct.
Love corrupts the rule of proper conduct, as it is written, "Avraham arose early and saddled his ass" (Bereishit 22:3) – did he
not have a number of servants [who should have done this task]?
Rather, love corrupts the rule of proper conduct. And hatred corrupts the rule of proper conduct, as it says, "Bilam arose in the
morning and saddled his ass" (Bamidbar 22:21) – Did he not have
a number of servants? Rather, hatred corrupts the rule of proper
conduct.   (Midrash Bereishit Rabbah 55:8)

מדרש בראשית רבה נה:ח

"וישכם אברהם בבוקר ויחבוש את חמורו" (בראשית כב:ג), אר"ש בן יוחai אהבה
מקלקלת את השורה ושנאה מקלקלת את השורה, אהבה מקלקלת את השורה
דכתיב "וישכם אברהם בבוקר וגו'" (בראשית כב:ג) ולא היה לו כמה עבדים אלא
אהבה מקלקלת את השורה, ושנאה מקלקלת את השורה, שנא' "ויקם בלעם
בבוקר ויחבוש את אתונו" (במדבר כב:כא) ולא היה לו כמה עבדים אלא שנאה
מקלקלת את השורה.

153

Our sages make clear the subjectivity by which all are influenced, if not indeed blinded.

Both Avraham the righteous and Bilaam the wicked act in a manner which is inappropriate to the situation, one because of love, the other because of hate. Avraham is instructed by G-d to bring his beloved son Yitzchak as a sacrifice, and he personally saddles his animal rather than asking the servant who would normally perform this menial task. Avraham is so involved with G-d's command that he departs from the norm and thus performs a task otherwise performed by a servant.

Bilaam is intent on cursing the Children of Israel, thus his objectivity is distorted and he too performs a menial task unbecoming to a man of his station.

Our sages illustrate the inherent limitation of objectivity when involved on some level of self-interest, be it for good or evil. We know, for example, that brothers may not give witness for one another, or with one another. Thus even brothers Moshe and Aharon would not have been permitted to be witnesses in the same case. The Torah prohibits it on the grounds this midrash presents, that it is possible to lose one's objectivity, even the most righteous.

How important it is in our relationships to understand the limitations of objectivity, even for the ethical individual, when matters of self-interest are involved.

Leaders in Every Generation

וַיִּקְרָא אֵלָיו מַלְאַךְ ה' מִן־הַשָּׁמַיִם וַיֹּאמֶר
אַבְרָהָם אַבְרָהָם וַיֹּאמֶר הִנֵּנִי: (בראשית כב:יא)

Then an Angel of the Lord called to him from
heaven: "Avraham! Avraham!" And he answered,
"Here I am." (Bereishit 22:11)

Rabbi Eliezer ben Yaakov said: [The angel] said [the first "Avraham"] to him, and [the second "Avraham"] to future generations [to teach us that] there is no generation that lacks someone like Avraham, no generation that lacks someone like Yaakov, no generation that lacks someone like Moshe, and no generation that lacks someone like Samuel (all of whom G-d called by repeating their name).   (Midrash Bereishit Rabbah 56:7)

מדרש בראשית רבה נו:ז

ר' אליעזר בן יעקב אמר לו ולדורות, אין דור שאין בו כאברהם ואין דור שאין בו
כיעקב ואין דור שאין בו כמשה ואין דור שאין בו כשמואל.

Each generation develops its own great leaders. There is no generation without its own Avraham, Moshe, and Shmuel. Each generation must look to its leaders as earlier generations looked to Avraham, Moshe, and Shmuel.[1]

---

1. Our sages comment further on this concept: יפתח בדורו כשמואל בדורו (Yiftach in his generation was like Shmuel in his generation.) Yiftach goes into battle promising to bring a sacrifice to G-d of the first thing which comes out of his tent upon his victorious return. When his daughter emerges from the tent to greet him, he fails to seek absolution from his vow and kills his own child (Judges 11). Despite this horrible moral failure, the Rabbis insist that Yiftach was still a great man in his time, comparing him to the great prophet and leader Shmuel.

This theme is also expressed in the statements of our sages regarding the verse:

זה ספר תולדות אדם. "This is the book of the generations of Adam." (Bereishit 5:1)

> Resh Lakish said, "Did the first human being posses a book?" [Rather,] this teaches that the Holy One, blessed is He, showed the first human being each generation and its interpreters, each generation and its sages, each generation and its communal leaders. (Babylonian Talmud, Avodah Zara 5a)

עבודה זרה ה.

אמר ריש לקיש וכי ספר היה לו לאדם הראשון? מלמד שהראה לו הקב"ה לאדם הראשון דור דור ודורשיו, דור דור וחכמיו, דור דור ופרנסיו.

Each generation must seek leaders and endow them with authority and influence. No one would suggest that a Moshe of the 21st century would be comparable to the Moshe of Sinai; however, we must allow our teachers to teach and guide as did our ancient leaders. This principle is the bedrock of the halachic process, which allows today's scholars to make halachic rulings for our time, based upon the judgments of earlier scholars. This is not unlike the U.S. Judicial system, where the judge cites precident from earlier decisions.

The midrash states, each generation has its own Avraham, Moshe, and Shmuel, this would suggest that our generation has its Avraham, Moshe, and Shmuel, thus, are as qualified in their decisions and judgment as were their predecessors.

Israel as Role Model

וַיֹּאמֶר אַבְרָהָם אֱ-לֹהִים יִרְאֶה-לּוֹ הַשֶּׂה לְעֹלָה
בְּנִי וַיֵּלְכוּ שְׁנֵיהֶם יַחְדָּו: (בראשית כב:ח)

Then Avraham said, "G-d will seek out for Himself the Lamb for the offering, my son" and the two of them went together. (Bereishit 22:8)

Whenever Israel performs acts of kindness (*tsedakah*), the nations of the world are blessed on its behalf, as it says, "All the nations of the earth shall bless themselves by your descendants" (Bereishit 22:18).   (Midrash Tanaim Devarim 15:9)

מדרש תנאים דברים טו:ט
כל זמן שישראל עושין צדקה אומות העולם מתברכין בשבילו שנאמר "והתברכו
בזרעך כל גויי הארץ" (בראשית כב:יח).

The influence that the People of Israel can have upon humankind is in proportion to our practice of *tsedakah*/"acts of righteousness and kindness." Our righteousness is our source of influence. History will clearly demonstrate the catalytic power of Torah and Jewish moral values upon society.

What better illustration than a sovereign Jewish state – in a part of the world lacking in democratic traditions, justice and education – serving as a role model to free the people of the Middle East from totalitarianism and ignorance. Israel as a land of justice and freedom and universal education perfectly fulfills this Midrash, in which the nations of the world will "bless themselves" through Avraham's descendents' righteousness.

Honoring Age

וְאַבְרָהָם זָקֵן בָּא בַּיָּמִים וַה' בֵּרַךְ אֶת־אַבְרָהָם
בַּכֹּל: (בראשית כד:א)

*Avraham was now old, advanced in years, and
the Lord had blessed Avraham in all things.*
(Bereishit 24:1)

Rabbi Levitas a man of Yavneh says: Like a crown that adorns the
head of a king, so white hair is an adornment and honor for elders
as it says, "The glory of youths is their strength; the majesty of old
men is their white hair" (Mishlei 20:29).
(Pirkei deRabbi Eliezer 52)

פרקי דר' אליעזר פרק נב
רבי לויטס איש יבנה אומר ככתר שהוא הדור הראשו של מלך כך השיבה הדור
וכבוד לזקנים שנאמר "תפארת בחורים כחם והדר זקנים שיבה" (משלי כ:כט).

Age is to be honored. White hair is as beautiful and elegant as a
crown on the head of a king. This and other physical hallmarks of
aging are to be viewed as symbols of the elegance and dignity of
our elders, as well as marks of survival that should be celebrated
rather than masked.

Greeting the Stranger

וַתֹּאמֶר שְׁתֵה אֲדֹנִי: (בראשית כד:יח)

"Drink my lord," she said. (Bereishit 24:18)

The Torah has taught you good manners, that a person should greet all people with joy and call them "my master," or "my lord." For Rebecca our mother said to Eliezer (Avraham's servant), "Drink my lord" (Bereishit 24:18).   (Midrash HaGadol)

מדרש הגדול

לימדתך התורה דרך ארץ שיהא אדם מקבל את כל האדם בשמחה וקורא לו
רבי ואדוני שהרי רבקה אמנו אומרת לאליעזר "שתה אדוני" (בראשית כד:יח).

Derech eretz / Respect is to be extended to everyone you encounter, even to a stranger. The midrash notes that Rivka, upon seeing Eliezer for the first time, said to him "Sir, have a drink." She promptly made water available to him from the pitcher she was carrying. The Midrash concludes from her action that we are to greet each person with respect and a pleasant demeanor. The Midrash goes so far as to say that you should even address them as Teacher, Sir, or my lord. Greet the stranger with respect, offer whatever basic necessity (e.g., water) might be appropriate at the moment, and only then judge the person and the situation.

The Good Eye

וַתְּכַל לְהַשְׁקֹתוֹ וַתֹּאמֶר גַּם לִגְמַלֶּיךָ אֶשְׁאָב עַד
אִם־כִּלּוּ לִשְׁתֹּת: (בראשית כד:יט)

When she had let him drink his fill, she said, "I
will also *draw for your camels, until they finish*
drinking." (Bereishit 24:19)

Come and see the spirit of generosity [literally "good eye"] that
[Rebecca] possessed, for it was not sufficient that she gave him to
drink, but she [also] said "'I will also draw water for your camels"
(Bereishit 24:19).   (Midrash HaGadol)

מדרש הגדול

בוא וראה עין טובה שהיתה בה, לא דיה שהשקתה אותו אלא שאמרה "גם
לגמליך אשאב" (בראשית כד:יט).

This midrash praises Rivka again, for not only did she provide
water for the stranger, but she also provided water for his animals.
"Come and see," says the Midrash, "the good eye," by which is
meant the fine and good manner in which she saw the situation
and responded with kindness even to the animals. The Midrash
Lekach Tov makes the observation that this response was נציבות של
עצמה, i.e., giving of herself. In other words, she gave more than
what was called for, being motivated by her own values of kindness and caring.

Gratitude

וַיִּקֹּד הָאִישׁ וַיִּשְׁתַּחוּ לַה': (בראשית כד:כו)

The man bowed low in homage to the Lord.
(Bereishit 24:26)

From this we learn that we give thanks [to G-d] for good news.
(Midrash Bereishit Rabbah 60:26)

מדרש בראשית רבה ס:כו
מכאן שמודים על בשורה טובה.

One needs to acknowledge good news with gratitude. One needs
to say *Baruch Hashem*/Thank G-d, when one is privileged to
receive a message which brings happiness and, as in the case of
Eliezer, the realization that a mission has been accomplished.

Any experience of goodness, when either ignored or taken for
granted, is diminished in its impact. Life is filled with moments
which may either enrich us or pass unnoticed. The midrash re-
minds us of the necessity of acknowledging these moments; for if
they pass unrecognized they may well be lost as a source of blessing.

We also note that our sages teach us the deeper significance of
הודאה or מודים, that there is a form of thanksgiving/acknowledge-
ment even for tragic or painful moments in life. As the Talmud
states:

"For good news we say 'Blessed be He who is good and does
good.' For bad news we say, 'Blessed is the righteous Judge.'"
(Babylonian Talmud Brachot 54a)

ברכות נד.
ועל בשורות טובות, אומר: ברוך הטוב והמטיב. על בשורות רעות אומר: ברוך
דיין האמת.

161

We are commanded to say ברוך/"Blessed" for a simcha and
ברוך/"Blessed" for a tragedy. The imperative to acknowledge
our relationship with G-d at every critical moment in life is what
binds the individual to G-d in a profound and intimate way.

The Treatment of Animals

וַיָּבֹא הָאִישׁ הַבַּיְתָה וַיְפַתַּח הַגְּמַלִּים וַיִּתֵּן תֶּבֶן
וּמִסְפּוֹא לַגְּמַלִּים . . . וַיּוּשַׂם לְפָנָיו לֶאֱכֹל . . . :
(בראשית כד:לב-לג)

So the man entered the house, and the camels
were unloaded, and he gave the camels straw
and feed...And food was set before him...
(Bereishit 24:32–33)

"The camels were given straw and feed" (Bereishit 24:32). [The verses] first mention the animal food, and only afterward "food was set before him" (Bereishit 24:33), which concurs with the words of Rabbi Judah, for Rabbi Judah says: It is forbidden for a person to [even] taste any [food] until he gives straw to his animal, as it is written, "I will also provide grass in the field for your cattle" (Devarim 12:15), and afterwards, "and thus you shall eat your fill" (Ibid.).   (Midrash HaGadol)

מדרש הגדול

"ויתן תבן ומספוא לגמלים" (בראשית כד:לב). הקדים מזון הבהמה תחילה ואחר
כך "ויושם לפניו לאכול" (שם כד:לג) כדרבי יהודה, דאמר רבי יהודה אמר רב,
אסור לו לאדם שיטעום כלום עד שיתן תבן לבהמתו דכתוב "ונתתי עשב בשדך
לבהמתך" (דברים יב:טו) והדר "ואכלת ושבעת" (שם).

According to this midrash, a person may not eat until the animals have been fed. With this teaching, our sages evince a remarkable standard of sensitivity toward animals. While it is only in recent history that society at large has demonstrated any moral obligation of compassion and respect for animals, Torah and our sages have taught a consistent imperative of kindness towards animals.

Judaism allows for the slaughter of certain animals for human consumption. There are many laws governing the manner of slaughter, and an entire body of law under the rubric of צער בעלי חיים – i.e., the prohibition against causing pain to any living being. Thus the slaughter of animals is strictly defined within an ethic of humane treatment. Violations of that ethic render the animal unfit for human consumption, even at great economic cost to the owner. This is in fact a fundamental principle of the laws of kashrut. Though many laws of kashrut may appear to the laymen to be without reason, this one has profound reason.

The Talmud (Bava Metziah 32b) teaches that צער בעלי חיים דאורייתא – i.e., the prohibition against cruelty to animals is "Torah law:"

> Just as the mercy of the Holy One, blessed is He is upon humans, so too His mercy is upon animals.
>
> (Midrash Devarim Rabbah 6:1)

מדרש דברים רבה ו:א
וכשם שרחמיו של הקב"ה על האדם כך רחמיו על הבהמה.

Our Rabbis said: When Moshe our Rabbi, of blessed memory, was tending Yitro's flock, a kid ran away from him, and he ran after it until it reached a shady place. When it reached the shady place, it chanced upon a pool of water, and the kid stood to drink. When Moshe reached the kid, he said, "I did not know that you were running because you were thirsty. Now you are tired." He placed him on his shoulders and walked. The Holy One, blessed is He said, "You have the compassion to tend to a person's flock, by your life, thus you will tend to My flock Israel." This is what it says, "Moshe tended the flock" (Shemot 3:1). (Midrash Shemot Rabbah 2:2)

מדרש שמות רבה ב:ב
אמרו רבותינו כשהיה משה רבנו ע"ה רועה צאנו של יתרו במדבר ברח ממנו גדי ורץ אחריו עד שהגיע לחסית כיון שהגיע לחסית נזדמנה לו בריכה של מים ועמד הגדי לשתות, כיון שהגיע משה אצלו אמר אני לא הייתי יודע שרץ היית מפני צמא עיף אתה אתה הרכיבו על כתיפו והיה מהלך, אמר הקב"ה יש לך רחמים

לנהוג צאנו של בשר ודם חייך כך אתה תרעה צאני ישראל, הוי אומר "ומשה
היה רועה" (שמות ג:א).

This midrash attributes G-d's selection of Moshe to Moshe's quality of mercy, demonstrated while he was a shepherd. The story is told that he sought out a lost sheep, found it, and carried it back to the flock. Rather than judging the sheep as undisciplined, he understood that it was simply seeking water to quench its thirst. It was this quality of kindness and compassion which was necessary in the individual who would lead the Jewish people.

It is further taught:

> One is not permitted to take [i.e. purchase] a domesticated animal, wild animal, or bird unless one has first prepared food for them. (Jerusalem Talmud Ketubot 4:8)

תלמוד ירושלמי מסכת כתובות פרק ד הלכה ח

אין אדם רשאי ליקח בהמה חיה ועוף אלא אם כן התקין להן מזונות.

There is a remarkable dispute between Maimonides (*Guide to the Perplexed* 3:48) and Sa'adia Ga'on concerning the mitzvah of שילוח את הקן/ "sending away the mother bird." The Torah commands us to send away a mother bird before we take her young birds or eggs from the nest.[1] Obviously we are permitted to eat eggs, thus there should be no problem with a person taking eggs from a nest. However, the Torah prohibits us from taking the young birds or eggs in the presence of the mother bird.

The question is then posed: Are we concerned with the feelings of the mother bird, or with the impact of the act upon the individual taking the eggs? Rambam (Maimonides 1135–1204 CE) argues that the mother bird has emotional sensitivity, and thus removing the eggs in her presence would be an act of cruelty.

---

1. The text reads: "If a bird's nest happens to be before you on the road on any tree or on the ground, young birds or eggs, and the mother is roosting on the young birds or eggs, you shall not take the mother with the young. You shall surely send away the mother and take the young for yourself, so that it will be good for you and will prolong your days" (Devarim 22:6–7).

Sa'adia Ga'on (882–942 CE) argues that although the bird has no mental capacity for such an emotional response, the Torah prohibits the act in order that the person avoid becoming de-sensitized to committing acts of cruelty. Even though the bird may not "emotionally" sense the "pain" of separation, nonetheless, a human being *should* sense that pain.

There are many other illustrations concerning the prohibition against cruelty to animals, all demonstrating the Torah's imperative of kindness to animals.

A True Blessing

וַה' בֵּרַךְ אֶת־אֲדֹנִי מְאֹד וַיִּגְדָּל וַיִּתֶּן־לוֹ צֹאן
וּבָקָר וְכֶסֶף וְזָהָב וַעֲבָדִם וּשְׁפָחֹת וּגְמַלִּים
וַחֲמֹרִים: (בראשית כד:לה)

The Lord has greatly blessed my master, and he
has become rich: He has given him sheep and
cattle, silver and gold, male and female slaves,
camels, and asses. (Bereishit 24:35)

The Lord has greatly blessed my master (Bereishit 24:35) – not
from theft and not from violence.   (Midrash Lekach Tov)

מדרש לקח טוב
"ברך את־אדני מאד" (בראשית כד:לה) – לא מגזל ולא מחמס.

What is a true blessing? This midrash makes the point that Avraham is described as being *very* blessed as a result of his honesty
and integrity; i.e., none of his possessions were acquired either
through theft or violence. Possession alone does not lead to blessing; what is important is the manner in which possessions are
acquired.

Re-marrying

וַיֹּסֶף אַבְרָהָם וַיִּקַּח אִשָּׁה וּשְׁמָהּ קְטוּרָה:
(בראשית כה:א)

*Avraham took another wife, whose name was
Keturah.* (Bereishit 25:1)

Rabbi Yudan said: The Torah teaches good manners, that if a
widower [literally, 'a man'] has adult sons, he should first marry
them off and only then marry. From whom do we learn this? From
Avraham. First "Yitzchak brought her" (Bereishit 24:67) and afterwards "Avraham took another wife whose name was Keturah"
(Bereishit 25:1). (Midrash Bereishit Rabbah 60:67, Theodor-Al-
beck edition.)

מדרש בראשית רבה ס:סז

אמר ר' יודן לידמתך תורה דרך ארץ שאם יהיה לאדם בנים גדולים יהא משיאן
תחילה ואחר כך נושא לו אשה, ממי את למד מאברהם, תחילה "ויביאה יצחק"
(בראשית כד:סז) ואחר כך "ויוסף אברהם ויקח אשה ושמה קטורה" (בראשית כה:א).

According to this midrash, a widower with grown children should
not marry until his children marry and leave home. The implication is clear: In the case of young children, a step-mother may be
helpful and even necessary for the proper raising of the children.
However, with grown children, having "another woman" in the
home may lead to conflict. One may ponder this insight in the
light of modern societal norms.

A related teaching offers the following perspective:

And in the Midrash HaGadol this is taught in the name of Rabbi
Akiva – if he had children from the first marriage, he is not permitted to marry another until he marries off his sons, as it is

written "Yitzchak brought her into her tent" (Bereishit 24:67) and afterwards "Avraham took another wife" (Bereishit 25:1). (Torah Shelemah note 1 to Bereishit chapter 25)

מדרש הגדול, מובא בתורה שלמה, הערה 1 על בראשית כה

ובמדרש הגדול מביא בשם ר' עקיבא – היה לו בנים מן הראשונה אינו רשאי
לישא אחרת עד שישיא בניו דכתיב "ויביאה יצחק האהלה" (בראשית כד:סז)
ולבסוף "ויוסף אברהם ויקח אשה" (בראשית כה:א).

This text is even more restricting than that of the previous text. Here, Rabbi Akiva does not distinguish between young children and grown children. Apparently, the whole notion of a step-mother is repugnant to him. This viewpoint was never accepted either into Jewish law or practice. Nonetheless, this midrash offers a provocative, radical perspective on re-marriage and its potential consequences under certain circumstances.

Grandchildren

וְאֵלֶּה תּוֹלְדֹת יִצְחָק בֶּן־אַבְרָהָם: (בראשית כה:יט)

This is the story of Yitzchak, son of Avraham.
(Bereishit 25:19)

"Grandchildren are the crown of their elders, [and the glory of the children is their parents]" (Mishlei 17:6). The parents are the crown of the children, and the children are the crown of the parents. The parents are the crown of their children, as it is written, "and the glory of the children is their parents" (ibid.); Children are the crown of their parents as it is written, "Grandchildren are the crown of their elders" (ibid.). (Midrash Bereishit Rabbah 63:2)

מדרש רבה בראשית סג:ב

"עטרת זקנים בני בנים וגו'" (משלי יז:ו) האבות עטרה לבנים והבנים עטרה
לאבות, האבות עטרה לבנים דכתיב "ותפארת בנים אבותם" (שם), הבנים
עטרה לאבות דכתיב "עטרת זקנים בני בנים" (שם).

The "crown of the elders" is their children's children, for grandchildren demonstrate that parental values have been cherished and then transmitted to the third generation. Parents may best judge the efficacy of their parenting when their values and commitments are transmitted by their children to *their* children.

When values are appreciated and successfully transmitted, children are proud of their parents, as the Midrash says, "the parents are the crown of their children." The relationship is clearly positive when parents sense, too, that their "crown" is their children. A relationship of this quality allows for the transmission of values to the point when grandchildren become the crown of grandparents. There is no greater blessing than that of grandparents and grandchildren sharing and cherishing similar values and commitments. The sharing by three generations of the common language of tradition is truly a source of נחת / *nachas*, ultimate parental fulfillment.

Parent and Child

אַבְרָהָם הוֹלִיד אֶת־יִצְחָק: (בראשית כה:יט)

Avraham begot Yitzchak. (Bereishit 25:19)

For when Avraham would pass with Yitzchak his son behind him, everyone would say: "blessed are you Avraham that Yitzchak is your son and blessed are you Yitzchak that Avraham is your father." (Midrash Hagadol)

מדרש הגדול

שכשהיה אברהם עובר ויצחק בנו אחריו היו הכל אומרין אשריך אברהם שבנך יצחק ואשריך יצחק שאביך אברהם.

When parent and child are equally blessed in their relationship and in their sharing of values and commitments, and this is obvious to those who behold them, this indeed is the fulfillment of the parent and child relationship.

Nature or Nurture

וַיְהִי יִצְחָק בֶּן־אַרְבָּעִים שָׁנָה בְּקַחְתּוֹ אֶת־
רִבְקָה בַּת־בְּתוּאֵל הָאֲרַמִּי מִפַּדַּן אֲרָם אֲחוֹת
לָבָן הָאֲרַמִּי לוֹ לְאִשָּׁה: (בראשית כה:כ)

Yitzchak was forty years old when he took
Rebekah, daughter of Bethuel the Aramean of
Paddan-aram, sister of Laban the Aramean, for
a wife. (Bereishit 25:20)

Rabbi Yitzchak said: If the verse means to teach that [Laban] was
from Aram Nahraim, it already says "from Padan Aram," so why
does the verse state [redundantly] "the Aramean [Arami]" and
"daughter of Bethuel the Aramean"? And why does it state "the
sister of Laban the Aramean"? Rather, it teaches that her father
was a deceiver [ramai, a pun on Arami], and her brother was a
deceiver, and so too the people of the place of her home. And yet
this righteous woman emerged from among them. To what can
this be compared? To a "rose among thorns" (Song of Songs 2:2).
(Midrash Bereishit Rabbah 63:4)

בראשית רבה סג:ד

א"ר יצחק אם ללמד שהיא מארם נהרים והלא כבר נאמר "מפדן ארם", מה ת"ל
ארמי בת בתואל הארמי מה ת"ל אחות לבן הארמי אלא בא ללמדך אביה רמאי
ואחיה רמאי ואף אנשי מקומה כן, והצדקת הזו שהיא יוצאה מביניהם למה היא
דומה ל"שושנה בין החוחים" (שיר השירים ב:ב).

Is it nature or nurture? What is it that determines a person's values? Rivka is raised in a warped society: Her father is a liar, her
brother is a liar, she is raised in a culture of liars. Nonetheless, she
grows up to be a righteous, sensitive, spiritual individual destined

173

to become one of our matriarchs. As the Midrash says, she was a "rose among thorns." A person may, with great determination, transcend the corrupt society and environment in which he or she is raised. In the final analysis, one may never blame others for one's own actions.

Conflict and Criticism

וַיֹּאמֶר אֲלֵהֶם יִצְחָק מַדּוּעַ בָּאתֶם אֵלָי וְאַתֶּם
שְׂנֵאתֶם אֹתִי וַתְּשַׁלְּחוּנִי מֵאִתְּכֶם:
(בראשית כו:כז)

Yitzchak said to them, "Why have you come to
me, seeing that you have been hostile to me and
have driven me away from you?" (Bereishit 26:27)

Rebuke [or, criticism] leads to peace ... and similarly it says
regarding Yitzchak, "And Yitzchak said to them, 'Why have
you come to me seeing that you have been hostile to me and
have driven me away from you?'" (Bereishit 26:27) And it says,
"Yitzchak then bade them farewell, and they departed from him in
peace" (Bereishit 26:31).　　　　　　　　(Sifrei Devarim 2)

ספרי דברים ב

התוכחה מביאה לידי שלום - וכה"א ביצחק "ויאמר אלהם יצחק מדוע באתם
אלי ואתם שנאתם אותי ותשלחני מאתכם" (בראשית כו:כז) - ואומר "וישלחם
יצחק וילכו מאתו בשלום." (שם כו:לא)

In a conflict between people, our sages teach us, it is best to explore the issues. Here, Yitzchak confronts Avimelech: Why are
you coming to me now, when in the past you rejected me, hated
me, sent me away? Questioned in this way, Avimelech is compelled to face the past. Relationships must be based upon an open
and frank understanding of the past. Only then can there be hope
for the continuing of that relationship into the future.

We read in Mishlei 9:7 – אַל־תּוֹכַח לֵץ פֶּן־יִשְׂנָאֶךָּ הוֹכַח לְחָכָם וְיֶאֱהָבֶךָּ –
Don't criticize one who mocks, for he will hate you; criticize a
wise person and he will love you.

In Bereishit Rabbah (54) we read:

Yosi bar Chanina said: Any love that is not accompanied by rebuke
[or, criticism] is not love. Resh Lakish said: Rebuke leads to peace,
[as it says] "Then Avraham rebuked Abimelekh" (Bereishit 21:25).
This is the same as his view [in which] he states, "Any peace that is
not accompanied by rebuke is not peace."

(Midrash Bereishit Rabbah 54:3)

מדרש בראשית רבה נד:ג

יוסי בר חנינא דאמר כל אהבה שאין עמה תוכחה אינה אהבה, אמר ריש לקיש
תוכחה מביאה לידי שלום, "והוכיח אברהם את אבימלך" (בראשית כא:כה) היא
דעתה דאמר כל שלום שאין עמו תוכחה אינו שלום:

In addition, we find this remarkable teaching:

Rabbi [Judah the Patriarch] says: What is the straight path that a
person should choose? He should love rebuke, for when there is
rebuke in the world, peace of mind enters the world, goodness enters the world, blessing enters the world, and evil leaves the world,
as it says, "But it shall go well for those who admonish, blessings
of good things will rest upon them" (Mishlei 24:25).

(Babylonian Talmud Tamid 28a)

תמיד כח.

רבי אומר איזה הוא דרך ישרה שיבור לו האדם, אהב את התוכחות שכל זמן
שהתוכחות בעולם נחת רוח באה לעולם טובה באה לעולם ברכה באה לעולם
ורעה מסתלקת מן העולם שנאמר "ולמוכיחים ינעם ועליהם תבא ברכת טוב"
(משלי כד:כה).

Is it proper to offer criticism to everyone? The answer is no,
based on the passage in Mishlei cited above. The question is then
raised: "To what extent may you criticize?" The Talmud answers:

To what extent may you criticize? Rav says until your subject
strikes you; Shmuel says until he curses you; Rabbi Yochanan says
until he insults you! (Talmud Erchin 16b)

ערכין טז:
עד היכן תוכחה? רב אמר: עד הכאה, ושמואל אמר: עד קללה, ורבי יוחנן
אמר: עד נזיפה

The sages are not suggesting some naive approach. Rather, they
are suggesting that there are limits which should be accepted
when expressing criticism to an individual. It may be more prudent to remain silent in a volatile situation in which words of
chastisement might elicit negative consequences.

Rabbi Acha said in the name of Rabbi Yochanan: Just as it is a
mitzvah to speak about a matter that will be done, so too it is a
mitzvah not to speak about a matter that will not be done. (Jerusalem Talmud, Chagigah 1:8)

תלמוד ירושלמי חגיגה פרק א הלכה ח
רבי אחא בשם רבי יוחנן כשם שמצוה לומר על דבר שהוא נעשה כך מצוה
שלא לומר על דבר שאינו נעשה.

The Talmud here actually prohibits words of chastisement when
it is known *a priori* that the chastisement will be rejected.

Just as it is a mitzvah for a person to say something that will be
listened to, so too it is a mitzvah for a person not to say something
that will not be listened to. Rabbi Abba says: It is an "obligation"
as it says, "Do not rebuke a scoffer, for he will hate you; reprove a
wise man and he will love you" (Mishlei 9:8). (Babylonian Talmud
Yevamot 65b)

יבמות סה:
כשם שמצוה על אדם לומר דבר הנשמע, כך מצוה על אדם שלא לומר דבר
שאינו נשמע. רבי אבא אומר: חובה, שנאמר: "אל תוכח לץ פן ישנאך הוכח
לחכם ויאהבך" (משלי ט:ח).

There is yet an additional dimension of chastisement: Who is responsible in a specific role, and what are the consequences when
one fails to assume that responsibility? We read in the midrash:

"Speak to the Children of Israel . . ." (Bamidbar 6:2) – these are
those who vow to become a nazir. ". . . and say to them . . ." (Ibid.)
– to warn the court not to allow the nazir to violate his nazirhood.
For if they see that he wishes to cease his nazirhood, they should
force him to keep to his words. This is to teach you that greater
ones [i.e. courts] are responsible for [the actions of] smaller ones
[ie. individuals] and that they are punished on their account if they
do not admonish them. Similarly it says, "they shall stumble over
one another" (Vayikra 26:37) – this teaches that all of Israel are
responsible for one another. (Midrash Bamidbar Rabbah 10:5)

מדרש במדבר רבה י:ה
"דבר אל בני ישראל" (במדבר ו:ב) אלו הנודרים בנזיר, "ואמרת אליהם" (שם)
להזהיר ב"ד על כך שלא יניחו לנזיר לעבור על נזירותו שאם יראו שירצה לבטל
נזירותו יכופו אותו כדי לקיים דבריו ללמדך שהגדולים מוזהרין ע"י הקטנים והם
נענשים על ידיהם אם לא יוכיחו אותם וכה"א "וכשלו איש באחיו" (ויקרא כו:לז)
איש בעון אחיו מלמד שכל ישראל ערבים זה בזה.

Parents, teachers, and adult friends are obligated to correct the
behavior of a young person. In addition, peers should challenge
peers. All people, in fact, should challenge a person whose behavior is immoral, unethical, or irreverent. If one is silent in the face
of evil, one shares the guilt with the perpetrator. It is always the
silence of the majority which allows the evil of the minority. It is
not acceptable to keep silent, thinking "who am I to speak up?"

Parents have a special role to play in chastising their children,
difficult though the task may be.

Whoever chastises his son – this causes the son to love the father
more and to honor him. (Midrash Shemot Rabbah 1:1)

מדרש שמות רבה א:א
וכל המייסר את בנו מוסיף הבן אהבה על אביו והוא מכבדו.

Conversely, when parents seek "peace at any price," the silence
of parents in the face of their child's misbehavior will ultimately
result in the wasting of the child's life.

Learning from Failure

וַיֹּאמֶר אֲלֵהֶם יִצְחָק מַדּוּעַ בָּאתֶם אֵלָי
וְאַתֶּם שְׂנֵאתֶם אֹתִי וַתְּשַׁלְּחוּנִי מֵאִתְּכֶם:
(בראשית כו:כז)

Yitzchak said to them, "Why have you come to
me, seeing that you have been hostile to me and
have driven me away from you?" (Bereishit 26:27)

This is what scripture states, "though your beginning be small
(*mitz'ar*)," (Job 8:7) to teach you that whoever suffers (*mitzta'er*)
at the beginning will be at ease in the end. And there is no one
who suffered more than Avraham, who was cast into the fiery
furnace, was exiled from his father's house, sixteen kings chased
after him, was tested with ten trials, and buried Sarah, and in the
end he was at ease, "Avraham was now old, advanced in years,
and the Lord had blessed Avraham in all things" (Bereishit 24:1).
Yitzchak suffered in his youth – "And the Philistines envied him"
(after Bereishit 26:14), [as it is written] "And Abimelech said to
Yitzchak, 'Go away from us, for you have become far too big for
us'" (Bereishit 26:16). [And] in the end they sought him out, [as it
is written], "And Yitzchak said to them, 'Why have you come to
me?'" (Bereishit 26:27).   (Midrash Tanchuma, Ekev 5:5)

מדרש תנחומא עקב ה:ה

זש"ה "והיה ראשיתך מצער וגו'" (איוב ח:ז), ללמדך שכל המצטער מתחילתו נוח
לו בסופו, ואין לך שמצטער יותר מאברהם, שהושלך בכבשן האש, וגלה מבית
אביו, ורדפו אחריו ששה עשר מלכים, ונתנסה בעשר נסיונות, וקבר את שרה,
ולבסוף נחה, "ואברהם זקן בא בימים וה' ברך וגו'" (בראשית כד:א). יצחק נצטער
בנערותו, ויקנאו בו פלשתים, [שנאמר] "ויאמר אבימלך אל יצחק לך מעמנו כי
עצמת ממנו מאד" (שם כו:טז), לסוף בקשו ממנו [שנאמר] "ויאמר אליהם יצחק
מדוע באתם אלי" (שם כו:כז).

179

Do not be discouraged when at first you meet with defeat or rejection. Early difficulty need not be interpreted as failure. Giving the example of Yitzchak, who is at first rejected by the Philistines – they tell him "leave us" and then later seek him out to establish a covenant with him – the midrash teaches that a painful beginning may yet result in a successful conclusion.

Ethical Wills

וַיִּקְרָא יִצְחָק אֶל־יַעֲקֹב וַיְבָרֶךְ אֹתוֹ וַיְצַוֵּהוּ
וַיֹּאמֶר לוֹ לֹא־תִקַּח אִשָּׁה מִבְּנוֹת כְּנָעַן:
(בראשית כח:א)

So Yitzchak sent for Yaakov and blessed him. He
instructed him saying, You shall not take a wife
from among the Canaanite women. (Bereishit 28:1)

Rabbi Shimon said: "Happy are the righteous who do not depart
this world until they give instruction to their children [who will
live] after them in matters of Torah . . ." And similarly Yitzchak
commanded Yaakov, as it says "So Yitzchak sent for Yaakov and
blessed him and instructed him . . ." (Bereishit 28:1).

(Midrash Tanaim, Devarim 1:1)

מדרש תנאים דברים א:א

אמר ר' שמעון אשריהם לצדיקים שאין נפטרין מן העולם עד שהן מצווין את
בניהם אחריהם על דברי תורה וכו' וכן יצחק צוה את יעקב שנאמר "ויקרא יצחק
אל יעקב ויברך אותו ויצוהו" (בראשית כח:א).

What is it that a parent considers vital for their children, and
indeed for the generations to come, to perpetuate in their lives?
What personal, familial, and communal obligations and traditions need they cherish, manifest, and teach?

The world is accustomed to the practice of writing a will regarding one's material possessions. Most countries demand a legal
document for this purpose or else the law of the state imposes its
own method of division and distribution of assets. Rabbi Shimon
here praises Yitzchak (and by extension all parents) who leave
an "ethical will" instructing their children and grandchildren as
to their religious, ethical, and spiritual heritage and values. No

responsible individual would fail to leave a legal will regarding material possessions. Rabbi Shimon teaches the moral obligation to carefully prepare an ethical will as well.

In the Talmud we find several citations which describe how the Rabbis dealt with the ethical facets of a will. For example:

> The Rabbis taught [in a baraita]: At the time of Rabbi [Judah the Prince's] death, he said, "I am in need of my sons." His sons came to him. He said to them, "be careful to honor your mother, let a candle remain lit in its proper place, let the table be set in its proper place, and let the bed be made in its proper place. Yoseph Chophni and Shimon Ephrati attended to me in my lifetime, and they shall attend to me in my death." . . . [And] he said to them, "I am in need of the sages of Israel." The sages of Israel came to him. He said to them, "Do not eulogize me in the towns, and establish a session after thirty days. Shimon my son will be *Chacham*, Gamliel my son will be *Nasi*, and Chanina bar Chama will be *Yoshev Rosh*." (Babylonian Talmud, Ketubot 103a-b)

כתובות קג.-קג:

ת"ר: בשעת פטירתו של רבי, אמר: לבני אני צריך, נכנסו בניו אצלו. אמר להם: הזהרו בכבוד אמכם אמר נר יהא דלוק במקומו, שולחן יהא ערוך במקומו, מטה תהא מוצעת במקומה יוסף חפני, שמעון אפרתי, הם שמשוני בחיי והם ישמשוני במותי . . . אמר להן: לחכמי ישראל אני צריך, נכנסו אצלו חכמי ישראל. אמר להן: אל תספדוני בעיירות, והושיבו ישיבה לאחר שלשים יום שמעון בני חכם , גמליאל בני נשיא, חנינא בר חמא ישב בראש.

Thus did Rabbi Yehudah the Prince, the head of the community, instruct his children and his students regarding how they were to behave after his death, including how to treat his wife, how his funeral was to be carried out, and which of his disciples was to carry on in his place.

In another comment, we find the Rabbis harsh in their judgment of a parent who disowns a child:

> One who bequeaths his property to others, passing over his children – what he has done is done (and cannot be undone), but the sages are not pleased with him.
>
> (Babylonian Talmud, Bava Batra 133b)

בבא בתרא קלג:
הכותב את נכסיו לאחרים והניח את בניו – מה שעשה עשוי, אלא אין רוח
חכמים נוחה הימנו.

Nonetheless the Rabbis are willing to give moral support to such a will when, in the words of Rabbi Shimon,

> But if his children do not behave properly, may he be remembered for good [for disinheriting them]! (Ibid.)

בבא בתרא קלג:
אם לא היו בניו נוהגים כשורה זכור לטוב.

A parent does have the right to reflect upon and judge the behavior of their children in the context of preparing a will. One must however be scrupulous in such action, and proceed with extraordinary care and sensitivity. In such a document, words of chastisement or negative judgments may have a devastating effect. Words of challenge and guidance are far more beneficial. To express admiration rooted in faith in the potential of your heirs is a proper and wholesome legacy. To express love and affection from which then flows a challenging agenda of positive and creative behavior and Jewish values is a catalytic legacy one might hope to bestow upon one's children and grandchildren.

Again, the careful preparation of both a material and an ethical will should be the concern of each individual, regardless of the extent of one's economic resources.

The Place

וַיִּפְגַּע בַּמָּקוֹם וַיָּלֶן שָׁם כִּי־בָא הַשֶּׁמֶשׁ וַיִּקַּח
מֵאַבְנֵי הַמָּקוֹם וַיָּשֶׂם מְרַאֲשֹׁתָיו וַיִּשְׁכַּב בַּמָּקוֹם
הַהוּא: (בראשית כח:יא)

He came upon a certain place and stopped there
for the night, for the sun had set. Taking one of
the stones of that place, he put it under his head
and lay down in that place. (Bereishit 28:11)

"And he came upon a certain place" (Bereishit 28:11) and there
he encountered the Holy One, blessed is He [as it says, "angels
of G-d encountered him" (Bereishit 32:2)] [and] as it says, "He
came upon a certain place" (Bereishit 28:11). And why is His name
"place (*makom*)"? Because in every place in which there are righteous people, He is there with them, as it says, "In every place
where I cause My name to be mentioned I will come to you and
bless you" (Shemot 20:21).   (Pirkei deRabbi Eliezer 35)

פרקי דרבי אליעזר פרק לה

"ויפגע במקום" (בראשית כח:יא) ופגע בו הקב"ה בו, שנאמר "ויפגע במקום"
(בראשית כח:יא). ולמה נקרא שמו מקום? שבכל מקום שהצדיקים שם, שם
הוא נמצא עמהם, שנאמר "בכל המקום אשר שאזכיר את שמי אבוא אליך
וברכתיך" (שמות כ:כא).

G-d is called *haMakom*/ the Place, for in every place where G-d
will find righteous people, there will G-d find His Place, and His
name shall be present among them. We also find this theme developed in a Midrash regarding Rivka. Disturbed by the inner,
physical struggle she feels during her pregnancy, she turns to G-d:

"But the children struggled in her womb, and she said, "If so why
do I exist?" She went to inquire of the Lord." (Bereishit 25:22)

(בראשית כה:כב)
וַיִּתְרֹצֲצוּ הַבָּנִים בְּקִרְבָּהּ וַתֹּאמֶר אִם־כֵּן לָמָּה זֶּה אָנֹכִי וַתֵּלֶךְ לִדְרֹשׁ אֶת־ה':

The midrash comments:

> Were there [not] synagogues and study-houses in those days? Yet
> she only went to the academy of Eber. This teaches you that who-
> ever greets an elder it is as if that person has greeted the Divine
> Presence. (Midrash Bereishit Rabbah 63:11)

מדרש בראשית פרק סג:יא
וכי בתי כניסיות ובתי מדרשות היו באותן הימים, והלא לא הלכה אלא למדרשו
של עבר, אלא ללמדך שכל מי שמקביל פני זקן כאילו מקביל פני שכינה.

According to this Midrash, when the Torah says that Rivka went
to seek G-d, it means that she went in search of a scholar. *HaMakom*/the Place, is where you can find a scholar. A Jewish scholar,
a תלמיד חכם, should be a person of knowledge and also a person of
manifest piety. It does not suffice to *know* Torah – one must *live*
Torah.

The Tsaddik

וְהִנֵּה ה' נִצָּב עָלָיו וַיֹּאמַר אֲנִי ה' אֱ-לֹהֵי
אַבְרָהָם אָבִיךָ וֵא-לֹהֵי יִצְחָק הָאָרֶץ אֲשֶׁר אַתָּה
שֹׁכֵב עָלֶיהָ לְךָ אֶתְּנֶנָּה וּלְזַרְעֶךָ: (בראשית כח:יג)

And the Lord was standing beside him and
He said, "I am the Lord, the G-d of your father
Avraham and the G-d of Yitzchak: The ground
on which you are lying I will assign to you and to
your offspring." (Bereishit 28:13)

Rabbi Shimon bar Yochai said: The Holy One, blessed is He does
not confer His name on the righteous in their lifetime, but only
after their death, as it says, "As to the holy ones that are in the land
. . ." (Psalms 16:3) – when are they "holy ones"? When they are
buried "in the land" meaning that while they are alive the Holy
One, blessed is He does not confer His name on them. Why to
such an extent? Because the Holy One, blessed is He does not have
faith in them that the evil inclination will not cause them to stray;
but once they die the Holy One, blessed is He confers His name
upon them. But have we not already found that the Holy One,
blessed is He conferred His name upon Yitzchak the righteous
during his lifetime? For thus He says to Yaakov: "The G-d of your
father Avraham and the G-d of Yitzchak" (Bereishit 28:13). Rabbi
Berekhia and the Rabbis say: He sees his ashes, as if he were [still]
heaped upon the altar. . . .   (Midrash Tanchuma Toldot 7)

מדרש תנחומא תולדות ז

אמר רשב"י אין הקב"ה מיחד שמו על הצדיקים בחייהן אלא לאחר מיתתן
שנאמר "לקדושים אשר בארץ המה וגו'" (תהלים מז:ג), אימתי הן קדושים כשהן
קבורים בארץ שכל זמן שהן חיין אין הקב"ה מיחד שמו עליהן, כל כך למה
שאין הקב"ה מאמין בהן שלא יטעה אותן היצר הרע, וכיון שמתים הקב"ה

מיחד שמו עליהן, והרי מצינו שיחד הקב"ה שמו על יצחק הצדיק בחייו שכן הוא
אומר ליעקב "אלהי אברהם אביך ואלהי יצחק" (בראשית כח:יג), רבי ברכיה ורבנן
אמרי רואה את אפרו כאלו הוא צבור על גבי המזבח.

This midrash cautions us not to be smug in our self-righteousness. Who can foretell the destiny of any individual? G-d does not
call even a true *tsaddik* by that name while he is alive. G-d waits
to bestow the title of *tsaddik* until there can be no doubt as to the
individual's ultimate status. Someone who acts righteously today
may forfeit his integrity and fall prey to human failure and folly
at any moment. Thus no individual may feel secure and smug in
self-righteousness. To live a righteous life is a constant challenge.

In *Pirkei Avot* / Ethics of the Fathers 2:4 we read:

> Hillel said, do not be sure of yourself until the day of your death
> and don't judge your friend until you reach his place.
>
> (Pirkei Avot 2:4)

אבות ב:ד
הלל אומר . . . אל תאמן בעצמך עד יום מותך. ואל תדין את חברך עד שתגיע
למקומו.

Hillel's admonition is two-fold. First, he cautions us against
smugness – for indeed, as the Midrash above suggests, even G-d
does not assume that someone is a true *tsaddik* during their lifetime. At the same time, Hillel admonishes us not to pass judgment on anyone until we have been in similar circumstances and
fared better.

It is not until you are quite old, having reached a point where
your moral destiny is (hopefully) clear and assumed, that you may
safely make any judgments regarding your level of righteousness.
The Midrash does, however, allow for the possibility that one
who has actually looked death in the face and survived and developed an intimate relationship with both man and G-d – such
an individual might indeed be called a *tsaddik* without any anxiety
that he might change and forfeit his title. Yitzchak, at the age of
37 having experienced the *akedah*, was such a man.

The "Akedah:" when his father Avraham placed Yitzchak upon

the "altar" to sacrifice him, at G-d's behest. In fact the actual sacrifice did not occur, for at the very last moment (Bereishit 22:12) Avraham was told "do not stretch out your hand against the lad nor do anything to him, for now I know you are a G-d-fearing man." Thus the Torah forever rejected the practice of human sacrifice.

I would suggest that the Klausenberger Rebbe who lived in our time, was an individual whose status as *tsaddik* was unassailable. Rabbi Yekusiel Yehuda Halberstam z"l, having lost his entire family (including his wife and 11 children) in the Holocaust, came to the United States in 1945 and established an institution through which he adopted thousands of Jewish boys and girls, all Holocaust orphans. He brought them to the U.S. and provided them with both Torah and vocational education, housing, and all the necessities of life. As they grew, he helped with marriages, paid for weddings and housing, and assisted them in job training and placement.

Eventually the Klausenberger Rebbe moved to Israel, settled in the mostly secular city of Netanya, and built a community known as Kiryat Sanz. He then built and supported Netanya's major hospital, Laniado Hospital.

Such a man is indeed a Yitzchak of our time, whose neck was on the altar ready to be slaughtered, and who miraculously survived and went on to live a remarkable life of *kiddush haShem* / sanctification of G-d's name for all to behold and emulate. Such is a *tsaddik*, whose status is not in question even during his lifetime.

Other Holocaust survivors who have demonstrated faith in G-d and man after having faced death in its cruelest terms, may also have earned during their lifetime the title of *tsaddik*.

The Limits of Tsedakah

וְהָאֶבֶן הַזֹּאת אֲשֶׁר־שַׂמְתִּי מַצֵּבָה יִהְיֶה בֵּית
אֱ-לֹהִים וְכֹל אֲשֶׁר תִּתֶּן־לִי עַשֵּׂר אֲעַשְּׂרֶנּוּ לָךְ:
(בראשית כח:כב)

And this stone, which 1 have set up as a pillar,
shall be G-d's abode; and of all that You give me,
1 will set aside a tithe for You. (Bereishit 28:22)

Rabbi Ila'a said: In Usha they decreed that whoever gives liberally
[to charity] must not give away more than one-fifth (of his wealth).
Similarly it is taught: Whoever gives liberally [to charity] must not
give away more than one-fifth (of his wealth) lest he become dependent on others (for charity). (Babylonian Talmud Ketubot 50a)

כתובות נ.

א"ר אילעא: באושא התקינו, המבזבז – אל יבזבז יותר מחומש. תניא נמי הכי:
המבזבז – אל יבזבז יותר מחומש, שמא יצטרך לבריות.

We are obligated to give *tsedakah* (charity), to take of our earnings
and to give to the needy and to worthy institutions. The Torah
expects us to tithe (10%) our income, as was the case in antiquity when the Israelites were expected to tithe their produce, etc.
Yet our sages place an upper limit on our charitable contributions. While 10% is obligatory, the midrash here states that 20%
should be the maximum, lest we impoverish ourselves and then
become a burden, rather than a contributor, to the well-being of
the community at large.

Moreover, one dare not underestimate the impact of one's act
of *tsedakah*, since each individual contribution, no matter how
small, makes an impact when pooled with every other contribution.

The Talmud comments on the verse in Isaiah 59:17 וילבש צדקה כשרין/"For he put on righteousness as a breastplate":

> "Just as each shell, shell-by-shell, contributes towards the making of a large and effective breastplate, so indeed each individual contribution, coin-by-coin, ultimately adds up to a large sum." (Babylonian Talmud Bava Batra 9b)

בבא בתרא ט:

לומר לך, מה שריון זה – כל קליפה וקליפה מצטרפת לשריון גדול, אף צדקה – כל פרוטה ופרוטה מצטרפת לחשבון גדול.

Thus, no one should ever deprecate the amount of their own or anyone else's contribution, so long as it represents a true act of generosity.

Greetings

וַיֹּאמֶר לָהֶם יַעֲקֹב אַחַי מֵאַיִן אַתֶּם וַיֹּאמְרוּ
מֵחָרָן אֲנָחְנוּ: (בראשית כט:ד)

Yaakov said to them, "My friends, where are you
from?" And they said, "We are from Charan."
(Bereishit 29:4)

From here they said: A person should always have a pleasant dis-
position toward others, and they should call them "brothers" and
"friends," and be the first to greet them.   (Midrash Hagadol)

מדרש הגדול
מכאן אמרו לעולם תהא דעתו של אדם מעורבת עם הבריות וקורא להם אחים
ורעים ויקדים בשלום.

To greet a person in a pleasant and peaceful manner is an obligation incumbent upon each of us. Do not wait for the other
person to say *Shalom*. Yaakov is portrayed as greeting strangers
with the title "my brothers" which obviously is not a designation
of family but rather a common greeting of friendship. Thus our
sages teach, extend the hand of friendship to a stranger without
waiting on formal grounds of status or ego. Extend the hand of
friendship with a simple *Shalom*.

Bringing Blessings

וַיֹּאמֶר אֵלָיו לָבָן אִם־נָא מָצָאתִי חֵן בְּעֵינֶיךָ
נִחַשְׁתִּי וַיְבָרְכֵנִי ה' בִּגְלָלֶךָ: (בראשית ל:כז)

But Laban said to him, "If you will indulge me,
I have learned by divination that the Lord has
blessed me on your account." (Bereishit 30:27)

"The Lord has blessed me on your account" (Bereishit 30:27).
Let your house be a place of meeting for sages for whenever sages
and their students enter a person's house, the house is blessed on
their account. For thus we find regarding Yaakov our forefather:
When Yaakov entered Laban's house, the house was blessed on
[Yaakov's] merit, as it says, "For the little you had before I came
[has grown to much, since the Lord has blessed you wherever
I have turned] . . ." (Bereishit 30:30), and Laban says, "I have
learned by divination that the Lord has blessed me on your account" (Bereishit 30:27).

(Avot D'Rabbi Natan, version B, chap. 1)

אבות דרבי נתן נוסחא ב פרק א

"ויברכני ה' בגללך" (בראשית ל:כו). יהי ביתך בית ועד לחכמים שכל זמן שהחכמים
ותלמידיהן נכנסין לתוך ביתו של אדם הבית מתברך בזכותן שכן מצינו ביעקב
אבינו בשעה שנכנס יעקב לתוך ביתו של אדם נתברך הבית בזכותו שנאמר "כי
מעט אשר היה לך לפני ויפרץ לרב ויברך ה' אתך לרגלי וכו'" (שם ל:ל), כן לבן
אומר "נחשתי ויברכני ה' בגללך" (שם ל:כו).

"For the little you had before I came has grown to much, since the
Lord has blessed you wherever I turned. And now, when shall I
make for my own household?" (Bereishit 30:30)

192

(בראשית ל:ל)

כי מעט אשר־היה לך לפני ויפרץ לרב ויברך ה' אתך לרגלי ועתה מתי אעשה גם־אנכי לביתי:

"For the Lord has blessed you wherever I have turned" (Bereishit 30:30) – wherever the righteous go, blessing goes with them . . . Yaakov went down to Laban, and blessing came to where his feet had gone, as it says, "The Lord has blessed you wherever I have turned [lit., to where my feet had gone]" (Bereishit 30:30).

(Midrash Bereishit Rabbah 73:12)

מדרש בראשית רבה עג:יב

"ויברך ה' אותך לרגלי" (בראשית ל:ל) – כל מקום שהצדיקים הולכים ברכה הולכת עמהם . . . . ירד יעקב אצל לבן ובאת ברכה לרגלו שנאמר "ויברך ה' אותך לרגלי" (שם).

Do Yaakov's feet indeed cause Laban's sheep to be fruitful and multiply? From this they say that the foot of some individuals blesses a house and the foot of other individuals destroys a house. And Yaakov's foot was one that blesses, as it says, "since the Lord has blessed you wherever I have turned" (Bereishit 30:30), and Laban says, "I have learned by divination that the Lord has blessed me on your account" (Bereishit 30:27). (Pirkei de-Rabbi Eliezer, 31)

פרקי דרבי אליעזר פרק לא

וכי רגליו של יעקב מפרות ומרבות צאנו של לבן מכאן אמרו יש רגל אדם מברכת בית ויש רגל אדם מחרבת בית והיה רגל יעקב מברכת – שנאמר ויברך ה' אותך לרגלי (בראשית ל:ל) וכן אמר לבן ליעקב "נחשתי ויברכני ה' בגללך" (בראשית ל:כז).

The presence of a righteous person brings blessings and peace to a home. Depending on one's attitude, any individual may bring blessings – or curses – into any environment.

Yaakov was, in the words of Lavan, a "blessing" in Lavan's home; i.e., his flocks increased, bringing prosperity. Yaakov sought to provide for his family, thus his hard work brought blessing both to him and to the entire household of Lavan. The Torah refers specifically to Yaakov's feet as the source of the blessing.

"Did Yaakov's feet really increase the flock?," asks Pirkei D'Rabbi Eliezar. Yes, the midrash answers – there are people who, wherever they step, bring blessings. Conversely, there are people who bring with them nothing but curses.

It is not the feet which have the power of blessing or curse, it is the attitude people bring with them into a given situation. Good people – kind people, people who cherish learning and seek meaning and purpose in their lives and who desire peace and well-being for themselves, their loved ones, and for all people – bring these hopes and aspirations wherever they go, and thus bring peace and blessings with them.

Right Livelihood

וַיֹּאמֶר מָה אֶתֶּן־לָךְ וַיֹּאמֶר יַעֲקֹב לֹא־תִתֶּן־
לִי מְאוּמָה אִם־תַּעֲשֶׂה־לִּי הַדָּבָר הַזֶּה אָשׁוּבָה
אֶרְעֶה צֹאנְךָ אֶשְׁמֹר: (בראשית ל:לא)

He said, "What shall 1 pay you?" And Yaakov
said "Pay me nothing! If you do this thing for
me, 1 will again pasture and keep your flocks."
(Bereishit 30:31)

Work is valued, for all the prophets engaged in it. Regarding Yaakov it says, "I will again pasture and keep your flocks" (Bereishit
30:31); regarding Moshe it says, "And Moshe was a shepherd"
(Shemot 3:1); regarding David it says, "And took him from the
sheepfolds" (Psalms 78:70); regarding Amos it says, "For I am a
sheepbreeder and a tender of sycamore figs." (Amos 7:14).
(Mishnat Rabbi Eliezer Ch. 8).

משנת רבי אליעזר פ"ח

חביבה היא המלאכה שכל הנביאים התעסקו בה. ביעקב כתיב "אשובה ארעה
צאנך וגו'" (בראשית ל:לא). במשה הוא אומר "ומשה היה רועה וגו'" (שמות ג:א),
דוד ע"ה "ויקחהו ממכלאות צאן" (תהלים עח:ע). עמוס, "כי בוקר אנכי וכולם
שקמים" (עמוס ז:יד).

Yaakov is portrayed as a laborer, a simple shepherd. We are re-
minded of the other great men in Tanach who are also described
as shepherds. There is no shame in working for one's livelihood;
in fact, G-d sanctifies the labor of human beings. This theme is
well developed in the Talmud, for example:

Just as the Torah was given in a covenant, so too work was given
in a covenant, as it says, "Six days you shall labor and do all your

work, but the seventh day is a sabbath of the Lord your G-d" (Shemot 20:9–10). (Avot D'Rabbi Natan, 11)

אבות דרבי נתן יא

כשם שהתורה נתנה בברית כך המלאכה נתנה ברית שנאמר "ששת ימים תעבוד ועשית כל מלאכתך ויום השביעי שבת לה' א-להיך" (שמות כ:ט-י).

Work is considered to be noble, and we have a plethora of sources which confirm this concept. Work is a holy, covenantal obligation, as sacred as the obligation to rest on Shabbat.

In Pirkei Avot we read:

Shemaiah says: Love work and despise positions of power.

(Pirkei Avot 1:10)

פרקי אבות א:י

שמעיה אומר אהב את המלאכה ושנא את הרבנות.

Work is to be cherished, the *rabbanut* is to be despised. Here, the word *rabbanut* does not mean the rabbinate as we use the term; rather, it refers to the glory and honor hence the potential for pomposity that may accrue to someone in a position of power. Obviously, rabbis and scholars earn their livelihood as religious leaders and teachers. The Mishnah does not intend to deprecate the nobility of the profession. Rather, hard work – the exertion of energy – is necessary in *any* profession, including that of the rabbinate.

The Talmud bestows honor upon the laborer when it says:

Great is work for it brings honor to its masters. (Babylonian Talmud Nedarim 49b)

נדרים מט:

גדולה מלאכה שמכבדת את בעליה.

This attitude is further reflected in a host of comments concerning the honest labor of the individual. For example, Hillel the Elder was a hewer of wood (T. Yoma 35); Rabbi Yose ben Chalafta was a tanner (T. Shabbat 49); Shammai was a builder (T. Shabbat 31); Rabbi Yochanan was a shoemaker (Avot 4); Rav Chisda and Rav Papa were beer makers (Pesachim 113, Brachot 44). These are just a sample of the great Talmudic scholars who were engaged in physical labor without shame, for indeed they are referred to in the texts not only by name but also by trade.

Labor is understood by the sages to be a means of *imitatio Dei* – כמו הוא אף אתה/"As G-d is, so should you be." In attempting to imitate G-d, we manifest G-d's presence in our midst. Thus the Rabbis sought opportunities to demonstrate that G-d blesses us when we do our share of physical work. For example:

> Rabbi Shimon ben Elazar says: Even the first human being did not taste any [food] until he had worked, as it says, "and placed him in the garden of Eden to till it and tend it" (Bereishit 2:15) and [only] subsequently, "of every tree of the garden you are free to eat" (Bereishit 2:16). Rabbi Tarfon says: Even the Holy One, blessed is He did not cause the Divine Presence to rest on Israel until they had done work, as it says, "And let them make me a sanctuary that I may dwell among them" (Shemot 25:8).
>
> (Avot D'Rabbi Natan, 11)

אבות דרבי נתן יא
רבי שמעון בן אלעזר אומר אף אדם הראשון לא טעם כלום עד שעשה מלאכה שנא' "ויניחהו בגן עדן לעבדה ולשמרה" (בראשית ב:טו) והדר "מכל עץ הגן אכל תאכל" (שם ב:טז). רבי טרפון אומר אף הקב"ה לא השרה שכינתו על ישראל עד שעשו מלאכה שנאמר "ועשו לי מקדש ושכנתי בתוכם" (שמות כה:ח).

Life demands, in a moral sense, that we labor so that G-d's blessings will be bestowed upon that which we do.

Commenting on the verse ובחרת בחיים/"and you shall choose life" (Devarim 30:19), Rabbi Yishmael teaches that you should choose a means of livelihood through which you will be able to support yourself in the life you choose.

Moreover, one is not to wait for a miracle in order to provide for one's needs and the needs of one's family. Quite the contrary, as the Rabbis teach:

A person must [first] toil and work with his two hands and then the Holy One, blessed is He sends His blessing.

(Midrash Tanhuma, Vayetze, 13)

מדרש תנחומא ויצא יג
צריך אדם לעמול ולעשות בשתי ידיו והקב"ה שולח את ברכתו.

He should learn a trade and the Holy One, blessed is He will support him. (Midrash Ecclesiastes Rabbah 6:8)

מדרש קהלת רבה ו:ח
ילמד אדם אומנות והקב"ה מפרנסו.

The Rabbis dramatically reject the "manna from heaven" approach to life, i.e., that I don't need to do anything because "G-d will provide":

If a person does (i.e. works), he receives blessing, but if not, he does not receive blessing. (Midrash Tehillim 23:3)

מדרש תהלים כג:ג
אם עשה אדם הרי הוא מתברך, ואם לאו אינו מתברך.

He said to him: "This is the way of the world – a person works with his own hands, and then the Holy One, blessed is He blesses what [the person] has done, as it says, "so that the Lord your G-d may bless you in all the enterprises that you undertake" (Devarim 14:29). Perhaps [you might think] that a person should sit and be idle, this is why the verse states "that you undertake (asher ta'aseh)." (Midrash Tehillim 136:10)

מדרש תהלים קלו:י
א"ל זהו דרך ארץ עושה בידיו והקב"ה מברך מעשה ידיו, שנאמר "למען יברכך ה' אלהיך בכל מעשה ידך" (דברים יד:כט), יכול יהא יושב ובטל, ת"ל אשר תעשה.

Clearly, a "work ethic" is inherent in the Torah view of human values and behavior.

A Good Heart

וַיַּרְא יַעֲקֹב אֶת־פְּנֵי לָבָן וְהִנֵּה אֵינֶנּוּ עִמּוֹ
כִּתְמוֹל שִׁלְשׁוֹם: (בראשית לא:ב)

Yaakov also saw that Laban's manner toward him
was not as it had been in the past. (Bereishit 31:2)

Bar Sira said, "A person's heart will change one's face, both for good and for bad." (Midrash Bereishit Rabbah 73:14)

מדרש בראשית רבה עג:יד
בר סירא אמר לב אדם ישנה פניו בין לטוב ובין לרע.

One's outer appearance, particularly one's face, is the outer reflection of how one feels. The *lev* / heart referred to in this midrash is one's emotional state. If you feel good about yourself and others, that sense of well-being will manifest in your outer appearance as well. Just as you can tell from a person's face that they are physically in pain, so too can you gauge a person's emotional health from their face.

We find in Pirkei Avot an expression of the centrality of *lev*, of one's emotional state:

Rabbi Yohanan ben Zakkai said to [his students], "Go out and see: What is the right path to which a person should adhere?" Rabbi Eliezer says: good will. Rabbi Joshua says: a good friend. Rabbi Yose says: a good neighbor. Rabbi Shimon says: one who foresees what will be the outcome. Rabbi Elazar says: a good heart. He said to them, "I prefer the words of Rabbi Elazar ben Arakh to all of your words, for your words are included in his." (Pirkei Avot 2:9)

אבות ב:ט

אמר להם רבי יוחנן בן זכאי צאו וראו איזוהי דרך ישרה שידבק בה האדם. רבי
אליעזר אומר עין טובה. רבי יהושע אומר חבר טוב. רבי יוסי אומר שכן טוב. רבי
שמעון אומר הרואה את הנולד. רבי אלעזר אומר לב טוב. אמר להם. רואה אני
את דברי אלעזר בן ערך מדבריכם. שבכלל דבריו דבריכם.

Rabbi Yochanan ben Zakai asks of his disciples 'What is the most
important attribute one should develop'? After hearing their responses, he concludes that a "good heart" – i.e. a good attitude
– determines almost everything about an individual: not only
their outward demeanor, but also their values, the quality of their
interpersonal relationships, and their goals. Faith in oneself, in
others, and in G-d, are all part of one's attitude. Do you seek the
best in people and in situations, or do you always see the worst?
Are you appreciative or are you cynical? Your attitude will determine the quality of your life.

One may ask, are we predetermined to be slaves of our emotions? The midrash teaches:

> The wicked are under the control of their hearts . . . but the righ-
> teous – their hearts are under their control. (Midrash Bereishit
> Rabbah 67:8)

מדרש בראשית רבה סז:ח

הרשעים ברשות לבן . . . אבל הצדיקים לבן ברשותן.

Morally weak people are *controlled by* their emotions, whereas
righteous people are *in control of* their emotions. Everyone deals
with the inner struggle of id versus ego. Legitimate needs, as well
as avarice, fear, shame, etc. are all expressed within that struggle.
This midrash suggests that we are ultimately in control of our
own moral destiny. The moral quality of our lives is in our hands.

Giving Honor

וַיִּקְרָא־לוֹ לָבָן יְגַר שָׂהֲדוּתָא וְיַעֲקֹב קָרָא לוֹ
גַּלְעֵד: (בראשית לא:מז)

*Laban named it Yegar-sahadutha but Yaakov
named it Gal-ed. (Bereishit 31:47)*

Do not treat the Persian language [i.e. Aramaic] lightly, for in the Torah, the Prophets, and the Sacred Writings, we find that the Holy One, blessed is He gives it honor. In the Torah: "And Laban called it yegar sahaduta" (which means "the mound is a witness" – Rashi to Bereishit 31:47); in the Prophets: "Thus you shall say to them . . ." (Jeremiah 10:11, in Aramaic); in the Sacred Writings: "The Chaldeans spoke to the king in Aramaic" (Daniel 2:4).

(Midrash Bereishit Rabbah 74:14)

מדרש בראשית רבה עד:יד
א"ר שמואל בר נחמן אל יהא לשון פרסי הזה קל בעיניך שבתורה בנביאים
בכתובים מצינו שהקדוש ב"ה חולק לו כבוד, בתורה "ויקרא לו לבן יגר
שהדותא" (בראשית לא:מז), בנביאים "כדנה תאמרון להום וגו'" (ירמיה י:יא),
בכתובים "וידברו הכשדים למלך ארמית" (דניאל ב:ד).

In this midrash, G-d is described as "giving honor" to the Syrian language of antiquity. This is a powerful term, not used lightly, and it is all the more remarkable given that the Rabbis were not living in a culture which valued brotherhood, respect and tolerance when dealing with foreigners, or their religion and culture.

In the Face of the Enemy

וַיְצַו אֹתָם לֵאמֹר כֹּה תֹאמְרוּן לַאדֹנִי לְעֵשָׂו
כֹּה אָמַר עַבְדְּךָ יַעֲקֹב עִם־לָבָן גַּרְתִּי וָאֵחַר עַד־
עָתָּה: (בראשית לב:ה)

And he instructed them as follows, "Thus you shall say to my lord Eisav, 'thus says your servant Yaakov, I stayed with Laban and remained until now.'" (Bereishit 32:5)

Our Rabbi (Rabbi Judah the Patriarch) said to Rabbi Appas, "Write a letter in my name to our master the emperor [lit. 'King'] Antoninus." He went and wrote: From Judah the Patriarch [referring to the Patriarch who lived in Amoraic times] to our master Emperor Antoninus. He took it and read it and tore it up. He said to him, "Write: From your servant Judah to our Master Emperor Antoninus." He said to him, "Rabbi [my master], why are you disgracing your honor?" He replied, "Am I better than my ancestor? Did he not say [in a message to Eisav] 'thus says your servant Yaakov' (Bereishit 32:5)."

(Midrash Bereishit Rabbah 75:5)

מדרש בראשית רבה עה:ה

רבינו אמר לרבי אפס כתוב חד אגרא מן שמי למרן מלכא אנטונינוס, קם וכתב
מן יהודה נשיאה למרן מלכא אנטונינוס, נסבה וקרייה וקרעיה, אמר ליה כתוב
מן עבדך יהודה למרן מלכא אנטונינוס, אמר ליה רבי מפני מה אתה מבזה
על כבודך, אמר ליה מה אנא טב מן סבי לא כך אמר "כה אמר עבדך יעקב"
(בראשית לב:ה). . . .

A similar midrash is recorded elsewhere:

Great is modesty, for which Yaakov our forefather was praised, as it says, "your servant Yaakov" (Bereishit 32:5). (Mishnat Rabbi Eliezer chapter 10)

משנת רבי אליעזר פרק י
גדולה היא הענוה שבה נשתבח יעקב אבינו שנאמר "עבדך יעקב" (בראשית לב:ה).

This text also praises Yaakov for humbling himself before his brother. On the other hand, we find a contrary view expressed in similar sources. For example:

> When Yaakov called Eisav "my master" the Holy One, blessed is He said to him, "you humbled yourself and called Eisav 'my master' eight times; by your life, I will raise up eight kings from among his sons before [I raise any up from] your sons", as it says, "These are the kings [who ruled in the land of Edom before any king reigned over the Israelites" (Bereishit 36:31).
>
> (Midrash Bereishit Rabbah 75:11)

(מדרש בראשית רבה פרשה עה סימן יא)
באותה שעה שקרא יעקב לעשו אדוני אמר לו הקב"ה אתה השפלת עצמך
וקראת לעשו אדוני ח' פעמים, חייך אני מעמיד מבניו שמנה מלכים קודם
לבניך, שנאמר "ואלה המלכים אשר מלכו וגו'" (בראשית לו:לא).

Yaakov humbles himself by calling his brother Eisav "my lord" eight times. As a consequence of his doing so, says this midrash, eight kings will arise from Eisav's line before one king arises from Yaakov. Thus the Midrash harshly condemns what it sees as unnecessary humility in the face of an enemy.

Yet another midrash offers a more profound perspective of Yaakov's action:

> And Yaakov took the entire tenth of his property that he had brought from Padan Aram, sent it with his servants, and gave it to Eisav. He told them, "say to him: Thus says your servant Yaakov." The Holy One, blessed is He said to Yaakov, "You have made the sacred profane." He replied, "Master of all the worlds, I am flattering the wicked so that he does not kill me." Based on this the sages say: One flatters the wicked in this world for the sake of peace (lit. because of the ways of peace). (Pirkei de-Rabbi Eliezer 37)

פרקי דרבי אליעזר פרק לז

ולקח יעקב את כל מעשר קניינו שהביא מפדן ארם ושלח ביד עבדיו ונתן לעשו,
אמ' להם אמרו לו כה אמר עבדך יעקב, אמר הקב"ה יעקב עשית הקדש חול,
אמ' לפניו רבון כל העולמים אני מחניף לרשע בשביל שלא יהרגני, מכאן אמרו
חכמים מחניפין את הרשעים בעולם הזה מפני דרכי שלום.

Rather than judging Yaakov's actions, here the Midrash engages
Yaakov in a dialogue with G-d. G-d asks, "Why did you take that
which was holy and defile it by giving it to Eisav?" Yaakov responds, "It was necessary so that Eisav spare my life." Thus the
midrash points out that it is at times necessary to flatter one's
enemy in order to achieve peace.

Throughout Jewish history there has been a debate regarding
how to approach the enemy. Do you appease? Do you confront?
Contemporary Israeli politics reflect this conundrum. This debate is reflected in these conflicting rabbinic sources.

Economic Pragmatism

וַיִּירָא יַעֲקֹב מְאֹד וַיֵּצֶר לוֹ וַיַּחַץ אֶת־הָעָם
אֲשֶׁר־אִתּוֹ וְאֶת־הַצֹּאן וְאֶת־הַבָּקָר וְהַגְּמַלִּים
לִשְׁנֵי מַחֲנוֹת: (בראשית לב:ח)

Yaakov was greatly frightened; in his anxiety, he
divided the people with him, and the flocks and
herds, and camels, into two camps. (Bereishit 32:8)

"He divided the people" (Bereishit 32:8) – The Torah is teaching
you the way of the world (good business practice), that a person
should not put all of his money in one corner (i.e. in one investment). From whom do you learn this? From Yaakov, as it says, "he
divided the people."   (Midrash Bereishit Rabbah 76:3)

מדרש בראשית רבה עו:ג

"ויחץ את העם" (בראשית לב:ח), לימדך תורה דרך ארץ שלא יהא אדם נותן כל
ממונו בזוית אחד ממי אתה למד מיעקב, שנאמר "ויחץ את העם וגו."

A person should always divide his money into three: a third in
property (real estate), a third in business (goods), and a third at his
disposal (cash). (Babylonian Talmud Bava Metzia, 42a)

בבא מציעא מב.

לעולם ישלש אדם את מעותיו שליש בקרקע, שליש בפרקמטיא ושליש תחת יד.

The pragmatism evident in these Midrashic observations is serious and relevant to today's financial markets. Never put all your
assets in one investment, counsel the sages.

These observations help us understand and appreciate the sophistication of the rabbinic community in the Talmudic period
and even earlier. These men were not ivory tower scholars, de-

tached from the world. They engaged in every form of craft and trade.

While pragmatism informed the Rabbis' economic perspective, ethical and moral standards informed their economic view as it informed all else. We find in Ethics of the Fathers:

> Rabbi Yose says: Let your friend's money be as precious to you as your own. (Pirkei Avot 2:17)

אבות ב:יז
רבי יוסי אומר יהי ממון חברך חביב עליך כשלך.

While I need to be well informed concerning my financial assets and act wisely in their investment, I must treat the possessions of others with equal respect and concern.

At the same time, the Rabbis did not value wealth in and of itself. Intrinsic to the significance of wealth was its ultimate use in developing a life of meaning. What gives meaning to life?

The Rabbis teach:

> There are three things beloved to a person during his life: his children and the members of his household, his money, and good deeds. And at the time of his departing from the world, he calls to his children and the members of his household and says to them, "please save [lit. take] me from this evil judgment of death." And they reply, "have you not heard, 'There is no authority over the day of death' (Ecclesiastes 8:8), and is it not written, 'A brother cannot redeem a man' (Psalms 49:8). And even [the person's] money that he loves cannot redeem him, as it says, 'or pay his ransom to G-d'" (Ibid.). (Pirkei de-Rabbi Eliezer, 33)

פרקי דרבי אליעזר פרק לג
שלשה אהובים יש לו לאדם בחייו, ואלו הן, בניו ובני ביתו וממונו ומעשים
טובים, ובשעת פטירתו מן העולם קורא לבניו ובני ביתו ואומ' להם בבקשה מכם
"הוציאוני מדין המות הרע הזה", והם אומרים לו "והלא שמעת ואין שלטון ביום
המות" (קהלת ח:ח), ולא כך כתיב "אח לא פדה יפדה איש" (תהלים מט:ח), ואפילו
ממונו שהוא אוהב אותו אינו יכול לפדותו, שנ' "ולא יתן לא־לוהים כפרו" (שם).

At the end of life, neither family nor wealth can redeem from or transcend, death and its implications. Yet, say the Rabbis, one's acts of generosity and good deeds are "eternal," thus capable of transcending even death.

The Rabbis do not narrowly interpret "good deeds" as the distribution of one's wealth to charitable endeavors. Children, family members, and associates who have been inspired, taught and motivated to perform the mitzvah of *tsedakah* and who manifest the values of *tsedek* – "righteousness" in all their endeavors, become part of one's eternal legacy.

Don't Wait for a Miracle

קָטֹנְתִּי מִכֹּל הַחֲסָדִים וּמִכָּל־הָאֱמֶת אֲשֶׁר
עָשִׂיתָ אֶת־עַבְדֶּךָ כִּי בְמַקְלִי עָבַרְתִּי אֶת־הַיַּרְדֵּן
הַזֶּה וְעַתָּה הָיִיתִי לִשְׁנֵי מַחֲנוֹת: (בראשית לב:יא)

I am unworthy of all the kindness that You have
steadfastly shown Your servant; with my staff
alone I have crossed this Jordan, and now I have
become two camps. (Bereishit 32:11)

Rabbi Yanai said: A person should never stand in a place of danger and say, "a miracle will be performed for me," for perhaps a
miracle will not be performed for him. And even if you say that a
miracle will be performed for him, this will be deducted from his
merits. (Babylonian Talmud Ta'anit 20b)

תענית כ:
אמר רבי ינאי: לעולם אל יעמוד אדם במקום סכנה ויאמר עושין לי נס, שמא אין
עושין לו נס, ואם תימצי לומר עושין לו נס - מנכין לו מזכיותיו.

Our sages learn from Yaakov the pragmatic approach of a person
of faith. Yaakov says to G-d, "I am unworthy of even the least
of your mercies" – that is to say, Yaakov does not intend to rely
solely on G-d's intervention should Eisav decide to attack. We
dare not ignore the possibility of danger when we are capable of
making choices and respond in ways which may in fact protect
us. Miracles have occurred, and will occur – yet, say the Rabbis,
we must act in a responsible, pragmatic manner to the extent of
our G-d-given capabilities. Only then may we hope for a miracle.

This midrash is a wonderful companion to the previous cita-
tion. How one earns a livelihood, what one does with assets acquired honestly and justly, also requires an ethical and pragmatic

approach. The rabbinic admonition אין סומכין על הנס /"one does not rely upon a miracle" (Yannai Rabbah, Babylonian Talmud Shabbat 32a), informs all of Jewish thought and judgment. Even the Sea of Reeds did not yield to the Children of Israel until one man, Nachshon, stepped forward and demonstrated that prayer alone was not sufficient. The miracle of the Hanukkah Menorah began with the use of one real jug of oil. Do not wait for a miracle – we must do all that we can, and only then rely upon G-d to perform a miracle.

Everything is from G-d; yet there are moments and events which transcend the daily, indeed constant, miracles which enable us to function. There are moments or events which defy the norm, such as when a patient recovers after the doctor has said there is "no hope." These moments are truly miraculous.

The Transcendent Value of Tsedakah

קָטֹנְתִּי מִכֹּל הַחֲסָדִים וּמִכָּל־הָאֱמֶת אֲשֶׁר
עָשִׂיתָ אֶת עַבְדֶּךָ כִּי בְמַקְלִי עָבַרְתִּי אֶת הַיַּרְדֵּן
הַזֶּה הָיִיתִי לִשְׁנֵי מַחֲנוֹת: (בראשית לב:יא)

I am unworthy of all the kindness that You have
steadfastly shown Your servant; with my staff
alone I have crossed this Jordan, and now I have
become two camps. (Bereishit 32:11)

Yaakov is only praised on account of [his] *tsedakah* [acts of righ-
teousness] as it says, "I am unworthy [*katonti*] of all of the kindness" (Bereishit 32:11). "Unworthy [*katonti*]" is "little [*me'at*]" and
"little [*me'at*]" is *tsedakah*, as it says, "better a little [*me'at*] with
righteousness [*tsedakah*]" (Mishlei 16:8).   (Tanna de-Bei Eliyahu
Zuta 1:8)

תנא דבי אליהו זוטא א:ח

יעקב לא נשתבח אלא בצדקה, שנאמר "קטנתי מכל החסדים" (בראשית לב:יא),
אין קטנתי אלא מעט, אין מעט אלא צדקה, שנאמר "טוב מעט בצדקה"
(משלי טז:ח).

Yaakov is praised only because of his acts of *tsedakah*. Beyond all
his struggles, achievements, and nation-building efforts, his tsedakah transcends all other dimensions of his life.

Avraham, too, is praised for his acts of *tsedakah*:

For his greatness of *tsedakah* – "Acts of Kindness," Avraham our
father [forefather] is blessed. (Midrash Mishlei 14:15)

מדרש משלי יד:טו

גדולה צדקה שבה נשתבח אברהם אבינו.

Both Avraham and Yaakov are heralded not for their acts of faith or piety alone, rather, their claim to fame is attributed to *tsedakah*, understood here as acts of loving kindness and righteousness.

We find in the Talmud the following related teachings:

Tsedakah is equivalent to all of the commandments.

(Babylonian Talmud Bava Batra 9a)

בבא בתרא ט.
שקולה צדקה כנגד כל המצות.

Great is *tsedakah* for it brings the redemption closer.

(Babylonian Talmud Bava Batra 10a)

בבא בתרא י.
גדולה צדקה שמקרבת את הגאולה.

Jerusalem will only be redeemed through *tsedakah*.

(Babylonian Talmud Shabbat 139a)

שבת קלט.
אין ירושלים נפדה אלא בצדקה.

The unique merit of *tsedakah* lies in its intrinsic and transcending quality. Beyond the obvious fact that it requires the giving of one's self, one's time, and/or one's possessions, *tsedakah* impacts the giver in spiritual ways as well. At the same time, it has an impact upon the recipient that transcends the material, for it enhances the quality of life of that individual or community. Thus both giver and receiver are beneficiaries. Perhaps this dual nature of *tsedakah* is what prompted the sages to consider it to be the greatest attribute of both Avraham and Yaakov.

Knowing When and How to Respond

וַיְצַו אֶת־הָרִאשׁוֹן לֵאמֹר כִּי יִפְגָשְׁךָ עֵשָׂו אָחִי
וּשְׁאֵלְךָ לֵאמֹר לְמִי־אַתָּה וְאָנָה תֵלֵךְ וּלְמִי אֵלֶּה
לְפָנֶיךָ: (בראשית לב:יח)

When my brother Eisav meets you and asks
you whose man are you? Where are you going?
And whose [animals] are these ahead of you?
(Bereishit 32:18)

Yaakov instructs his servant how to answer the question his
brother Eisav is likely to pose. Most of the commentaries suggest
that the Torah here teaches us how to respond even to one who
may not have the most honorable intentions: Regardless of our
assumptions about the intentions of the questioner – דֶּרֶךְ אֶרֶץ –
Derech Eretz usually means "respect" (i.e. Have דֶּרֶךְ אֶרֶץ for elders, parents, teachers and all people), a civil attitude is necessary.

One source suggests:

> The Torah teaches good manners that if you meet a person on the
> road, ask him: Who are you? Where are you going? What is your
> trade? (Midrash Lekach Tov)

מדרש לקח טוב
למדתך תורה דרך ארץ שאם תפגע אדם בדרך שאל לו למי אתה ולאן אתה
הולך והאומנתך.

A respectful attitude would require answers to the questions
posed.

We find in the Peirush HaTur a sensitive and remarkable insight on the subject, quoted in *Torah Shlemah*:

212

My father Rabbi Asher of blessed memory said that [Yaakov] specifically told them [that] if they ask you then tell them "thus said . . ." but if they do not ask, then keep going and do not give them anything. (Yaakov ben Asher, Peirush HaTur, Cited in Torah Shelemah, n. 98 to Bereishit 32)

תורה שלמה בראשית פרק לב בהערה צח
אמר אדוני אבי הרא"ש ז"ל שאמר להם דווקא אם ישאלכם אז תאמרו לו "כה אמר וגו'" ואם לא ישאלכם אז תלכו לדרככם ולא תתנו לו מאומה.

Modern society loves to "tell all" – even when not asked. The Rosh (Asher ben Yechiel, father of the Tur) teaches that you need only answer when asked – otherwise, silence is most appropriate.

Personal Possessions

וַיִּוָּתֵר יַעֲקֹב לְבַדּוֹ . . . : (בראשית לב:כה)

"Yaakov was left alone . . ." (Bereishit 32:25)

Rabbi Elazar said: Because he remained behind for the sake of some small jars. From this we learn that righteous individuals hold their money more dear than their bodies. And why to this extent? Because they do not engage in [lit. put their hand in] theft.

(Babylonian Talmud Chullin 91a)

חולין צא.

אמר רבי אלעזר: שנשתייר על פכין קטנים, מכאן לצדיקים שחביב עליהם ממונם יותר מגופם וכל כך למה – לפי שאין פושטין ידיהן בגזל.

Moral enlightened self-interest is a right of moral people. The Midrash tell us that Yaakov, having moved his family to a place of safety in preparation for his brother Eisav's possible attack, now returns alone during the night – to retrieve some small jars he has left behind. The Rabbis are obviously perplexed by this move. Why does he endanger himself just for a few jars?! Says Rabbi Elazar, righteous and honest people cherish their possessions because they have worked hard to acquire them.

We find an interesting observation concerning money in a passage of the Jerusalem Talmud:

Rabbi Yochanan was robbed at Alei Kanyah. He went to the assembly house (study hall), and Rabbi Shimon ben Lakish asked him a question, but he did not respond. He asked him a question [again], and he did not respond. [R. Shimon ben Lakish] said to him, "why [are you acting] in this manner?" He said to him, "all of the limbs are dependent on the heart, and the heart is dependent on the wallet." (Jerusalem Talmud Terumot 8:4)

ירושלמי תרומות פרק ח הלכה ד
רבי יוחנן אמר איקפח בעלי קנייה סליק לבית וועדא והוה רבי שמעון בן לקיש
שאיל ליה ולא מגיב שאיל ליה ולא מגיב אמ' ליה מהו הכין א"ל כל האיברין
תלויין בלב והלב תלוי בכים.

A remark which seems materialistic even in our time. Yet, it is clear that our sages viewed poverty as a plague. We find in the Talmud, for example:

"Poverty in one's home is more painful than 50 plagues." (Babylonian Talmud Bava Batra 116a)

בבא בתרא קטז.
קשה עניות בתוך ביתו של אדם יותר מחמשים מכות.

Moreover, the Rabbis fully appreciated the demoralizing nature of poverty:

Whoever depends on the table of others – the world is dark for him, as it says "He wanders about for bread – where is it? He knows that the day of darkness has been readied for him" (Job 15:23). Rav Chisda said: His life is not even life.

(Babylonian Talmud Beitzah 32b)

ביצה לב:
כל המצפה על שלחן אחרים – עולם חשך בעדו, שנאמר "נדד הוא ללחם איה
ידע כי נכון בידו יום חשך" (איוב טו:כג). רב חסדא אמר: אף חייו אינן חיים.

For one who must depend upon the "table of others," i.e., who is economically dependent on others for food, the world is dark. Rav Hisda adds – "His life is not a life." Elsewhere, our sages say that a poor person is like a dead person.

Judaism clearly rejects the teaching of some other religious traditions i.e., poverty is intrinsically a virtue, a path to spiritual growth. Perhaps this rabbinic rejection of the supposed virtue of poverty is what led to the difficult concept quoted above from the Jerusalem Talmud, that "all is determined by the heart and the

heart is determined by the purse." Perhaps this is also the source
of the concept cited earlier that the righteous value their wealth
even above their very being. Thus neither wealth nor poverty are
considered automatic signs of virtue or piety.

One needs the material to allow the spiritual. The balance between possession and person is what leads to the ideal. This is
best stated in the Mishnah of *Ethics of our Fathers* 3:17:

אם אין קמח אין תורה, אם אין תורה אין קמח/ "If there is no bread there
can be no Torah, if there is no Torah there can be no bread."

The Sun Rises for You

וַיִּזְרַח־לוֹ הַשֶּׁמֶשׁ כַּאֲשֶׁר עָבַר אֶת־פְּנוּאֵל וְהוּא
צֹלֵעַ עַל־יְרֵכוֹ: (בראשית לב:לב)

The sun rose for him as he passed Penuel, limping
on his hip. (Bereishit 32:32)

Rabbi Akiva said: I asked Rabban Gamliel and Rabbi Joshua in the
fair of Emmaus, when they had gone there to purchase an animal
for Rabban Gamliel's son's wedding. It is written 'The sun rose for
him' (Bereishit 32:32) – did the sun rise for him alone? Did it not
rise for the entire world? Rabbi Yitzchak said: The sun which came
for his sake rose for his sake.   (Babylonian Talmud Chullin 91b)

חולין צא:

אמר ר' עקיבא: שאלתי את רבן גמליאל ואת רבי יהושע באיטליז של אימאום,
שהלכו ליקח בהמה למשתה בנו של רבן גמליאל, כתיב "ויזרח לו השמש"
(בראשית לב:לב), וכי שמש לו לבד זרחה? והלא לכל העולם זרחה אמר ר' יצחק:
שמש הבאה בעבורו, זרחה בעבורו.

The question posed by Rabbi Akiva here is obvious: Why does
the Torah suggest that the sun rose for Yaakov's sake, when the
sun rises for everyone equally? Rabbi Yitzchak responds, the sun
which came to heal Yaakov had a uniquely healing quality for
him in his moment of pain and fear. It was his personal and direct
sun for that moment. Note the comment of Rashi -לצרכו ולרפאות
את צלעתו – "the sun came to (Yaakov) for his needs and to heal
his limp" the sun's rays were of specific and personal comfort to
Yaakov and his injured hip.

We need to see the particular blessings or challenges which
occur in life as our specific and personal events.

Life may either be a continuous experience of humdrum

events which move us through day after day, unchallenged and unfulfilled – or we may see each day, each rising of the sun, as our call, our challenge, our healing.

The midrash insists that when Yaakov was in pain and in need of healing, the sun rose *for him* – though obviously it rose for all of humanity as well. The specificity with which the Torah describes the sun's appearance for Yaakov that day is indeed true for us as well. Each day brings each of us its unique blessings and challenges, if we but sense it and respond personally.

Completeness

וַיָּבֹא יַעֲקֹב שָׁלֵם עִיר שְׁכֶם אֲשֶׁר בְּאֶרֶץ כְּנַעַן
בְּבֹאוֹ מִפַּדַּן אֲרָם וַיִּחַן אֶת־פְּנֵי הָעִיר:

(בראשית לג:יח)

Yaakov arrived safe in the city of Shechem which
is in the land of Canaan-having come thus from
Paddan-aram-and he encamped before the city.

(Bereishit 33:18)

"Yaakov arrived unharmed [lit. whole]" (Bereishit 33:18) – and
Rav said "whole in body, whole in money, and whole in Torah."

(Babylonian Talmud Shabbat 33b)

שבת לג:

"ויבא יעקב שלם" (בראשית לג:יח) ואמר רב: שלם בגופו, שלם בממונו, שלם
בתורתו.

What does the Torah consider critical in a person's life? To be
shalem/ complete. In defining the word *shalem*, the Talmud gives
three criteria: first, completeness in body, i.e., being healthy. (I
would suggest that this refers both to physical as well as mental
health.) A sick person, through no personal failing, is limited.
Pain, incapacity, or suffering brought on by physical or mental
torment in some measure may impact upon the individual and
lessen objective judgment.

The second criterion is that of being complete economically.
The Talmud is not suggesting that wealth is a prerequisite for
human completeness. However, recognize that economic independence and stability give the individual greater latitude for
self-determination. You are more accountable for your actions

when you are in a position to choose without fear of interference or retribution from those who control your purse strings.

The third criterion for human completeness is completeness in Torah. Yaakov was said to be complete in his "Torah." Though wandering and lacking the support of community, bearing the complex burdens of family, travel, and fear of a hostile brother and father-in-law, nonetheless he was complete in his "Torah." The tradition given Yaakov by Yitzchak and Rivka guided him and enabled him to maintain the faith of his parents and grand-parents in a hostile, pagan world.

Health, economic stability, and loyalty to Torah – one's values and family tradition are what give one completeness in the human experience. No doubt one may argue that throughout history, in-dividuals who were not well and poor did in fact contribute much to society. Nonetheless, the text speaks of the average person.

Repaying Hospitality

וַיָּבֹא יַעֲקֹב שָׁלֵם עִיר שְׁכֶם אֲשֶׁר בְּאֶרֶץ
כְּנַעַן בְּבֹאוֹ מִפַּדַּן אֲרָם וַיִּחַן אֶת־פְּנֵי הָעִיר:
(בראשית לג:יח)

Yaakov arrived safe in the city of Shechem which
is in the land of Canaan – having come thus
from Paddan-aram – and he encamped before
the city. (Bereishit 33:18)

He began to set up shops and sell at cheap prices. This says that
a person must show gratitude to a place from which he benefits.
(Midrash Bereishit Rabbah 79:6)

מדרש בראשית רבה עט:ו
התחיל מעמיד הטליסין ומוכר בזול, הדא אמרת שאדם צריך להחזיק טובה
למקום שיש לו הנאה ממנו.

Yaakov comes to Shechem, is welcomed by its citizens, and is
offered the opportunity to settle in the city. He expresses his appreciation for this hospitality by establishing what appears to be
a butcher shop, in which he sells his products at greatly reduced
prices. Here the Rabbis teach that one needs to manifest one's
appreciation in a tangible manner when welcomed as a stranger
into a new community.

This value is especially pertinent to American Jewry. The com-
patibility and opportunity of American society, its institutions,
and its culture, are unprecedented in Jewish history. Although at
times we have been victims of discrimination, nonetheless Jews
ultimately reached a level of achievement never before experienced. In academia, finance, science, government, the arts – in

221

virtually every arena of American life – we have reached prominence, admiration, and success.

Yet, we dare not forget the tragic end of Yaakov's Shechem
experience. His daughter Dinah "goes out" from the secure environment of her father's camp, and the result is catastrophic: She is
violated, and then two of her brothers (Shimon and Levi) avenge
her honor by killing the men of Shechem. Yaakov says to Shimon
and Levi: "You have brought trouble on me to make me odious
among the inhabitants of the land" (Bereishit 34:30).

The relationship between Yaakov and the citizens of Shechem
was initially positive and productive, yet it ended in disaster. The
Rabbis teach that one must manifest an appreciation of a host
community, yet one needs to be cautious in relating to an alien
culture. How/where does one draw the line?

This distinction has yet to be drawn in the open and multi-cul-
tural society of the United States, and other democratic societies.
It is, however, at the core of the survival of a serious and vibrant
Jewish community involved in the academic, cultural, political
and economic life of a free and democratic country.

While one may argue that increasing the Jewish population in
Israel is critical, it is equally necessary to maintain significant and
proud Jewish communities in the diaspora. Modern Israel may
have as its destiny to be a "light unto the nations," but the light of
Jewish values must also emanate from Jewish communities in the
diaspora. This issue demands serious and sensitive deliberation.

Honoring the Deceased

וַיַּצֵּב יַעֲקֹב מַצֵּבָה עַל־קְבֻרָתָהּ הִוא מַצֶּבֶת
קְבֻרַת־רָחֵל עַד־הַיּוֹם: (בראשית לה:כ)

Over her grave Yaakov set up a pillar; it is a pillar
at Rachel's grave to this day. (Bereishit 35:20)

Rabban Shimon ben Gamliel taught: "one does not make monuments for the righteous [for] their words are their remembrance."
(Midrash Bereishit Rabbah 82:10)

מדרש בראשית רבה פב:י
תני ר' שמעון בן גמליאל אין עושין נפשות לצדיקים דבריהם הן זכרוניהם.

This midrash seems to dismiss the tradition of placing monuments on the graves of the righteous; yet clearly, throughout Jewish history, this has been our tradition. From the tomb of Rachel on the road into Bethlehem, to the tomb of the revered Rabbi Meir of Talmudic times in Tiberias, to the tomb of the Maharal of Prague – and in modern times as well – Jews have placed monuments of all shapes and sizes on the graves of the most revered personalities of our people. The words of this midrash obviously did not deter families or communities from erecting monuments in Jewish cemeteries throughout the world.

Rabbi Shimon ben Gamliel's objective seems to have been to compel us to understand that in a profound sense, monuments do not honor righteous people. The exclusive manifestation of honor is the continued role of that person's wisdom and values in our lives – that is the only honor we can bestow upon those we love, cherish and revere. Huge or elaborate monuments serve no one, neither the deceased nor the living.

We visit graves to recall and be inspired by the life, teachings, and accomplishments of the deceased, and thereby challenged to improve our lives. Jewish tradition does require that we place a tombstone, primarily to protect the grave and to assure that we know who is buried in this place. Thus it is obligatory to place a tombstone as a marker; yet the only honor for the deceased is the continued influence of their deeds upon our lives.

Conversion Through Education

וַיֵּשֶׁב יַעֲקֹב בְּאֶרֶץ מְגוּרֵי אָבִיו בְּאֶרֶץ כְּנָעַן:
(בראשית לז:א)

Now Yaakov was settled in the land where his
father had sojourned, the land of Canaan.
(Bereishit 37:1)

Another interpretation: "Yaakov was settled . . ." (Bereishit 37:1) –
Avraham converted people, as it is written, "Avraham took his wife
Sarai . . . [and the people they had made in Charan]" (Bereishit
12:5). Rabbi Elazar said in the name of Rabbi Yose ben Zimra: If
all of the people of the world got together to try to create, even
only a mosquito, they would not be able to do so. And you say "the
people they had made in Charan"? Rather, these are the converts
that Avraham had made. And why does the text say "made" rather
than "converted"? To teach you that whoever brings a convert
near [to G-d], it is as if he created him. Will you say that Avraham
converted people and Sarah did not convert people? The verse
says "the people they had made in Charan" – it does not say "he
made" but rather "that they had made." Rabbi Chunia said: Avraham converted the men and Sarah converted the women. And
why does it say, "that they had made"? It teaches that Avraham our
forefather brought them into his house, fed them, gave them what
to drink, brought them near [to G-d], and brought them under
the wings of the Divine Presence (Shechinah). Yaakov converted
people, as it is written, "Yaakov said to his household [and to all
who were with him, 'Rid yourselves of the alien gods in your midst
. . .']" (Bereishit 35:2) and "They gave to Yaakov [all the alien gods
that they had] . . ." (Bereishit 35:4). Regarding Yitzchak, we do not
hear [that he converted people]. And where have we heard with

respect to Yitzchak [that he converted people]? As Rabbi Hoshaya the great taught in the name of Rabbi Judah son of Rabbi Simon: Here it is written "Yaakov was settled in the land where his father had sojourned" (Bereishit 37:1) – what does "where his father sojourned (megurei)" mean? "Of the converts (*migiyurei*) of his father."   (Midrash Bereishit Rabbah 84:4)

מדרש בראשית רבה פד:ד

ד"א "וישב יעקב וגו'" (בראשית לז:א), אברהם גייר גיורים, הה"ד (בראשית יב:ה)
"ויקח אברם את שרי אשתו", א"ר אלעזר בשם ר' יוסי בן זימרא אם מתכנסין כל
באי העולם לבראות אפילו יתוש אחד אינן יכולין ואת אומר "ואת הנפש אשר
עשו בחרן" (שם), אלא אלו הגרים שגייר אותם אברהם ולמה אמר עשו ולא
אמר גיירו ללמדך שכל מי שהוא מקרב את הגר, כאלו בראו, תאמר אברהם
היה מגייר ושרה לא היתה מגיירת תלמוד לומר "ואת הנפש אשר עשו בחרן"
(שם) אשר עשה אין כתיב כאן אלא אשר עשו, א"ר חונ[י]א אברהם היה מגייר
את האנשים ושרה מגיירת את הנשים, ומה ת"ל "אשר עשו" אלא מלמד שהיה
אברהם אבינו מכניסן לתוך ביתו ומאכילן ומשקן ומקרבן ומכניסן תחת כנפי
השכינה, יעקב גייר גיורים דכתיב "ויאמר יעקב אל־ביתו ואל כל־אשר עמו
הסרו את־אלהי הנכר אשר בתככם": (שם לה:ב) "ויתנו אל יעקב וגו'" (שם לה:ד)
ביצחק לא שמענו והיכן שמענו רבי יצחק ותאני לה משום רבי הושעיא רבה
בשם ר' יהודה בר סימון כאן כתיב "וישב יעקב בארץ מגורי אביו" (שם לז:א) מאי
מגורי אביו מגיורי אביו.

This text adds to the plethora of rabbinic comments concerning converts and the Jewish historical perspective regarding conversion. It becomes increasingly clear that there is no consistent rabbinic attitude, and obviously one can not compare, the pre-Christian pagan world, to that of the Christian and Islamic world. The paradoxical positions held by the Talmudic/Midrashic scholars reflect the cultural tensions they experienced.

The text quoted here highlights the educational approach of the patriarchs and matriarchs towards potential converts: i.e., men instructed men, and women instructed women. The missionary effort was thus an educational effort. We do not sense in this description a charismatic, evangelical approach; the Midrash suggests that Avraham and Sarah persuaded through instruction rather than emotion. Their hospitality served as the vehicle for conversion, though not in a coercive manner.

Jealousy

וְיִשְׂרָאֵל אָהַב אֶת־יוֹסֵף מִכָּל־בָּנָיו כִּי־בֶן־זְקֻנִים
הוּא לוֹ וְעָשָׂה לוֹ כְּתֹנֶת פַּסִּים: (בראשית לז:ג)

Now Israel loved Yosef best of all his sons, for he
was the child of his old age; and he made him an
ornamented tunic. (Bereishit 37:3)

Resh Lakish said in the name of Rabbi Elazar ben Azariah: A person should not distinguish one child among his children, for on
account of the multi-colored coat that Yaakov our forefather made
for Yosef – "they hated him" (Bereishit 37:4).

(Midrash Bereishit Rabbah 84:8)

מדרש בראשית רבה פד:ח

ריש לקיש בשם רבי אלעזר בן עזריה אמר שלא צריך אדם לשנות בן מבניו שע"י
כתונת פסים שעשה אבינו יעקב ליוסף "וישנאו אותו וגו'" (בראשית לז:ד).

And Rava bar Mechasiah said [in the name of] Rav Chama bar
Goria [in the name of] Rav: A person should never distinguish one
child among his children, for on account of the wool weighing
[only] two sela that Yaakov gave Yosef above [what he gave] his
other sons, [Yosef's] brothers were jealous of him, and the matter
unfolded and our ancestors went down to Egypt. (Babylonian Talmud Shabbat 10b)

שבת י:

ואמר רבא בר מחסיא אמר רב חמא בר גוריא אמר רב: לעולם אל ישנה אדם
בנו בין הבנים, שבשביל משקל שני סלעים מילת שנתן יעקב ליוסף יותר משאר
בניו – נתקנאו בו אחיו, ונתגלגל הדבר וירדו אבותינו למצרים.

Our sages take this opportunity to teach the powerful lesson of

227

the potential evil of jealousy inherent in sibling rivalry, nourished by parent-child relationships.

Yaakov obviously loves his wife Rachel more than the other mothers of his children. He then favors Yosef, the firstborn of Rachel, and demonstrates his love with the gift of the infamous multi-colored coat.

The text in the Talmud is specific: "because of two *s'la'eem,*" i.e., the cost of the coat, Israel was exiled in Egypt.

Obviously, the Egyptian exile was foretold: The Israelites were destined to be in Egypt. Nonetheless, the Rabbis choose to focus upon this seemingly minor event – this failure of Yaakov to anticipate the consequences of his favoritism – to teach the significance of jealousy and the role that parents may play in the development of that jealousy. Indeed, parents may develop unique relationships with each child; yet, they dare not blatantly demonstrate special regard for any one child.

Our sages also teach us that there are conditions when jealousy would be unlikely:

A person is jealous of everything, except for his child and his student.   (Babylonian Talmud Sanhedrin 105b)

סנהדרין קה:
בכל אדם מתקנא, חוץ מבנו ותלמידו.

In a psychologically healthy relationship, a parent is not jealous of a child's accomplishments, nor is a teacher jealous of a student's scholarship, for in fact these achievements reflect honor upon the parent and the teacher. There exists a sharing in these experiences which precludes jealousy.

The Rabbis also observe:

The jealousy of scholars increases wisdom.
                                       (Babylonian Talmud Bava Batra 22a)

בבא בתרא כב.
קנאת סופרים תרבה חכמה.

The sense of rivalry among scholars will motivate them to acquire more knowledge and therefore increase wisdom. One observes this dynamic in the contemporary scene of scientific research. The Rabbis do caution, however, that envy or excessive ambition may destroy an individual:

Jealousy destroys a person.   (Pirkei Avot 4:21)

אבות ד:כא

הקנאה . . . מוציאין את האדם מן העולם:

This negative quality of jealousy is common in society, the need to have what the "other" possesses. It is this covetous attitude which the Rabbis condemn.

Being Wealthy

וַיֹּאמֶר לוֹ לֶךְ־נָא רְאֵה אֶת־שְׁלוֹם אַחֶיךָ וְאֶת־
שְׁלוֹם הַצֹּאן: (בראשית לז:יד)

And he said to him, "Go and see how your
brothers are and how the flocks are faring, and
bring me back word." (Bereishit 37:14)

Do flocks understand what *shalom* is that he asked him [to inquire
after] "the *shalom* of the flocks (i.e. how they are faring)" (Bereishit 37:14)? Rabbi Aibo said: A person must pray for whomever
sustains him; because Yaakov benefited from his flocks and ate the
fat and wore the fleece, therefore he was required to ask after their
welfare (*shelomam*). (Midrash Tanhuma, Vayeshev 13:14)

מדרש תנחומא וישב יג:יד

וכי הצאן יודעות, מהו שלום שאמר לו "ואת שלום הצאן" (בראשית לז:יד), אמר
ר' אייבו צריך אדם שיהא מתפלל על מי שהוא משביר אותו, לפי שהיה יעקב
משתכר מצאנו ואוכל החלב ולובש הגז, לפיכך נצרך לשאול בשלומן.

"How your brothers are faring" (Bereishit 37:14) makes sense, but
why "how the flocks are faring" (ibid.)? This says that a person
must ask after the welfare of something that benefits him. (Midrash Bereishit Rabbah 84:13)

מדרש בראשית רבה פד:יג

"את שלום אחיך" (בראשית לז:יד) ניחא אלא מאי "ואת שלום הצאן" (שם), הדא
אמר שאדם צריך לשאול בשלום דבר שיש בו הנייה ממנו.

Into the cistern from which you drink, do not throw dirt. (Babylonian Talmud Bava Kama 92b)

230

בבא קמא צב:
בירא דשתית מיניה לא תשדי ביה קלא

Once again, we find that our sages are sensitive to the value of material possessions, legitimately acquired. As noted in a previous passage, the Midrash tells of Yaakov risking his life to protect his possessions. From the rabbinic perspective, wealth is neither virtue nor vice – it is simply another dimension of the human experience. The Rabbis insist that one needs to appreciate that which has the potential to sustain life, and therefore guard the wealth which one has acquired. Wealth is thus understood as providing an opportunity to enhance life. If, however, one comes to be dominated by one's wealth, the result will be spiritual poverty.

The Rabbis insist that we respect, as well, the possessions of others. For example, we find in Pirkei Avot:

> Rabbi Yose says: Let your friends' money be as dear to you as your own. (Pirkei Avot 2:17)

אבות ב:יז
רבי יוסי אומר יהי ממון חברך חביב עליך כשלך.

The moral right – perhaps even obligation – to guard and cherish one's material possessions, requires one to protect the possessions of others. In fact, only appreciation of one's own possessions can instill a sense of respect and appreciation for the possessions of others. If I pay no heed to that which is mine, it is unlikely that I will be concerned with that which is yours.

An Evil Place

וַיִּשְׁלָחֵהוּ מֵעֵמֶק חֶבְרוֹן וַיָּבֹא שְׁכֶמָה:
(בראשית לז:יד)

So he sent him from the valley of Hebron, when
he reached Shechem. (Bereishit 37:14)

It is a place designated for calamities: In Shechem they raped Dinah, in Shechem they sold Yosef, [and] in Shechem the Kingdom
of the House of David was divided, "Jeroboam fortified Shechem
in the mountain of Ephraim" (1 Kings 12:25).

(Midrash Tanhuma, Vayeshev 2)

מדרש תנחומא וישב ב

מקום מוכן לפורענות, בשכם ענו את דינה, בשכם מכרו את יוסף, בשכם נחלקה
מלכות בית דוד "ויבן ירבעם את שכם בהר אפרים" (מלכים א יב:כה).

This midrash suggests the possibility that a community or a given
environment – perhaps geographical, perhaps sociological – may
be given to act in inherently evil ways, and should therefore be
avoided. Is it possible that the community of Shechem was corrupt to its core, which then impacted upon events throughout
history? The Rabbis remind us of all the painful and destructive
events which occurred in Shechem: the rape of Dinah, the sale of
Yosef into servitude,[1] etc.

We know that it was prohibited for Jews to return to Spain
after the 15th century expulsion and the tragic consequences of

---

1. The identical text is also cited in Babylonian Talmud, Sanhedrin 102a.
    with one interesting difference, i.e., in the Talmud, the text reads: בשכם
    מכרו אחיך את יוסף/"In Shechem they sold your brother Yosef." Thus the
    Gemara's version of the story makes it absolutely clear that the *brothers*
    were the perpetrators of this crime.

the Inquisition. Not until modern times did Jews again establish communities in Spain. One may wonder, too, about countries such as Germany and Russia. So much death and destruction brought upon our people – and others as well – born of unjustified hatred fostered and financed by church and state. How soon does one return to share the social experience of such nations?

The midrash's admonition concerning Shechem is clear: Shechem is an evil place and remains so for generations. The Rabbis thus voice their concern that there may be an inherent moral "pollution" in some societies. One dare not conclude, however, that "inherent" means unavoidable in the sense that they had no choice. To attribute a society's evil to "inherent" qualities would exonerate all evils perpetrated throughout history. What "inherent" may suggest, is that the values, sensibilities, agendas, and aspirations of a given society may foretell its actions and destiny.

Speaking Evil

וְעַתָּה לְכוּ וְנַהַרְגֵהוּ: (בראשית לז:כ)

Come now, let us kill him. (Bereishit 37:20)

Why is speaking ill of someone (*lashon hara*) called *lashon shlishi* (the third tongue)? Because it kills three people – the one who says it, the one who listens to it (lit. "accepts it"), and the one about whom it is spoken. (Midrash Devarim Rabbah 5:10)

מדרש דברים רבה ה:י
למה נקרא שמו של לשון הרע לשון שלישי שהוא הורג. שלשה שאמרו והמקבלו ושנאמר עליו.

Lashon harah – speaking evil of others, or simply speaking *about* others – is considered inherently evil, it leads to pain and suffering, to a degree at times unimaginable.

In this text, the Midrash observes the simple yet profound fact that speaking ill of someone in effect "kills" the speaker, the listener, and the subject of the statement. The Rabbis use the harsh term "kills" to emphasize upon us the broad impact and devastating consequences of this act. When one speaks evil of another – even when it is the *truth* (and this is critical to note) – there will inevitably be three victims: The speaker is diminished, for he has caused human suffering. The listener becomes a conduit of the evil spoken, and is thereby diminished. And of course, the subject of the *lashon harah* is diminished, having been compromised and libeled.

Throughout rabbinic literature, *lashon harah* is condemned in the harshest language. First the Torah's admonition:

You shall not be a gossiper among your people, you shall not stand aside while your fellow's blood is shed. I am Hashem (Vayikra 19:16).

ויקרא יט:טז

לֹא־תֵלֵךְ רָכִיל בְּעַמֶּיךָ לֹא תַעֲמֹד עַל־דַּם רֵעֶךָ אֲנִי ה':

In this text a connection is made between *lashon harah* and standing by as "your fellow's blood is being spilled," immediately followed by "I am the Lord." A dramatic and poignant message! When the blood (metaphorical or actual) of the innocent and vulnerable is shed, G-d is a caring witness.

Examine more critical observations of the Rabbis concerning *lashon harah*:

> *Lashon Hara* that is spoken in Rome kills in Syria.
>
> (Midrash Bereishit Rabbah 98:19)

לשון הרע דאמור ברומי וקטיל בסוריא.

This midrash suggests that there is no limit to the potential harm of *lashon harah*: i.e., "someone speaking ill of another in Rome, kills in Syria" (both places very much a part of the early rabbinic world). The Rabbis also compare *lashon harah* to an arrow which travels considerable distance from its source; i.e., while *lashon harah* may be spoken at a great distance from its subject, its painful and destructive impact will nevertheless be felt.

One might imagine that speaking ill of another is condemned only if the talebearer speaks lies. Not so! The Rabbis teach:

> Any *lashon hara* that does not contain a grain of truth at first, will not stand up in the end. (Babylonian Talmud Sotah 35a)

סוטה לה.

כל לשון הרע שאין בו דבר אמת בתחילתו – אין מתקיים בסופו.

When one speaks ill of another, the comment must have some

element of truth or else it will not be heard or accepted. Hence *lashon harah* is an effective tool of defamation precisely because it carries at least a grain of truth, and even if *completely* true, it is still *lashon harah*, and evil.

Facing the Finality of Death

וַיָּקֻמוּ כָל־בָּנָיו וְכָל־בְּנֹתָיו לְנַחֲמוֹ וַיְמָאֵן
לְהִתְנַחֵם: (בראשית לז:לה)

*All his sons and daughters sought to comfort
him, but he refused to be comforted.* (Bereishit 37:35)

A matron asked Rabbi Jose: It is written, "For Judah prevailed
above his brethren" (1 Chronicles 5:2), and yet we read, "And Judah was comforted" (Bereishit 38:12) while this man (Yaakov) the
father of them all refused to be comforted: He said to her – you
can be comforted for the dead, but not for the living.

(Midrash Bereishit Rabbah 84:21)

מדרש בראשית רבה פד:כא

מטרונה שאלה את ר' יוסי אמרה לו כתיב "כי יהודה גבר באחיו" (דברי הימים א'
ה:ב), וכתיב "וינחם יהודה" (בראשית לח:יב) וזה אביהם של כלם וימאן להתנחם,
אמר לה מתנחמים על המתים ואין מתנחמים על החיים.

A Roman matron asks a perceptive question: The Torah tells us
that after suffering the loss of his two sons, Yehudah was eventually consoled; yet when Yaakov was told that he had lost Yosef,
Yaakov refused to be consoled.

Rabbi Yosi responds: "One can be consoled for the dead, but
not for the living." Rabbi Yosi understands human nature. Unless a mourner is willing/able to confront the reality of the loved
one's death and its devastating finality, the mourner cannot hope
to heal and go on with life. So long as the mourner rejects that
finality, the deceased remains alive in the psyche of the mourner.
In the case of the Torah narrative, Yosef was indeed still alive!

It is interesting to observe in this context that the Halachah of

238 / *Middot le-Dorot*

the burial of next-of-kin requires the actual completion of internment in the presence of the immediate family. *Kaddish* may not be
recited until the casket is covered and the grave is literally "in the
shape of a grave," i.e., with a mound of earth above the grass line.
Thus a proper Jewish burial demands what psychologists refer
to as "closure": confrontation with the reality of death and loss.
The *halachah* thus anticipates the problem of dealing with the
finality of death; for its acceptance allows the onset of consolation
and ultimately healing. Without this sense of the reality of death,
acceptance and consolation become difficult, if not impossible.

We are aware of the tormenting trauma experienced by many
survivors of the Shoah who have been unable to bring the horror
to "closure." The overwhelming memories of what occurred have
been repressed either consciously or unconsciously, thus making
closure forever elusive.

Extended Family

וַיָּקֻמוּ כָל־בָּנָיו וְכָל־בְּנֹתָיו לְנַחֲמוֹ:
(בראשית לז:לה)

All his sons and daughters sought to comfort him. (Bereishit 37:35)

According to Rabbi Nehemiah: A person does not refrain from calling his son-in-law his son and his daughter-in-law his daughter. (Midrash Bereishit Rabbah 84:21)

בראשית רבה פד:כא
על הדא דר' נחמיה . . . אין אדם נמנע מלקרוא לחתנו בנו ולכלתו בתו.

The Torah text states that Yaakov was consoled by his "sons and daughters;" yet we know that he had only one daughter, Dinah. This Midrashic explanation is most insightful: "One may call a son-in-law a son, and a daughter-in-law a daughter." The acceptance of the spouses of children, as children, is an essential quality of a positive and endearing extended family relationship. It is critical for *shalom bayit*, "a peaceful and harmonious" family, to respect and cherish those who become part of the family through marriage.

Family Matters

וַיֵּבְךְּ אֹתוֹ אָבִיו: (בראשית לז:לה)

... Thus his father bewailed him. (Bereishit 37:35)

"Thus his father bewailed him" (Bereishit 37:35) – this refers to
Yitzchak [i.e. Yaakov's father, Yitzchak, bewailed Yosef]. Rabbi Levi
and Rabbi Simon said: [when Yaakov was] with him [Yitzchak]
would cry, but when he [Yaakov] would leave he [Yitzchak] would
go and wash, anoint, eat, and drink. And why did he not reveal to
[Yaakov that Yosef was still alive]? He said [to himself], "The Holy
One, blessed is He did not reveal this to him, shall I reveal it to
him?"   (Midrash Bereishit Rabbah 84:21)

מדרש בראשית רבה פד:כא

"ויבך אותו אביו" (בראשית לז:לה), זה יצחק, רבי לוי ור' סימון אמרו אצלו היה
בוכה וכיון שיצא מאצלו היה הולך ורוחץ וסך ואוכל ושותה, ולמה לא גילה לו
אמר, הקב"ה לא גלה לו ואני מגלה לו.

This midrash teaches two profound and sensitive lessons: First,
it is neither your obligation nor your right to convey bad news
when there are others, closer to the situation who have not done
so. Second, do not tread where those greater and wiser have not.

According to this fascinating Midrash, Yitzchak was alive at
the time that Yosef was sold into slavery by his brothers, *knew* of
the situation and said nothing to his son Yaakov. Yitzchak then
visited Yaakov and joined him in mourning the death of Yosef.
Yet when Yitzchak departed, knowing that Yosef was actually
alive, he put aside his mourning. The midrash quotes Yitzchak as
saying, if G-d does not tell Yaakov that Yosef is alive, how dare *I*
do so?

240

One must be careful not to interfere in family matters without deliberate examination of all the issues, so that one does not further complicate an already painful situation. The best of intentions may lead to unforeseen conflict and misery. Beware before you enter into family conflicts.

Witnessing G-d's Presence

וַיַּרְא אֲדֹנָיו כִּי ה' אִתּוֹ וְכֹל אֲשֶׁר־הוּא עֹשֶׂה ה'
מַצְלִיחַ בְּיָדוֹ: (בראשית לט:ג)

*And when his master saw that the Lord was with
him and that the Lord lent success to everything
he undertook.* (Bereishit 39:3)

Rabbi Avin the Levite said: Yosef would bless the Holy One,
blessed is He on every single thing that he would do, and his master saw him whispering and said to him, "What are you saying?"
And he would respond, "I am blessing the Holy One, blessed is
He." His master said, "I want to see him." Yosef said to him, "the
sun is one of His servants and you are unable to look at it, how will
you be able to look at His glory?" The Holy One, blessed is He
said to him, "By your life! Because of your glory I am revealed to
him," as it says, "And his master saw that the Lord was with him"
(Bereishit 39:3).   (Midrash Bamidbar Rabbah 14:3)

מדרש במדבר רבה יד:ג

אמר רב אבין הלוי - יוסף מברך להקב"ה על כל דבר ודבר שהיה עושה והיה
אדניו רואה אותו מלחש בפיו, והוא אומר לו מה אתה אומר. והוא משיבו ואומר
אני מברך להק"בה. אמר לו אדניו מבקש אני לראותו. אמר לו יוסף הרי חמה,
אחת מכמה שמשין שלו, ואין אתה יכול להסתכל בו. והאיך תוכל להסתכל
בכבודו. אמר לו הקב"ה חייך בשביל כבודך אני נגלה עליו שנאמר "וירא אדוניו
כי ה' אתו" (בראשית לט:ג).

This remarkable midrash tells us that G-d allows himself (as it
were) to be revealed to a pagan Egyptian, so that the pagan might
appreciate the G-d to whom Yosef constantly prays. The pagan
first senses and then in fact experiences G-d due to Yosef's piety
and manifest relationship with G-d.

A profound lesson: It is the role of the pious and praying Jew to be a manifest example of how prayer changes and enhances a person's life. When a non-believing and non-praying person beholds the impact of prayer and faith, she is challenged to seek this path personally. This midrash attests that G-d is only too happy to aid in the process of bringing the non-believer closer, so long as the individual takes the first step.

And what is our responsibility in this process? When our ethical behavior, speech, and attitude reflect a commitment to Torah values, we thereby demonstrate a Torah and mitzvot standard of living. Thus we become the role model for others to admire and emulate.

Bad Times Lead to Alienation
and Catastrophe

וְהִנֵּה שֶׁבַע פָּרוֹת אֲחֵרוֹת: (בראשית מא:ג)

But presently, seven other cows . . . (Bereishit 41:3)

Why does it say "others?" Because in a time when catastrophe comes upon the world, everyone becomes "others" and strangers to one another. How so? A person comes from a distant place and enters the city and his friend is sitting in the town square. But when he sees him, he turns his face the other way and pretends that he never saw him and never knew him. What causes this? Famine and catastrophe in the world. (Midrash Hagadol)

מדרש הגדול

מה תמצא לומר "אחרות" - שבשעה שהפורענות באה לעולם הכל עשוין "אחרים" ונכרים זה מזה כיצד אדם בא ממקום רחוק נכנס לעיר ואהבו יושב ברחובה כיון שראה אותו הפך את פניו לאחוריו ושם את עצמו כמי שלא ראהו ולא ידעו מעולם מי גרם כך רעבון ופורענות שבעולם.

This midrash observes human nature and concludes, in times of suffering and depravation, everyone becomes "Other." Even the best of friends may avoid their responsibility to one another. In fact, we may deny knowing one another: When a friend arrives in town, says the Midrash, we turn away and make believe we never saw him; and even if our eyes meet, we pretend we have no idea who it is and thus deny any responsibility.

The Talmud offers this related teaching:

Rabbi Shemuel bar Nachmani said in the name of Rabbi Yonatan: Catastrophe only comes upon the world when there are wicked people in the world. (Babylonian Talmud Bava Kama 60a)

244

בבא קמא ס.

אר"ש בר נחמני א"ר יונתן: אין פורענות באה לעולם אלא בזמן שהרשעים בעולם.

Bad times come to a society only as a result of evil people who become catalysts for further evil, which then leads to catastrophe. The Talmud goes on to say:

> And [catastrophe] begins with the righteous. (Babylonian Talmud Bava Kama 60a)

בבא קמא ס.

ואינה מתחלת אלא מן הצדיקים תחלה.

Where does the catastrophe strike first, if not among the righteous people? For they are the most vulnerable members of a society. History has demonstrated all too often the victimization of good people at the hands of evil-doers. In our own lifetimes, we have witnessed events such as those described in this midrash: During the Holocaust, Jews were betrayed by the very people who had been friends, classmates, associates.

"Evil times" are often attributed to G-d, when in fact *humans* bring about most human suffering and devastation. Witness the second World War, when the forces of evil were blatantly ignored and appeased in a narrow-minded effort to protect "turf." Many powerful nations were prepared to appease the tyrant, until it became self-evident that evil would never be satisfied with anything less than world conquest and domination.

Catastrophe is initiated by evil people, and fueled by those who avert their eyes or look on in silence.

Anti-Semitism

וְשָׁם אִתָּנוּ נַעַר עִבְרִי עֶבֶד לְשַׂר הַטַּבָּחִים
וַנְּסַפֶּר־לוֹ וַיִּפְתָּר־לָנוּ אֶת־חֲלֹמֹתֵינוּ אִישׁ
כַּחֲלֹמוֹ פָּתָר: (בראשית מא:יב)

A Hebrew youth was there with us, a servant of
the chief steward; and when we told him our
dreams, he interpreted them for us, telling each
of the meaning of his dream. (Bereishit 41:12)

Cursed are the wicked, for [when they do something good], they
do not do a good thing completely. "A youth" (Bereishit 41:12) – a
fool; "Hebrew" – hated; "slave" – for it is written in Pharaoh's
secret writings [or: shrines] that a servant of the king cannot wear
clothing of splendor. (Midrash Bereishit Rabbah 89:7)

מדרש בראשית רבה פט:ז

א"ר שמואל בר נחמן ארורים הם הרשעים שאין עושים טובה שלימה, "נער"
(בראשית מא:יב), שוטה, עברי, שונא, עבד, שכך מוכתב בסקרידין של פרעה שאין
עבד מולך ולא לובש כלידים.

"A Hebrew youth, a slave" (Bereishit 41:12) – cursed are the
wicked, for their good acts are not completely good. He mentions him in denigrating language: "a youth" – a fool who is not
worthy of greatness; "Hebrew" – he does not even recognize our
language; "slave" – and it is written in Egyptian law that a slave
cannot be king and cannot wear the clothing of princes.
(Rashi to Bereishit 41:12)

רש"י, בראשית מא:יב

"נער עברי עבד" (בראשית מא:יב) - ארורים הרשעים, שאין טובתם שלמה,
מזכירו בלשון בזיון: נער. שוטה, ואין ראוי לגדולה: עברי. אפילו לשוננו אינו

מכיר: עבד. וכתוב בנימוסי מצרים, שאין עבד מולך ולא לובש בגדי שרים.

While in prison, Yosef accurately predicts that Pharaoh's chief butler will be restored to his place of prominence. The butler promises to speak to Pharaoh on behalf of Yosef, but he forgets. When he finally recalls his debt, he refers to Yosef as: "a boy," which the midrash points out is a way of saying Yosef is a fool of no significance; "a Jew," i.e., our enemy; and "a slave," who according to Egyptian tradition could never aspire to nobility.

Thus is Yosef rewarded for his prediction of the butler's good fortune, and for his encouraging words during the butler's dark time of despair.

Both the Midrash and Rashi teach what Jewish history has demonstrated repeatedly: Jews were always called upon to serve the ruling power, yet Jews could never trust they would be rewarded for their loyal service to ruler and country. The most devastating example in our own day: Jews had been loyal citizens of Austria and Germany for centuries; yet these countries ultimately turned against and viciously annihilated millions of Jews.

The Midrash directs our attention to the subtle hints of the butler's words, which were intended to degrade and thus destroy the very person who had saved him and helped restore him to his royal service and stature. A classic demonstration of the persistent disease of anti-semitism. Jews have contributed to many countries and cultures, yet again and again past service and loyalty have not protected them from hatred and destruction.

The United States, one may argue, has a tradition of law tested in the crucible of conflict and has remained true to its democratic values. These United States may serve as an exception to the rule of history. The unique challenge for Jews in this land may well be the very equality we are guaranteed under the Constitution. Will a dynamic, successfully integrated American Jewish community retain its loyalty and commitment to the Jewish People, the State and People of Israel, the study of Torah, and the observance of Mitzvot? This is the historic unprecedented opportunity of our time: two vibrant and serious Jewish communities, one in our homeland, Israel, with a population of some 6 million Jews and the other in the United States, also 6 million Jews, living in freedom with an unprecedented dynamic religious, academic, cultural, economic, and political community. Each community, Israel and the United States, compliment one another yet are in fact unlike one another. Israel – the first sovereign Jewish state in 2,000 years, with a Jewish calendar, culture, language, population, army, and police, indeed all the particulars which makes a "nation state" sovereign.

In the United States, we enjoy all the rights and privileges as do all citizens, and we have established religious, academic, and cultural institutions as never before in the diaspora experience. Moreover, we are a powerful political presence in this nation with, at present, 10% of both the U.S. Senate and House of Representatives identifying themselves as Jewish, though demographically we represent significantly less than 6% of the American population. Virtually every major university in the United States boasts of a Judaic studies department with doctoral programs.

This is a remarkable moment in Jewish history, indeed some may say "it is the best of times" and some may say "it is the worst of times." On the one hand, assimilation is on the rise, and on the other, two unprecedented Jewish communities exist, Israel and North America.

A Dignified Appearance

וַיִּשְׁלַח פַּרְעֹה וַיִּקְרָא אֶת־יוֹסֵף וַיְרִיצֻהוּ מִן־
הַבּוֹר וַיְגַלַּח וַיְחַלֵּף שִׂמְלֹתָיו וַיָּבֹא אֶל־פַּרְעֹה:
(בראשית מא:יד)

Thereupon Pharaoh sent for Yosef, and he was rushed from the dungeon. He had his hair cut and changed his clothes and he appeared before Pharaoh. (Bereishit 41:14)

"He had his hair cut" (Bereishit 41:14) – for the honor of the kingship. (Rashi to Bereishit 41:14)

רש"י. בראשית מא:יד

"ויגלח" (בראשית מא:יד) – מפני המלכות.

Rashi suggests, when one appears in the presence of royalty, one must be properly attired. Rashi's focus is the royalty one is visiting; yet there is a Midrash which is more concerned with the individual who has been demeaned and degraded as a result of imprisonment:

"He had his hair cut and changed his clothes" (Bereishit 41:14) – based on this source they said: a captive who was redeemed, a prisoner who left prison, and an excommunicated person whom they permitted, cut their hair and washed their clothes, even during the intermediate days of the festival [when haircutting and washing clothing is forbidden], because all their days of imprisonment they have been like a mourner. (Midrash Hagadol)

מדרש הגדול

"ויגלח ויחלף שמלתיו" (בראשית מא:יד) מכאן אמרו – שבוי שנפדה וחבוש שיצא
מבית האסורים ומנודה שהתירוהו – מגלחין ומכבסין אפילו בחולו של מועד –
מפני שכל ימיהן כאבל.

249

Rashi is concerned with the respect due royalty. The midrash on the other hand is more concerned with the emancipated prisoner.

While imprisoned, the individual is degraded by his environment and his keepers. No one, eventually not even the prisoner, cares about appearance – in fact this neglect of appearance is part of the process of degradation which is the intent of the authority.

Thus the Midrash teaches that a newly emancipated prisoner should be given a haircut and a shave even during Chol Hamoed, because his days in prison have been "days of mourning." Giving him a haircut will begin to restore his sense of well-being and self-respect, hence his proper place in society. The midrash recognizes the importance of self-respect born of a sense of dignified appearance. Similarly, the Talmud teaches that a scholar who appears in public with a spot on his garment is guilty of a capital offense (Shabbat 113b). Obviously, the Talmud is not to be taken literally, its point is to dramatize the importance of a dignified and neat appearance.

Power and Reconciliation

וַיִּשְׁאַל לָהֶם לְשָׁלוֹם וַיֹּאמֶר הֲשָׁלוֹם אֲבִיכֶם
הַזָּקֵן אֲשֶׁר אֲמַרְתֶּם הַעוֹדֶנּוּ חָי: (בראשית מג:כז)

He greeted them, and he said, "How is your aged father of
whom you spoke? Is he still in good health?" (Bereishit 43:27)

There are some people who, until they come to power they greet
everyone, but once they come to power, arrogance overcomes
them and they do not concern themselves with greeting the people
of the city. But Yosef was not like this. Even though he had come
to power, his custom was to greet his brothers, as it says, "He
greeted them" (Bereishit 43:27). (Midrash Tanchuma, Vayeshev 7)

תנחומא ישן וישב ז

יש לך אדם עד שלא נכנס לשררה הוא שואל בשלום בני אדם, אבל משנכנס
לשררה רוחו גסה עליו ואינו משגיח לשאול לשלום בני העיר – אבל יוסף לא
היה כן, אף על פי שנכנס לשררה הוא מנהגו לשאול בשלום אחיו שנאמר
"ושאל להם לשלום" (בראשית מג:כז).

What happens to a person who reaches high office or great power
or significant wealth? This midrash provides one answer: Before
attaining wealth and power, a simple person is friendly, concerned
about others, and greets everyone with a pleasant and sensitive
demeanor. Once attaining wealth and power, this same person
becomes unreachable, aloof, and unconcerned.

Yet there are those whose wealth and high status do not alter
their values and sensitivities: Yosef, the midrash points out, greets
his estranged brothers with words of *shalom*. The lesson of the
midrash is clear: Wealth and power should not alter long-stand-
ing relationships of family and friends. If there is to be a change,

it should be one of reaching out to seek an even stronger and more profound relationship.

One with new-found wealth and power may fear being exploited and abused. While that may be a legitimate concern, nonetheless it is the mark of a good person to risk exploitation rather than seek the safety of distance and alienation.

Yosef's brothers betray him: They abandon him, cast him into a pit, consider murdering him, and finally sell him into slavery. Yet when Yosef eventually comes face-to-face with them again, he speaks words of *shalom*. What a remarkable lesson. Obviously, Yosef could have opted to protect his blood-brother Binyomin while punishing the other brothers with imprisonment or worse. Yet he chooses to look beyond the narrow opportunity for vengeance and instead seeks reconciliation with words of peace.

Family discord is not unusual; rather, it is a fact of life. Whether it is initially a matter of ego, or inheritance, or jealousy, or perhaps even simple nonsense, family discord has a way of escalating out of control, with ever-increasing venom. Who can even recall the original source of these destructive conflicts? This is why the midrash focuses on Yosef's action: By speaking words of peace, he opens the door to a new relationship. Clearly Yosef has every reason to be vengeful; yet he freely chooses to concern himself with the well-being of his brothers.

There comes a time, suggests the Midrash, when the past – no matter how painful – ought not to be the focus. Though Yosef has a right to seek justice, he understands in this moment it is necessary to seek peace in order for true healing to occur.

Truth and Falsehood

וַיִּשְׁאַל לָהֶם לְשָׁלוֹם וַיֹּאמֶר הֲשָׁלוֹם אֲבִיכֶם
הַזָּקֵן אֲשֶׁר אֲמַרְתֶּם הַעוֹדֶנּוּ חָי: (בראשית מג: כז)

He greeted them, and he said, "How is your aged
father of whom you spoke? Is he still alive?"
(Bereishit 43:27)

"Ask to the point and respond [to the point]" (Avot 5:7), as it is
written, "He greeted them and said, 'How is your aged father of
whom you spoke? Is he still in good health?' They replied, 'It is
well with your servant our father; he is still in good health'" (Bereishit 43:27–28).   (Tractate Kallah Rabbati chap. 3)

מסכת כלה רבתי פרק ג
"שואל כענין ומשיב" (אבות ה:ז), דכתיב "וישאל להם לשלום, ויאמר השלום
אביכם הזקן אשר אמרתם העודנו חי, ויאמרו, שלום לעבדך, אבינו עודנו חי"
(בראשית מג:כז-כח).

When asked a question, says the Talmud, be specific in your answer – and keep your answer to the subject about which you have
been asked. The Talmud also demands of the inquirer that the
question be as specific as possible, for then the answer may be
equally specific and accurate.

Elsewhere the Talmud states:

A person should always be careful in his responses.
(Babylonian Talmud Megillah 25b)

מגילה כה:
לעולם יהא אדם זהיר בתשובותיו.

"Always be careful with your answer." One must be very careful how one answers a question. An ambiguous answer, or an attempt to evade the truth with complex technical or legalistic language, may lead to an erroneous impression. The truth may be preserved, yet the "moral" truth will be destroyed.

Our sages are extremely sensitive concerning the use of language. Telling the truth and avoiding falsehood are highly valued. A classic illustration is provided in the following text:

> All your ways should be for the sake of heaven. You should love heaven and fear heaven. You should tremble and rejoice over all the mitzvot. Sit before the elders, incline your ear to hear their words, and listen to the words of your friends and do not be afraid to respond. Consider every matter in accordance with its general subject. Speak first about what is first and last about what is last. Admit to what is true and do not speak before one who is greater than you in wisdom. If you desire to learn, then do not say "I have heard a tradition" about something which you have not heard a tradition. And if they ask you about a minor matter and you do not know about it, do not be embarrassed to say, "I don't know." If you taught something but did not hear it as a tradition, do not be embarrassed to say, "I taught it," but do not favor yourself to say, "I have not heard this as a tradition." Do things for the sake of doing them and for the sake of heaven. (Tractate Derekh Eretz Zuta [the "minor" tractate of "proper manners"], chap. 2)

מסכת דרך ארץ זוטא פרק ב

כל דרכיך יהיו לשם שמים הוי אוהב את השמים וירא מן השמים הוי חרד ושש על כל המצוות שב לפני הזקנים והטה אזנך לשמוע את דבריהם והקשב אזניך לדברי חבירך אל תהי נבהל להשיב ותהא מחשב דברים כענין ואומר על ראשון ראשון ועל אחרון אחרון והוי מודה על האמת ואל תדבר בפני מי שגדול ממך בחכמה ואם חפצת ללמד אל תאמר על מה שלא שמעת שמעתי ואם שאלוך דבר קטן ואי אתה יודע בו אל תבוש לומר איני יודע ואם שנית לך ולא שמעת אל תבוש לומר שנה לי ואל תשא פנים לעצמך לומר לא שמעתי עשה דברים לשום פעולתן לדבר בהם לשמים:

Concerning the issue of truth and falsehood, we find that our sages allow falsehood to be spoken when the truth would inflict pain upon an innocent individual. It must be noted that any deviation from the Torah's insistence upon absolute truth may be invoked only when the falsehood does not cause suffering or economic loss to anyone.

The first such instance in the Torah occurs when G-d tells Sarah that she will bear a child,[1] and in her incredulous response she mentions that her husband is old. When G-d tells Avraham of Sarah's response, G-d does not repeat her statement verbatim. Our sages teach that this is done so as not to tell Avraham that Sarah blames her childlessness on his old age. Thus, our sages teach, G-d establishes the principle that a lie in the service of a higher purpose – in this case that of maintaining "shalom bayit"/peace in the home – is morally acceptable.

Again, the Talmud emphasizes that shalom bayit, and the avoidance of human suffering, are legitimate justifications for falsehood *only if* the falsehood will cause no harm or loss to anyone.

The Talmud records an intriguing dispute regarding the question of how to praise a bride:

Our Rabbis taught: How should one dance before the bride? The House of Shamai say: "The bride as she is." And the House of Hillel say: "A beautiful and gracious bride." The House of Shamai said to the House of Hillel: If she is lame or blind, you would say "a beautiful and gracious bride"? But the Torah says, "Keep far from a false matter" (Shemot 23:7). The House of Hillel said to the House of Shamai: According to your opinion, if someone made a bad purchase in the market, should we praise it or debase it in his eyes? You must say: We should praise it in his eyes. From this the sages say: A person should always act pleasantly with other people. (Babylonian Talmud Ketubot 17a-b)

כתובות יז.-יז:

תנו רבנן: כיצד מרקדין לפני הכלה? בית שמאי אומרים: כלה כמות שהיא, ובית הלל אומרים: כלה נאה וחסודה. אמרו להן בית שמאי לבית הלל: הרי שהיתה חיגרת או סומא, אומרי' לה, כלה נאה וחסודה? והתורה אמרה: (שמות

---

1. Bereishit 18:10.

כג:ז) מדבר שקר תרחק. אמרו להם בית הלל לבית שמאי: לדבריכם, מי שלקח
מקח רע מן השוק, ישבחנו בעיניו או יגננו בעיניו? הוי אומר: ישבחנו בעיניו,
מכאן אמרו חכמים: לעולם תהא דעתו של אדם מעורבת עם הבריות.

Ought one to praise her "as she is," i.e., say only what is true about
her? Or is one obligated to say, "a beautiful and gracious bride"
regardless of what you perceive to be true about her? Again, our
sages were sensitive to the possibility of there being a higher purpose for expressing a falsehood under certain circumstances.

Then we find:

> And Rabbi [Judah the Prince] said: All lies are prohibited, but it
> is permitted to lie for the sake of bringing peace between people.
> (Tractate Derekh Eretz Zuta ["minor" tractate of "proper man-
> ners"], chapter of peace).

מסכת דרך ארץ זוטא - פרק השלום
ואמר רבי כל השקרים אסורים ומותר לשקר בשביל להטיל שלום בין אדם
לחבירו.

Here again is the principle that peace among people is a transcending value which may override truth – if, and only if, any
falsehood expressed causes no harm to any innocent person or
group.

> Come and see what good and comforting news can cause: Yaakov
> and his sons were like the dead on account of Yosef, but once they
> received the news and were comforted, it says, "The spirit of their
> father Yaakov revived" (Bereishit 45:27). (Midrash Hagadol)

מדרש הגדול
בוא וראה כמה בשורות טובות ונחמות גורמים יש הרי היו יעקב ובניו כמתים
בשביל יוסף וכיון שנתבשרו ונתנחמו מהיה אומר "ותחי רוח יעקב אביהם"
(בראשית מה:כז).

This Midrash teaches that an entire family may be emotionally
destroyed by tragedy. Yet is it not true that Yosef's brothers knew
that he was alive (having themselves sold him into slavery)? And

if that was the case, why would the midrash say that Yaakov's *sons* were "as if dead" – i.e., emotionally distraught – and were now revived with the news of Yosef's survival?

No doubt the sons of Yaakov, guilty of the betrayal of their brother Yosef and causing their father to mourn Yosef's death, carried the guilt of this act every moment of their lives. They had betrayed their brother *and* devastated their father with a lie. Being confronted with the reality of Yosef's survival must have relieved them of the constant burden of guilt.

Truth

וַיַּגִּדוּ לוֹ לֵאמֹר עוֹד יוֹסֵף חַי וְכִי־הוּא מֹשֵׁל
בְּכָל־אֶרֶץ מִצְרָיִם וַיָּפָג לִבּוֹ כִּי לֹא־הֶאֱמִין
לָהֶם: (בראשית מה:כו)

And they told him, "Yosef is still alive; yes,
he is ruler over the whole land of Egypt." His
heart went numb, for he did not believe them.
(Bereishit 45:26)

Rabbi Shimon says: This is the punishment of a liar – even when
he speaks the truth no one believes him, for this is what we have
found with the sons of Yaakov who lied to their father. In the beginning he believed them, as it says, "Then they took Yosef's tunic
and slaughtered a kid . . . ." (Bereishit 37:31) and "He recognized
it and said, 'My son's tunic!'" (Bereishit 37:33). But in the end,
even though they spoke the truth, he did not believe them, as it
says, "And they told him, 'Yosef is still alive . . .' and his heart went
numb for he did not believe them" (Bereishit 45:26).

(Avot D'Rabbi Natan, 30)

אבות דרבי נתן ל

ר' שמעון אומר כך עונש של בדאי שאפי' דובר אמת אין שומעין לו שכן מצינו
בבניו של יעקב שכיזבו לאביהן בתחלה האמין להם שנאמר "ויקחו את כתונת
יוסף וישחטו שעיר עזים" (בראשית לז:לא) וכתיב "ויכירה ויאמר כתונת בני" (שם
לז:לג) אבל באחרונה אע"פ שדברו אמת לפניו לא האמין להם שנאמר ("[ויפג
לבו כי לא האמין להם]) ויגידו לו לאמר עוד יוסף חי ולא האמין להם" (שם מה:כו).

Truth has the power to foster justice and progress. Only reality
born of truth can challenge and motivate the individual and society to make choices and to act morally.

Family relationships must also be structured upon a foundation of truth. As developed in the previous text, there are those rare occasions when truth must be avoided to preserve family peace. Nonetheless, those instances must be the unique exception. In the words of Mishlei, "the language of truth shall be established forever" (12:19).

Truth must be an expression of integrity. One must speak only what one believes to be true. The Talmud states:

> One should not speak one thing with one's lips and another thing in one's heart. (Babylonian Talmud Bava Metziah 49a)

בבא מציעא מט.

שלא ידבר אחד בפה ואחד בלב.

The Talmud makes an interesting observation about the liar:

> The punishment of a liar is that even when he tells the truth, he is not believed. (Babylonian Talmud Sanhedrin 89b)

סנהדרין פט:

עונשו של בדאי שאפילו אומר אמת אין שומעין לו.

Prayer and Despair

וַיְדַבְּרוּ אֵלָיו אֵת כָּל־דִּבְרֵי יוֹסֵף אֲשֶׁר
דִּבֶּר אֲלֵהֶם וַיַּרְא אֶת־הָעֲגָלוֹת אֲשֶׁר־שָׁלַח
יוֹסֵף לָשֵׂאת אֹתוֹ וַתְּחִי רוּחַ יַעֲקֹב אֲבִיהֶם:
(בראשית מה:כז)

But when they recounted all that Yosef had said
to them, and when he saw the wagons that Yosef
had sent to transport him, the spirit of their
father Yaakov was revived. (Bereishit 45:27)

The holy spirit (prophecy) does not rest upon a person in a state
of laziness, sadness, laughter, frivolity, or vanities, but only on account of a matter of joy, as it says "Now then, get me a musician,
and as the musician played the [hand of the Lord] came upon him"
(II Kings 3:15), and similarly "Yaakov's spirit revived" (Bereishit
45:27), [and] "G-d called to Israel (Yaakov) in a night vision"
(Bereishit 46:2), which the Aramaic translation translates as "the
sacred spirit rested [upon him]."   (Midrash Tehillim, 24:3)

מדרש תהלים כד:ג

אין רוח הקודש שורה לא מתוך עצלות, ולא מתוך עצבות, לא מתוך שחוק,
ולא מתוך קלות ראש, לא מתוך דברים בטלים, אלא מתוך דבר שמחה, שנאמר
"ועתה קחו לי מנגן והיה כנגן המנגן ותהי עליו יד ה'" (מלכים ב ג:טו) וכן "ותחי
רוח יעקב" (בראשית מה:כז), "ויאמר א-להים לישראל במראות הלילה" (בראשית
מו:ב), ותרגם 'ושרת רוח קודשא'.

The state of mind most suited for a profound spiritual relationship with G-d is that of spiritual joy: דבר שמחה, "a matter of joy."
The Talmud states:

One must not stand to pray in a state of sadness or in a state of
laziness . . . .   (Babylonian Talmud Berakhot 31a)

ברכות לא.

אין עומדין להתפלל לא מתוך עצבות, ולא מתוך עצלות . . . .

The Rabbis require a positive and hopeful mindset for one who
seeks to pray and reach G-d. The mood of the worshipper must
be neither sad nor irreverent; rather, one ought to be hopeful,
with faith in one's ability to reach G-d strengthened in the very
act of seeking G-d.

Elsewhere, the Talmud states:

There is no sadness before the Holy One, blessed is He, as it
says, "Glory and majesty are before Him; strength and joy in His
place." (1 Chronicles 16:26)   (Babylonian Talmud Chagigah 5b)

חגיגה ה:

אין עציבות לפני הקב"ה שנאמר "הוד והדר לפניו עוז וחדוה במקומו." (דברי
הימים א טז:כו)

In the presence of G-d there is no sadness. Rather, what is manifest in G-d's presence is "strength and gladness." No matter what
event or experience one is facing, with trust and faith one can
aspire to cope and persevere.

The well-known song of the Partisans of WWII, "Never say
you are going on your last journey,"[1] is a historic demonstration
of this classic Jewish article of faith. Survivors of the Shoah testify
that the power of faith, the rejection of despair, and the uncompromised determination to overcome whatever is yet to occur,
enabled them to survive even Auschwitz.

In the words of the psalmist (118:17), "I will not die, for I will
live and tell of the works of G-d"/לא אמות כי־אחיה ואספר מעשי יה.
This is a uniquely Jewish perspective which has been the Jews'

---

1.   זאג נישט קיינמאל אז דו גייסט דעם לעצטעם וועג – The original Yiddish.

262 / *Middot le-Dorot*

companion throughout history: the quintessential optimism born
of profound faith. How else did the Jews survive?

The 20th century civil rights song "We Shall Overcome" no
doubt has its roots in the Jewish faith in the future and the ultimate vindication of truth and justice.

Parents and Grandparents

וַיִּסַּע יִשְׂרָאֵל וְכָל־אֲשֶׁר־לוֹ וַיָּבֹא בְּאֵרָה שָּׁבַע
וַיִּזְבַּח זְבָחִים לֵאלֹהֵי אָבִיו יִצְחָק: (בראשית מו:א)

So Israel set out with all that was his, and he
came to Beer-Sheba, where he offered sacrifices
to the G-d of his father Yitzchak. (Bereishit 46:1)

"And he offered sacrifices to the G-d of his father Yitzchak" (Bereishit 46:1) – Rabbi Joshua ben Levi said: I went around to all the
masters of aggadah in the South to tell me [an aggadah associated
with] this verse, but they did not tell me, until I stood with Judah ben Pedaiah the nephew of ben Hakapar, and he said to me,
"When a teacher [Rabbi] and student are walking on the road,
at first one should greet the student and subsequently greet the
teacher." Rabbi Huna said: When Rabbi Joshua ben Levi reached
Tiberias he asked Rabbi Yochanan and Resh Lakish. Rabbi Yochanan said that a person is obligated to honor his father more
than he is obligated to honor his elder [ie. grandparent].

(Midrash Bereishit Rabbah 94:5)

מדרש בראשית רבה צד:ה
"ויזבח זבחים לאלהי אביו יצחק" (בראשית מו:א), אמר רבי יהושע בן לוי חזרתי
על כל בעלי אגדה שבדרום שיאמרו לי פסוק זה ולא אמרו לי עד שעמדתי עם
יהודה בן פדייה בן אחותו של בן הקפר, ואמר לי הרב והתלמיד שהיו מהלכין
בדרך, בתחלה שואלים בשלום התלמיד ואח"כ שואלים בשלום הרב, א"ר הונא
כד אתא רבי יהושע בן לוי לטבריה שאליה לרבי יוחנן ולריש לקיש, רבי יוחנן
אמר שחייב אדם בכבוד אביו יותר מכבוד זקינו.

This Midrash teaches that the commandment "honor your father
and mother," explicitly stated in the Torah, is the primary obliga-

tion of the child. The honor due a grandparent is based upon and related to the honor due the parent. This midrash suggests that in honoring the parent first, we demonstrate the proper relationship between child, parent, and grandparent.

Grandparents are, in most instances, not the direct source of influence on the child. It is the parents who are directly responsible, who convey life's values to the child. (Obviously, grandparents may derive great honor and *nachas* (a sense of joy) in the fulfillment of their influence upon their grandchildren.) The test of the efficacy of parenting is whether children transmit parental values and traditions to *their* children. Thus Jewish law does demand a direct acknowledgment of the role of the grandparent even if it is only after the honor due the parent.

Regarding Rabbi Yochanan's statement that one honors the (worthy) student before one honors the teacher, this is somewhat analogous to honoring the parent prior to honoring the grandparent. Obviously, the parent enjoys a unique role, for having given life to the child and thus a higher status than the grandparent and are therefore to be honored first; yet in a sense, by honoring the parent, the grandparent is thereby honored.

That the student is to be honored prior to the teacher may be based upon the assumption that teachers derive great joy and pride when their students are honored. Ideally the goal of a teacher is to seek honor for their students, as good parents seek honor for their children rather than for themselves.

The Midrash thus establishes a standard for both parent and teacher. Child and student reflect honor upon parents and teachers as they are honored. There is no greater pride than that of parent and teacher who witness the fruit of their labors as manifest in the success of their children and students.

Who Can Do the Job Best?

וַיִּקְרְבוּ יְמֵי־יִשְׂרָאֵל לָמוּת וַיִּקְרָא לִבְנוֹ לְיוֹסֵף
וַיֹּאמֶר לוֹ אִם־נָא מָצָאתִי חֵן בְּעֵינֶיךָ שִׂים־נָא
יָדְךָ תַּחַת יְרֵכִי וְעָשִׂיתָ עִמָּדִי חֶסֶד וֶאֱמֶת אַל־
נָא תִקְבְּרֵנִי בְּמִצְרָיִם: (בראשית מז:כט)

And when the time approached for Israel to die,
he summoned his son Yosef and said to him, "Do
me this favor, place your hand under my thigh
a pledge of your steadfast loyalty: Please do not
bury me in Egypt." (Bereishit 47:29)

"He summoned his son Yosef" (Bereishit 47:29) – Why did he
not call Reuven or Judah? Reuven was the firstborn and Judah
was king, and he left them aside, and called Yosef; why? Because
[Yosef] had the means to accomplish, therefore "he summoned
his son Yosef." And said unto him "Do not bury me in Egypt"
(Bereishit 47:29) "Because of you I came down to Egypt...."
(Midrash Bereishit Rabbah 96:5)

מדרש בראשית רבה צו:ה
"ויקרא לבנו ליוסף" (בראשית מז:כט), למה לא קרא לא לראובן ולא ליהודה וראובן
הוא הבכור ויהודה הוא המלך והניחן וקרא ליוסף, למה כן, בשביל שהיה סיפק
בידו לעשות לפיכך "ויקרא לבנו ליוסף", ולפי שהשעה מסורה לו, "אל נא
תקברני במצרים" (שם מז:כט), בשבילך ירדתי למצרים בשבילך אמרתי ....

Yaakov assigns the responsibility for his burial (in his native Canaan rather than in Egypt) to Yosef. Why Yosef? Why not Reuven the eldest, or Yehudah the one destined to produce kings and
even now the leader of Yaakov's sons?

The Midrash reveals Yaakov's thinking: While Reuven is

indeed the eldest, and Yehudah may one day be the ancestor to kings, in this moment it is only Yosef who has both the authority and the ability to fulfill Yaakov's wish to be buried in Canaan.

Status is not the criterion by which to assign vital tasks. A parent (or anyone, for that matter) must determine who is most suited for a given task. Yaakov demonstrates by his choice that *ability* transcends all other considerations.

This Midrash offers a lesson in parenting as well as in leadership: First determine the essence of the assignment, the nature and demands of the task, and then select the most capable person.

Maintaining Boundaries in the Family

וְעַתָּה שְׁנֵי־בָנֶיךָ הַנּוֹלָדִים לְךָ בְּאֶרֶץ מִצְרַיִם
עַד־בֹּאִי אֵלֶיךָ מִצְרַיְמָה לִי־הֵם אֶפְרַיִם וּמְנַשֶּׁה
כִּרְאוּבֵן וְשִׁמְעוֹן יִהְיוּ־לִי: (בראשית מח:ה)

Now your two sons, who were born to you in the
land of Egypt, before I came to you in Egypt; shall
be mine. Ephraim and Menasheh shall be mine
no less than Reuben and Simeon. (Bereishit 48:5)

Rav Chaviva said: People call a grandchild a child.
(Babylonian Talmud Bava Batra 143b)

בבא בתרא קמג:

רב חביבא אמר: קרו אינשי לבר ברא - ברא.

A person does not hesitate to call his son-in-law his son and his
daughter-in-law his daughter.   (Midrash Bereishit Rabbah 84:21)

מדרש בראשית רבה פד:כא

אין אדם נמנע מלקרוא לחתנו בנו ולכלתו בתו.

Both the Midrash and Talmud ascribe to grandchildren the status of children, based upon Yaakov's statement that Yosef's sons
Ephraim and Menasheh will be "as Reuven and Shimon unto
me." Perhaps Yaakov is simply assigning special status to his
beloved Yosef once again? Yet we also find a talmudic reference
suggesting that one may call a son-in-law a son and a daughter-
in-law a daughter.

While there are specific cases such as these where some transfer
of status is apparently permitted, the Rabbis are also clear about
maintaining boundaries in the parent-child relationship:

Our Rabbis taught: There are three who cry out (pray) but are not answered, and these are they: The one who has money and lends it without witnesses, the one who acquires a master for himself. Who is "the one who acquires a master for himself?" Some say: the one who legally transfers (in writing) his property to his children during his lifetime. . . . (Babylonian Talmud Bava Metzia 75b)

בבא מציעא עה:

תנו רבנן: שלשה צועקין ואינן נענין, ואלו הן: מי שיש לו מעות ומלוה אותן שלא בעדים, והקונה אדון לעצמו, . . . קונה אדון לעצמו מאי היא? . . . איכא דאמרי: הכותב נכסיו לבניו בחייו . . . .

One does not relinquish control of one's assets even to good children, the Talmud cautions, for one may then become subservient to them "as if you have acquired a master unto yourself." What a keen understanding of human nature. Even "good" children may become too concerned with your possessions (i.e., their potential inheritance) if given too much power over your affairs.

Place no temptations in their path. Maintain control of your assets. Moreover, based upon the Talmud's admonition, it seems important that one provide properly and objectively for the control of one's assets should one become disabled. Children, even loving children, may not be able to think objectively about their parents' assets.

Thus it appears that our sages would prefer the assignment of "power of attorney" to an uninvolved third party. This need not demonstrate a lack of faith, love, or respect; rather, it is a prudent way of avoiding potential conflicts of interest in the family. Particularly in a family with more than one child, the question of assigning authority over assets may become a major source of conflict.

Obviously, most children would serve the best interests of their parents as well as their siblings. However, the caveat of our sages is worthy of consideration. One might respond to these Rabbinic admonitions as a cynical judgment on the part of the Talmudic sages. Can one not judge children with a positive estimation of their response to economic gain as a result of parental limitations? However, the Torah in Vayikra 19:14 admonishes us וְלִפְנֵי עִוֵּר לֹא תִתֵּן מִכְשֹׁל / "Do not put a stumbling block before the blind," meaning that one ought not create a situation which under unpredictable circumstances of extraordinary pressure one might not be perfectly objective. Thus the Rabbinic admonition, should you give someone a loan, do so with a signed and witnessed document. Equally so prepare a legal document, signed and witnessed, according to *Halachah*, Jewish Law, and according to the "Law of the Land" which directs the distribution of your assets when that time arrives.

Of equal importance, it would seem appropriate that one prepares a document which would determine the appropriate "Powers of Attorney" should one become mentally incompetent (ח"ו/ G-d forbid.)

לִפְנֵי עִוֵּר לֹא תִתֵּן מִכְשֹׁל / "Do not put a stumbling block before the blind" is a profound admonition by the *Torah* which endeavors to admonish us to avoid any action which by its unique nature of "blindness" might cause harm to us and others (G-d forbid).

G-d Needs Us

וַיְבָרֶךְ אֶת־יוֹסֵף וַיֹּאמַר הָאֱ־לֹהִים אֲשֶׁר הִתְהַלְּכוּ
אֲבֹתַי לְפָנָיו אַבְרָהָם וְיִצְחָק הָאֱ־לֹהִים הָרֹעֶה
אֹתִי מֵעוֹדִי עַד־הַיּוֹם הַזֶּה: (בראשית מח:טו)

And he blessed Yosef saying, "The G-d in whose
ways my fathers Avraham and Yitzchak walked,
the G-d who has been my shepherd from my
birth to this day." (Bereishit 48:15)

"And he blessed Yosef, saying . . ." (Bereishit 48:15) – Rabbi
Berekhiah said in the name of Rabbi Yochanan and Resh Lakish:
Rabbi Yochanan said: Like a shepherd who stands and watches
his flock. Resh Lakish said: Like a prince who is walking and the
elders are before him. According to Rabbi Yochanan's opinion, we
require His honor, and according to Resh Lakish's opinion, He
requires our honor.   (Midrash Bereishit Rabbah 97:2)

מדרש בראשית רבה צז:ב

"ויברך את יוסף ויאמר" (בראשית מח:טו), ר' ברכיה ואמרי לה בשם ר' יוחנן וריש
לקיש, ר' יוחנן אמר לרועה שהוא עומד ומביט בצאנו, ריש לקיש אמר לנשיא
מהלך והזקנים לפניו, על דעתיה דר' יוחנן אנו צריכין לכבודו, על דעתיה דריש
לקיש הוא צריך לכבודנו.

A classic Jewish insight is expressed in this midrash. The text states
two distinct and perhaps contrary perceptions of our relationship
with G-d: The G-d before whom Avraham and Yitzchak walked,
and the G-d who is Yosef's shepherd. Using the shepherd metaphor, Rabbi Yochanan says that G-d is the shepherd who stands
and looks after his flock. Resh Lakish, on the other hand, picks up

on the image of a royal procession in which the elders precede the prince. According to Rabbi Yochanan's view, we are dependent upon G-d as sheep are dependent upon their shepherd. Yet from Resh Lakish's perspective, it is G-d who is dependent upon us, as a monarch is dependent upon his royal court to proceed *before* him as a sign of honor.

G-d is thus, "as it were," in need of humanity. "As it were," because how may one attribute the quality of "need" to G-d? Yet how else would G-d's attributes of justice, truth, mercy, and wisdom be manifest if not through humanity? His very act of creation of the world and of humankind may be seen as support for Resh Lakish's view that G-d is in need of all of humanity for his manifestation on earth. The universe itself (at least as far as we know) has no cognitive quality. The planets, stars, etc. have no ability to choose to act kindly or harshly, or to appreciate their creator. Thus our sages assert that G-d needs conscious beings in order for all of G-d's unique qualities to be manifest through them.

The concept of *tikkun olam* / "fixing the world" is meant to challenge the Jew (and in fact all of humanity) to transform the world into a just and peaceful community, manifesting G-d's qualities. A world populated with moral beings would be the royal procession of Resh Lakish's vision. Once we recognize G-d's gracious gift of freedom of choice, and choose as G-d would have us choose, our interdependence becomes a blessing to G-d and to us.

An interesting discussion is reported in the Talmud between the pagan philosophers and the Jewish sages in Rome:

> The Philosophers asked the Elders in Rome, "If your G-d does not desire idol worship (lit. the worship of the celestial bodies), why does he not nullify it?" They replied, "If it were something that the world did not need, then he would get rid of it, but they worship the sun, the moon, the planets, and the constellations. Should the world be destroyed because of fools? Rather, the universe operates the way it does, and the fools who have gone astray will be called to account in the future." (Babylonian Talmud Avodah Zarah 54b)

עבודה זרה נד:

שאלו פלוסופין את הזקנים ברומי: אם א-להיכם אין רצונו בעבודת כוכבים,
מפני מה אינו מבטלה? אמרו להם: אילו לדבר שאין העולם צורך לו היו עובדין
הרי הוא מבטלה, הרי הן עובדין לחמה וללבנה ולכוכבים ולמזלות, יאבד עולם
מפני השוטים? אלא עולם כמנהגו נוהג, ושוטים שקלקלו עתידין ליתן את הדין.

The Rabbis' metaphor is profound. Humans were put on earth
to establish a civilization of moral, G-d-revering, creative beings.
The universe was endowed with certain properties, qualities, and
potentialities. G-d's ultimate goal was to establish a human civilization which would reflect the glory and blessing of its Creator.
As we observe history from our contemporary perspective, we
must admit that humankind has made some leaps toward a more
civilized and responsible society. Even within a mere century,
many more individuals have opportunities for a life of health,
freedom, education, and personal growth than has been available
to any previous generation. While it is obvious that war, hunger,
disease, poverty, persecution, and human suffering persist, nonetheless a mere century ago the human experience was in every
sense less promising for most of humankind.

Thus the Rabbis affirm the centrality of freedom of choice in
Jewish theology. No, G-d will not destroy idolatry (including
power, greed, etc.); human society must destroy its own idols,
each in its own generation. We have been endowed with freedom
of choice which is the essence of our belief in and relationship
with G-d.

Shalom

וַיִּקְרָא יַעֲקֹב אֶל־בָּנָיו וַיֹּאמֶר הֵאָסְפוּ וְאַגִּידָה
לָכֶם אֵת אֲשֶׁר־יִקְרָא אֶתְכֶם בְּאַחֲרִית הַיָּמִים:
(בראשית מט:א)

And Yaakov called his sons and said, "Come together so that I may tell you what is to befall you in days to come." (Bereishit 49:1)

The Rabbis say: He commanded them regarding disagreement. He told them: Be like one gathering, for this is what is written, "And you, O mortal, take a stick and write on it, ['Of Judah and the other Israelites associated with him'; and take another stick and write on it, 'Of Yosef – the stick of Ephraim – and all the House of Israel associated with him']" (Ezekiel 37:16). The word is written *chaveiro* ("his friend," in the singular). When the Children of Israel become one brotherhood, prepare yourselves for the redemption. What is written subsequently [in Ezekiel]? "I will make them a single nation . . . ." (Ezekiel 37:22).

(Midrash Bereishit Rabbah 98:2)

מדרש בראשית רבה צח:ב
רבנן אמרי צוה אותן על המחלוקת אמר להון תהון כולכם אסיפה אחת, הדא
הוא דכתיב "ואתה בן אדם קח לך עץ אחד וכתוב עליו ליהודה ולבני ישראל
חברו ולקח עץ אחד וכתוב עליו ליוסף עץ אפרים וכל־בית ישראל חברו" (יחזקאל
לז:טז), חבירו כתיב נעשו בני ישראל אגודה אחת, התקינו עצמכם לגאולה מה
כתיב אחריו "ועשיתי אתכם לגוי אחד וגו'" (שם לז:כב) . . . .

"Prepare yourselves for the redemption" – if the Children of Israel become one brotherhood, they have thus prepared themselves for the redemption. And in Midrash Hagadol, the text reads "In being one group, they will prepare themselves for the redemption." (Torah Shelemah to Bereishit 49, note 7)

תורה שלמה בראשית פרק מט בהערה ז
התקינו עצמכם לגאולה, אם נעשו בני ישראל אגודה אחת בזה התקינו עצמן
לגאולה ובמדרש הגדול גורם מתוך שנעשו חבורה אחת יתקנו עצמן לגאולה.

As it is written:

> In Midrash Hagadol: Rabbi Eliezer ben Yaakov says: A house in
> which there is disagreement will be destroyed in the end. If there
> is disagreement in the house, there is licentiousness in the house.
> A city in which there is disagreement will in the end have murder
> and will be scattered. A synagogue in which there is disagreement
> will be laid to waste in the end. If there is disagreement in law (or
> verdict; or adjudication) – there is destruction in the world. Great
> is peace and hated is disagreement. This is why Yaakov our fore-
> father commanded [the tribes] not to take hold of disagreement.
> (Torah Shelemah, to Bereishit 49 note 8)

תורה שלמה בראשית פרק מט בהערה ח
ובמדרש הגדול כאן ר' אליעזר בן יעקב אומר בית שיש בו מחלוקת סופו ליחרב,
מחלוקת בבית, זמה בבית, עיר שיש בה מחלוקת סופה שיבא בה שפכת דמים
וסופה להפזר, בית הכנסת שיש בה מחלוקת סופה להשתומם מחלוקת בדין
חרבן בעולם, גדול הוא השלום ושנואה המחלוקת לכך צוה יעקב אבינו שלא
יחזיקו במחלוקת.

Peace is all too often thought of in terms of international affairs,
racial conflict, conflict between haves and have-nots, warring
social, economic and political groups. Peace in Torah terms is
elevated to relationships within the family and the community.
The most critical, ancient, and contemporary structure of civilization – the family – is the focus of this midrash. A family wherein
conflict becomes normative is destined for self-destruction, as it
implodes from the force of its conflict.

A community with internal conflict, the Midrash cautions,
results in self-destructive and immoral behavior of irreparable
consequences. The Torah views *shalom* as a transcending value,
a moral force without which family, community and nation will
not survive.

Our sages had profound respect for the power of *shalom*:

> Rabbi Elazar son of Rabbi Eliezer Hakapar says: Great is peace, for even if Israel worships idols, but there is peace among them, the Holy One, blessed is He, as it were, said, "the Satan cannot touch them," as it is written, "Ephraim is addicted to images – Let him be" (Hosea 4:17). But when they engage in argument (dissension), what does it say? "When their heart is divided, now they are guilty" (Hosea 10:2). (Sifrei, Bamidbar 42)

ספרי במדבר מב

ר' אלעזר בנו של ר' אליעזר הקפר אומר גדול השלום שאפילו ישראל עובדין עבודה זרה ושלום ביניהם כביכול אמר המקום אין השטן נוגע בהם שנאמר "חבור עצבים אפרים הנח לו" (הושע ד:יז) אבל משנחלקו מה נאמר בהם "חלק לבם עתה יאשמו" (הושע י:ב).

This midrash extrapolates from the verse in Hosea (10:2) that when peace is manifest in a community, even idolatry may be tolerated by G-d, since G-d's ultimate goal is a peaceful community. Obviously, there is a good measure of hyperbole in this comment, nonetheless the point is clear. Peace is G-d's highest standard for the human community. Peace allows each person to live unafraid to pursue a life which in turn fosters a peaceful family, community, nation and world.

> It was taught: Great is peace, for the world is supported by it, as it was taught in a Mishnah: "The world exists on account of law (or: the judicial system), truth, and peace." It is written in the book of Ben Sira: "Love peace, for the world exists because of it." (Tractate Kallah Rabbati chap. 3)

מסכת כלה רבתי פרק ג

תנא גדול הוא השלום שהעולם עומד עליו דתנן על "שלשה דברים העולם קיים על הדין ועל האמת ועל השלום" כתיב בספר בן סירא "הוי רחים לשלמא דעליה קם עלמא."

Once again, a classic rabbinic text speaks of the power of *shalom*: Here, the universe itself is said to exist because of the power of *shalom*.

We are familiar with the statement in Avot:

Hillel says: Be among the students of Aharon, loving peace and pursuing peace; loving all creatures and bringing them near to the Torah. (Pirkei Avot 1:12)

אבות א:יב
הלל אומר הוי מתלמידיו של אהרן. אוהב שלום ורודף שלום. אוהב את הבריות
ומקרבן לתורה:

This mishnah suggests that the way to bring people closer to Torah (i.e., to G-d, Judaism, mitzvot, and relationships reflective of Torah values) is to pursue peace. Peace is the *compass* which should be directing all human activity.

Non-Conformity

הֵקָּבְצוּ וְשִׁמְעוּ בְּנֵי יַעֲקֹב וְשִׁמְעוּ אֶל־יִשְׂרָאֵל
אֲבִיכֶם: (בראשית מט:ב)

Assemble and hearken, O sons of Yaakov,
Hearken to Israel your father. (Bereishit 49:2)

"Hearken" (Bereishit 49:2) twice – hearken to the criticisms and
hearken to the blessings.

(Otzar Hamidrashim, Ya'akov Avinu 109:13)

אוצר המדרשים יעקב אבינו קט:יג

"ושמעו" (בראשית מט:ב) שני פעמים שמעו הקנטורין שמעו הברכות.

The word *listen* is repeated in this Torah text to teach that Yaakov
wanted his sons to listen not only to his words of praise but also
to his words of criticism and chastisement.

Parents must convey to children not only commendations
for their worthy achievements and attributes, but must equally
convey an objective and critical analysis of their deeds so that a
credible and challenging vision may be set forth to enhance their
future years.

Rav Amram the son of Rabbi Shimon bar Abba said in the name of
Rabbi Shimon bar Abba in the name of Rabbi Chanina: Jerusalem
was only destroyed because they did not rebuke one another, as it
says, "Her leaders were like rams that found no pasture" (Lamen-
tations 1:6). Just as one ram's head is next to another's tail, so too
Israel in that generation – they pressed their faces to the ground
(they hid) and did not rebuke one another. (Babylonian Talmud
Shabbat 119b)

שבת קיט:

אמר רב עמרם בריה דרבי שמעון בר אבא אמר רבי שמעון בר אבא אמר רבי
חנינא: לא חרבה ירושלים אלא בשביל שלא הוכיחו זה את זה, שנאמר "היו
שריה כאילים לא מצאו מרעה" (איכה א:ו). מה איל זה ראשו של זה בצד זנבו
של זה – אף ישראל שבאותו הדור, כבשו פניהם בקרקע ולא הוכיחו זה את זה.

Here, the Talmud uses an apt metaphor to describe the leaders of
the generation of the Temple's destruction: They were like ram
or sheep, one following another with the head of one at the tail
of the other, all facing the ground. In other words, none walking
"head to head" where they might have challenged one another
openly.

A society which no longer has the leadership to challenge its
citizens to seek a higher moral ground is a society of sheep who
simply follow where they are led. For them, there is neither a
view of higher ground nor a view of alternate paths. They see
only the ground.

Conformity is a common plague of modern society. It is more
convenient, and seemingly less painful, just to conform. Judaism
demands, however, that we be – *Am Segulah* – "a unique" and
special people, who set new paths and seek higher ground – for
our head is, metaphorically, soaring to the heavens while our feet
are planted firmly on the ground.

Thus Yaakov says to his sons: Listen to the praise for your past
achievements and listen as well to the criticism, so that you may
move forward with an objective view of life and its challenges.

Is Silence Ever Justified?

רְאוּבֵן בְּכֹרִי אַתָּה כֹּחִי וְרֵאשִׁית אוֹנִי יֶתֶר שְׂאֵת
וְיֶתֶר עָז: (בראשית מט:ג)

Reuben, you are my first born, my might and
first fruit of my vigor, exceeding in rank, and
exceeding in honor. (Bereishit 49:3)

. . . This teaches that he only chastised them near his death. From
whom did he learn this? From Yaakov, who only chastised his sons
near his death, as it says, "And Yaakov called his sons and said,
'Come together that I may tell you what is to befall you in days to
come'" (Bereishit 49:1), and he said to him, "Reuven you are my
first born" (Bereishit 49:3). He said to him, "My son, I will tell you
why I have not rebuked you all of these years, so that you not leave
me aside and join my brother Eisav."   (Sifrei Devarim 2)

ספרי דברים ב

מלמד שלא הוכיחם אלא סמוך למיתה ממי למד מיעקב שלא הוכיח לבניו אלא
סמוך למיתה שנאמר "ויקרא יעקב אל בניו ויאמר האספו ואגידה לכם את אשר
יקרא אתכם באחרית הימים" (בראשית מט:א) אמר לו "ראובן בכורי אתה" (שם
מט:ג). אמר לו בני אומר לך מפני מה לא הוכחתיו כל השנים הללו כדי שלא
תניחני ותלך ותדבק בעשו אחי.

According to this midrash, Yaakov refrains from chastising his
sons until he is close to death, for fear of losing them. Perhaps,
he reasons, they might abandon him and "attach" themselves to
his brother Eisav.

One may question Yaakov's judgment. While it is obvious that
criticizing adult children is a complicated and sensitive matter,
should one refrain from speaking one's mind to one's adult chil-

dren for fear of rejection? Is a parent to be intimidated from speaking the truth for fear of losing a popularity contest? Are love and loyalty purchased at the cost of silence and acceptance?

Perhaps one may argue for silence, in the spirit of the Talmud:

> Just as it is a mitzvah to speak if the matter will be done, so too it is a mitzvah not to speak if the matter will not be done. (Jerusalem Talmud Terumot 5:3)

ירושלמי תרומות פרק ה הלכה ג

כשם שמצוה לומר על דבר שהוא נעשה כך מצוה שלא לומר על דבר שאינו נעשה.

Or, as the Babylonian Talmud states:

> Just as it is a mitzvah for a person to say something that will be heard, so too it is a mitzvah not to say something that will not be heard. Rabbi Abba says: It is an obligation, as it says, "Do not rebuke a scoffer, for he will hate you; Reprove a wise man and he will love you" (Mishlei 9:8). (Babylonian Talmud Yevamot 65b)

יבמות סה:

כשם שמצוה על אדם לומר דבר הנשמע, כך מצוה על אדם שלא לומר דבר שאינו נשמע. רבי אבא אומר: חובה, שנאמר: "אל תוכח לץ פן ישנאך הוכח לחכם ויאהבך" (משלי ט:ח).

There are undoubtedly circumstances in which silence is the proper response. One must nonetheless be careful that silence not be construed as approval. The Talmud warns:

> Silence is like an admission [or: confession].
> (Babylonian Talmud Yevamot 87b)

יבמות פז:

שתיקה כהודאה דמיא.

Silence in a "legal" sense, according to the Talmud, is an affirmation. Thus one must be prudent and learn when to speak up or respond in the face of evil or untruth. This midrash, in what seems to be a rather unusual portrayal of Yaakov, suggests that there may be circumstances in which a parent, in fear of losing a child, may be justified in keeping silent.

Conveying One's Values
to the Next Generation

וַיְכַל יַעֲקֹב לְצַוֹּת אֶת־בָּנָיו וַיֶּאֱסֹף רַגְלָיו אֶל־
הַמִּטָּה וַיִּגְוַע וַיֵּאָסֶף אֶל־עַמָּיו: (בראשית מט:לג)

When Yaakov finished his instructions to his sons,
he drew his feet into the bed and, breathing his
last; he was gathered to his people. (Bereishit 49:33)

Rabbi Shimon said: Happy are the righteous who do not depart
from this world before they give instruction to their children who
come after them . . . And similarly, Yaakov instructed his sons, as
it says, "Yaakov finished his instructions to his sons" (Bereishit
49:33).   (Midrash Tanaim Devarim 1:1)

מדרש תנאים דברים א' א'
אמר ר' שמעון: אשריהם לצדיקים שאין נפטרין מן העולם עד שהן מצווין את
בניהם אחריהם וכו' וכן יעקב צוה את בניו שנאמר "ויכל יעקב לצוות את בניו"
(בראשית מט:לג).

Every responsible person knows the importance of having a will
(formal legal document) concerning one's assets and their distribution among one's heirs. For a person to pass away intestate
(i.e., having made no legal will) may leave heirs in a state of legal chaos, and closure becomes time-consuming, expensive, and
more traumatic.

The same is true of a person who leaves no "ethical" will. An
ethical will allows parents to convey in precise terms those ethical and religious values and imperatives which they hope will be
carefully and seriously considered by their children and future
generations. An ethical will states, in effect, "Here is what has

been important in my life, which I hope I have already conveyed to you, my family, and which I hope you will consider important and convey to your children in turn."

Obviously, an ethical will may not be taken seriously if one's life was a contradiction to the values now set forth in writing. A parent (or grandparent) may in good faith set forth hopes and dreams for their descendants to envision as a challenge. Thus, the unique qualities and values of the deceased may live on, and perhaps their meaningful unfulfilled dreams realized.

Every Human is a World

וַיָּבֹאוּ עַד־גֹּרֶן הָאָטָד אֲשֶׁר בְּעֵבֶר הַיַּרְדֵּן
וַיִּסְפְּדוּ־שָׁם מִסְפֵּד גָּדוֹל וְכָבֵד מְאֹד וַיַּעַשׂ
לְאָבִיו אֵבֶל שִׁבְעַת יָמִים: (בראשית נ:י)

When they came to Goren Ha-atad, which is
beyond the Jordan, they held there a very great
and solemn lamentation, and he observed a
mourning period of seven days for his father.
(Bereishit 50:10)

"And he observed a mourning period of seven days for his father"
(Bereishit 50:10) – corresponding to the seven days of creation,
for a person departs from the world that contains the seven days
of creation, therefore we mourn over him for seven days.

(Midrash Lekach Tov)

מדרש לקח טוב

"ויעש לאביו אבל שבעת ימים" (בראשית נ:י) כנגד שבעת ימי בראשית שאדם
נפטר מן העולם שיש בו שבעת ימי בראשית לפיכך מתאבל עליו שבעת
ימים וכו'.

Mourning for seven days is reflective of the seven days of creation. Each person, according to this Midrash, has within himself
or herself the very process and significance of creation. Every
human is a world unto themselves. With the birth of each human being, creation becomes significant as it was at the original
creation. We mourn for each human being for seven days (*shiva*),
to demonstrate that a person is a world. Just as the world was
created in seven days, thus we are to mourn for this person, i.e.,
this world, for seven days. When a person dies, it is as if a world
has died, for the Talmud says:

Each person is obligated to say, "For me, the world was created."
(Babylonian Talmud Sanhedrin 37a)

סנהדרין לז.
כל אחד ואחד חייב לומר בשבילי נברא העולם.

Peacemaking

וַיְצַוּוּ אֶל־יוֹסֵף לֵאמֹר אָבִיךָ צִוָּה לִפְנֵי מוֹתוֹ
לֵאמֹר: כֹּה־תֹאמְרוּ לְיוֹסֵף. . .
(בראשית נ:טז-יז)

So they sent this message to Yosef, "Before
his death your father left this instruction."
(Bereishit 50:16–17)

And Rabbi Ila'a said in the name of Rabbi Elazar son of Rabbi
Shimon: A person is permitted to modify his words [to tell a
"white" lie] when it is for peace, as it says, "Your father instructed
. . . So shall you say to Yosef, 'Please forgive now . . .'" (Bereishit
50:16–17).   (Babylonian Talmud Yevamot 65b)

יבמות סה:

וא"ר אילעא משום רבי אלעזר בר' שמעון: מותר לו לאדם לשנות בדבר השלום,
שנאמר "אביך צוה וגו' כה תאמרו ליוסף אנא שא נא וגו'" (בראשית נ:טז-יז).

Here we are compelled to confront an obvious distortion of truth,
or perhaps even a blatant lie: Nowhere do we find any statement
in Torah that Yaakov actually said the words attributed to him
in this text. However, this is clearly an opportunity for Yosef to
develop a positive relationship with his brothers now that their
father has died. Yosef can afford to be magnanimous, and chooses
to allay his brothers' fears now that they are no longer protected
by Yaakov.

As we have seen elsewhere, the Talmud makes it clear that *for
the purpose of making peace*, the distortion of truth – indeed, the
overt lie – is not only permissible but may in fact be desirable.
Shalom is a transcending value in Torah and rabbinic literature.

Of course, the Torah insists upon the distinction between truth and falsehood, between good and evil; nonetheless it is emphatic in its insistence upon the pursuit of peace among individuals, families, communities, and nations.

The rabbinic focus on domestic peace is of particular significance, since it evolved and was first articulated in an era and civilization when such domestic concerns were not the norm. The following text is instructive on this matter:

> If regarding the stones of the Altar, which do not see, hear, or speak, the verse says "Do not wield an iron tool over them" (Devarim 27:5) because they bring peace between Israel and their Father in Heaven, then a human being who brings peace between a husband and wife, between one family and another, between one city and another, between one country and another, and between one nation and its neighbor, how much more so will calamities not come upon him [if they are careful to promote peace in their life].
> (Sifra, Kedoshim 10)

ספרא פ' קדושים

אם אבני מזבח שאינן לא רואות ולא שומעות ולא מדברות על ידי שמטילות שלום בין ישראל לאביהן שבשמים אמר הכתוב "לא תניף עליהן ברזל" (דברים כז:ה) אדם שמטיל שלום בין איש לאשתו בין משפחה למשפחה בין עיר לעיר ובין מדינה למדינה ובין אומה לחברתה על אחת כמה וכמה שלא תבואהו הפורעניות:

Yet the rabbinic mind is not naive in its pursuit of peace:

> Any peace that is not accompanied by rebuke is not [true] peace.
> (Midrash Bereishit Rabbah 54:3)

מדרש בראשית רבה נד:ג

כל שלום שאין עמו תוכחה אינו שלום.

At times, suggests this midrash, chastisement or rebuke are necessary in order for peace to be lasting and effective. If conflict – be it domestic, economic, or political – is to come to a peaceful conclusion, dialogue is necessary as well as a clarification of the very issues which led to the conflict.

The transcending value of peace requires that all parties understand and accept the obvious truth that in peace, not all issues may or can be settled amicably. The settling of issues with mathematical precision and balance is not always attainable. The commitment required for a peaceful settlement of conflict is that each party sacrifice something of value to enable the structure of lasting peace to be built. All parties must contribute to this process.

Psalm 29:11 says it best:

G-d has given strength to his people, G-d has blessed his people with shalom.

תהלים כט:יא

ה׳ עֹז לְעַמּוֹ יִתֵּן ה׳ יְבָרֵךְ אֶת־עַמּוֹ בַשָּׁלוֹם:

Peace requires the strength and resolve to reach out to the "Other" and the strength to risk the implications of peace.

Seeking Forgiveness

כֹּה־תֹאמְרוּ לְיוֹסֵף אָנָּא שָׂא נָא פֶּשַׁע אַחֶיךָ
וְחַטָּאתָם כִּי־רָעָה גְמָלוּךָ וְעַתָּה שָׂא נָא לְפֶשַׁע
עַבְדֵי אֱלֹהֵי אָבִיךָ וַיֵּבְךְּ יוֹסֵף בְּדַבְּרָם אֵלָיו:

(בראשית נ:יז)

*So shall you say to Yosef. "Forgive, I urge you, the
offense and guilt of your brothers who treated you
so harshly. Therefore, please forgive the offense of
the servants of the G-d of your father." And Yosef
was in tears as they spoke to him.* (Bereishit 50:17)

Rabbi Yose bar Chanina said: Whoever seeks forgiveness from his
friend should not ask [for forgiveness] more than three times, as
it says, "Please forgive . . . now, please forgive" (Bereishit 50:17).
(Babylonian Talmud Yoma 87a-b)

יומא פז.-פז::

אמר רבי יוסי בר חנינא: כל המבקש מטו מחבירו אל יבקש ממנו יותר משלש
פעמים, שנאמר "אנא שא נא . . . ועתה שא נא" (בראשית נ:יז).

Torah obligates us to both seek and to grant forgiveness. Yom
Kippur, the most sacred day of the Jewish calendar, is the day set
aside to focus upon this imperative.

The liturgy of Yom Kippur includes, on ten separate occasions, the *Al Chet* – "confessional" relating exclusively to sins
committed בין אדם לחברו – by one person towards another. G-d
is not introduced as a party in these confrontations (other than
requiring that this initiative for reconciliation be a spiritual / religious imperative). Moreover, the *musar* / ethical teachings on the
observance of Rosh Hashannah and Yom Kippur focus heavily
upon the issue of people seeking forgiveness of one another.

Thus the theme of this particular Talmudic observation is significant. Yosef's brothers turn to him now that they no longer have the implied protection of their father Yaakov, and convey a message which they hope will win their brother's forgiveness. The Midrash points to three distinct phrases in the brothers' statement to Yosef as support for the teaching that a person must seek forgiveness three separate times in domestic or interpersonal conflicts.

Both the offender and the offended are responsible for engaging in a dialogue of forgiveness. Stubborn anger is not a healthy attitude for either party. There must be a limit to anger, even when it is legitimate. This text makes a distinction, as well, between an Amalek-type evil and the daily pains we inflict upon one another.[1]

The Talmud's admonition that one need not ask forgiveness more than three times refers to the interpersonal relationships of daily life. While one has a right to self-esteem and need not accept offensive and demeaning behavior or language, nonetheless when approached for forgiveness one must be gracious and forgiving, allowing of course for issues to be clarified. According to *Halachah*, one need not grovel; three attempts are the maximum required.

Beyond doubt, any quest for forgiveness must come only after all monetary issues or other pragmatic aspects of the dispute have been resolved in a just and amicable manner. Then there comes a time when the past must be set aside and healing allowed to commence.

---

1. The Torah does instruct us to "remember" Amalek as an eternal enemy for attacking us without cause (Shemot 17). Ancient Amalek remains forever the symbol of absolute evil, experienced in every generation, that must be destroyed root and branch. In the Passover Haggadah, we attest to the ever-present nature of Amalek, who seeks to destroy the People of Israel throughout history. The Holocaust is a manifestation of Amalek in our time.

Loving Criticism

וְאַתֶּם חֲשַׁבְתֶּם עָלַי רָעָה אֱ־לֹהִים חֲשָׁבָהּ
לְטֹבָה לְמַעַן עֲשֹׂה כַּיּוֹם הַזֶּה לְהַחֲיֹת עַם־רָב:
(בראשית נ:כ)

Besides, although you intended me harm, G-d
intended it for good, so as to bring about the
present result – the survival of many people.
(Bereishit 50:20)

From here [we learn] that rebuke is pleasant, for out of rebuke
comes love, as it says, "open reproof is better than concealed love"
(Mishlei 27:5).   (Midrash Lekach Tov)

מדרש לקח טוב
מיכן שהתוכחה נאה שמתוך התוכחה באה האהבה וכה"א "טובה תוכחת
מגולה מאהבה מסותרת" (משלי כז:ה).

There comes a time when words of chastisement are necessary.
Loving criticism may provide a significant opportunity for growth
and maturation. Words of praise and flattery may sooth, while
words of criticism may be painful and embarrassing. Nonetheless, criticism may often prove to be a positive experience.

There is of course the issue of limits. Just as there must be a
limit to praise, so there must be a limit to criticism. There must
also be a careful judgment on the part of the critic as to who will
respond positively to criticism. In addition, there are limits to
the critic's responsibility. What are these limits, asks the Talmud?
Some would say threat of physical attack, others suggest threat of
being cursed, while others set a very fine line of counter-rebuke,
to allow the critic to be silent and cease from further criticism.

There is yet an additional dimension of the mitzvah of תוכחה (*to-chachah*) – "chastisement:"

> Rabbi Yosee, son of Chaninah says, "a love which has no words of chastisement is not love." Resh Lakish says, "chastisement brings peace" as the Torah says "And Avraham chastised Avimelech" (Bereishit 21:25). After which he (Avraham) effected a treaty of peace between the two of them. (Midrash Bereishit Rabbah 54)

מדרש בראשית רבה פ' נד

ר' יוסי ב"ר חנינא אמר, כל אהבה שאין עמה תוכחה אינה אהבה. ריש לקיש אמר תוכחה מביאה לידי שלום. שנאמר: "והוכיח אברהם את אבימלך" (בראשית כא:כה) ואח"כ כרתו ברית שלום ביניהם.

> Do not rebuke a scoffer for he will hate you, reprove a wise man and he will love you.   (Mishlei 9:8)

משלי ט:ח

אל תוכח לץ פן ישנאך, הוכח לחכם ויאהבך.

Moreover the Talmud teaches:

> Until when (what point) does one rebuke someone? Rav says "un-til beating," and Shmuel says "until cursing," and Rabbi Yonatan "until rebuke." (Babylonian Talmud Erchin 16b)

ערכין טז:

עד היכן תוכחה רב אמר עד הכאה, ושמואל אמר עד קללה, ורבי יוחנן עד נזיפה.

There is a limit to one's responsibility of being a critic. What are the limits, asks the Talmud. Some say:

הכאה – "beating," until the threat of physical attack. Others suggest קללה – "cursing," chastising to the point of being cursed by the "disciplined" person, while others still, set a very fine line of נזיפה – "rebuke" or counter rebuke to allow the critic to be silent and cease any further criticism or chastisement.

It would seem from the Talmudic approach that the observer

has a moral and religious obligation, based upon Torah sources, to confront the offender and express criticism. There then comes a point when the observer has fulfilled his obligation and may remain silent, and perhaps must remain silent. Yet we must consider the question of silence in the face of absolute evil. What does the moral/religious person say or do in a society of self-evident immoral behavior? The prophets give us ample and dramatic role models for confronting evil on every level of society. Neither kings nor priests were spared the prophets' chastisements.

There is yet an additional dimension to chastisement. The Rabbis observe that honest, objective criticism is an element of effective relationships. A friend, a child, a spouse is more likely to appreciate criticism within the context of a relationship of profound love and trust. Who better than a dependable friend or relative to express criticism such that pain or failure may be minimized.

For there is no righteous man on earth who does good and does not sin. (Ecclesiastes 7:20)

קהלת ז:כ

כִּי אָדָם אֵין צַדִּיק בָּאָרֶץ אֲשֶׁר יַעֲשֶׂה־טּוֹב וְלֹא יֶחֱטָא:

The Torah teaches that even a righteous person may sin. No one is perfect, for even in the act of doing good one may inadvertently do evil. Thus a critical observation from one who is trusted, respected and admired might indeed be most effective. However, the criticism must be conveyed in an atmosphere and tone which minimizes the potential for embarrassment or offense. The venue must be private. A personal, sensitive discussion allows for a dialogue rather than a monologue. The critic must demonstrate respect, patience and understanding rather than judgment and rancor. In addition, focused inquiry and discussion will allow the facts to emerge and conclusions to be reached fairly.

Peace and Reconciliation

וְעַתָּה אַל־תִּירָאוּ אָנֹכִי אֲכַלְכֵּל אֶתְכֶם
וְאֶת־טַפְּכֶם וַיְנַחֵם אוֹתָם וַיְדַבֵּר עַל־לִבָּם:
(בראשית נ:כא)

"And so, fear not, I will sustain you and your
children." Thus he reassured them, speaking
kindly to them. (Bereishit 50:21)

Rabbi Benjamin bar Yefet said in the name of Rabbi Elazar: This
teaches that he told them things that are accepted by the heart.
(Babylonian Talmud Megillah 16b)

מגילה טז:

אמר רבי בנימין בר יפת אמר רבי אלעזר: מלמד שאמר להם דברים שמתקבלין
על הלב:

We are taught that even when we must confront another person
with a painful truth, if presented with wisdom and sensitivity, the
result may indeed be positive. Attitude, language, and manner are
often the critical components of an effective, positive confrontation.

There is yet another dimension of "confrontation." Each
person must be open to chastisement – מוסר – coming from a
teacher, relative, colleague and, in special circumstances, even a
stranger.

The ultimate objective of a confrontation must be growth, reconciliation and peace. Whether the conflict is being acted out in
a family, profession or community, we must always seek paths to
reconciliation and peace. As complex as the process of reconciliation may be, it is worth the effort.

Rabbi Shimon ben Gamliel says: The world is sustained by three things – law, truth, and peace [and these three are in fact one], – if justice is done, truth is done and peace is achieved. Rabba Mana said: And all three are in one verse – "render truth, justice of peace in your gates" (Zechariah 8:16). (Jerusalem Talmud Megillah Chapter 3 Halacha 6)

תלמוד ירושלמי מגילה פרק ג הלכה ו

רבי שמעון בן גמליאל אומר על שלשה דברים העולם עומד על הדין ועל האמת ועל השלום ושלשתן דבר אחד הם נעשה הדין נעשה אמת נעשה אמת נעשה שלום א"ר מנא ושלשתן בפסוק אחד "אמת ומשפט שלום שפטו בשעריכם" (זכריה ח:טז).

Rabbi Shimon here states the essential values which sustain a civilized world: truth, justice, and peace. It appears that the ultimate objective is peace. In a peaceful society, truth and justice serve as the catalysts which foster and sustain the peace.

In fact, these three values are the elements of a successful family. Family relationships guided by the values of truth, justice, and peace will strengthen the family and foster an environment in which family bonds will mature and deepen over time. These are not values that can be espoused without action. Parents are role models for their children; if children are to learn the imperative of truth, justice, and peace as foundational human values, then these values must be manifest in the *behavior* as well as in the attitudes and speech of significant adults in their lives. Otherwise, these values will remain hollow.

The values of Judaism, Torah and mitzvot are primarily taught by parental modeling. A commitment to Torah and mitzvot requires a daily life reflecting the values, traditions and aspirations inherent in Judaism.

In addition to behavioral modeling, parents constantly provide ethical lessons for their children through their use – and sadly, their abuse – of language. The words we use, the sensitivity with which we convey them, the truthfulness of our speech, even our tone of voice reflect our values, whether we are conscious of it or not. Far too many parents are guilty of addressing their children (or speaking to others in the presence of their children) with embarrassing, painful, and/or vulgar speech. The Torah considers publicly embarrassing someone to be a serious evil. Vulgarity, lies, and slander are all violent transgressions of the values of Torah and mitzvot.

The Talmudic commentary on our verse suggests not only the absence of vengeance on Yosef's part, but also a profound outreach to his brothers: "I will sustain you and your children." Yosef thus assures his brothers that they will be taken care of. The Talmud here seeks to emphasize the transcending value of forgiveness, and focuses our attention upon the word וינחם – a word which speaks of "consolation," not vengeance. Yosef spoke words of compassion which were sensed by his brothers to be conciliatory, and which they could therefore accept. Forgiveness must have been a complex and daunting task for the aggrieved Yosef. Yet what would he have gained by using his power to incarcerate or even kill these men? What profit is there in vengeance? Yosef rises above the treachery and betrayal of his brothers, and seeks peace and family harmony through words of consolation and reconciliation, and peace.

Peace, peace for the far and the near, said the
Lord, and I will heal him. (Isaiah 57:19)

ישעיה נז:יט

שָׁלוֹם שָׁלוֹם לָרָחוֹק וְלַקָּרוֹב אָמַר ה' וּרְפָאתִיו:

תם ונשלם בעזה"ית

יעקב חיים בן א'מ ר' משה הילסנרט וא'מ שיינדל זצ"ל

ירושלים עיר הקודש

ב' אני לדודי ודודי לי

תשמ"ז

Respecting the Elderly / כבוד לזקנים

וְאֵלֶּה שְׁמוֹת בְּנֵי יִשְׂרָאֵל הַבָּאִים מִצְרָיְמָה אֵת
יַעֲקֹב אִישׁ וּבֵיתוֹ בָּאוּ: (שמות א:א)

*And these are the names of Bnei Yisrael who
came to Egypt, with Yaakov; each man with his
household.* (Shemot 1:1)

Said Rabbi Shimon Ben Halafta: It is the way of the world with a
person who has children; as long as he has strength, his children
are secondary to him. However, once he ages he becomes secondary to his children. However, here – even in his old age – they
are involving themselves with the needs of their father, with [his
needs] first. This is why it says "with Yaakov" (Shemot 1:1) and
afterwards, "each man with his household" (ibid.).

(Midrash HaGadol)

מדרש הגדול
אמר רבי שמעון בן חלפתא – בנוהג שבעולם אדם שיש לו בנים כל זמן שיש
בו כח בניו נעשין טפילה לו. הזקן הוא נעשה טפילה לבניו, ברם הכא אפילו
בזקנותו שמתעסקין בצרכי אביהן תחלה, לכך נאמר – "אֵת יַעֲקֹב" (שמות א:א),
ואחר כך "אִישׁ וּבֵיתוֹ בָּאוּ" (שם).

The Midrash states the essence of the parent-child relationship.
When a parent is young and vibrant, the children are "attached"
to the parent; when the parent ages and strength wanes perhaps
the parent becomes "attached" to the child. The term "attached"
suggests "dependence." The very idea of "dependence" has over-
tones of "helplessness" and "vulnerability" and thus demeaning
for the parent.

Not so with Yaakov. Yaakov's relationship with his children

in old age, the Midrash suggests, never deteriorated to "being attached," thus helpless with loss of dignity. His children demonstrate כבוד אב, "respect for their father," they provide for Yaakov first and then for their family. Yaakov remains their concern and their responsibility, with respect.

From a practical aspect one may consider the manner in which adult children demonstrate respect for their parent. Symbolically, in a traditional Jewish home, the parent, father and mother are always seated at the head of either end of the table. Father at one end, and mother at the other.

Of course, our contemporary dining tables are often round or oval, which precludes an obvious "head of table," thus necessitating a designated place as "head of table." Nonetheless, the Halacha requires that a child (even adult) may not sit in the designated place of a parent. Nor may a child (of any age) call a parent by their given name. A parent may be referred to, either directly or indirectly, as Father and Mother in whatever language they converse, never by given name.

These overt demonstrations of respect for parents are particularly critical in contemporary society where respect for parents, the elderly, the scholar are often compromised.

We live longer and seek dignity and independence in advanced years, thus the historic Jewish value of respect for parent and the elderly are critical values which need to be prioritized, in schools and in family discussions.

Protection for the Family / הגנה למשפחה

וְאֵלֶּה שְׁמוֹת בְּנֵי יִשְׂרָאֵל הַבָּאִים מִצְרַיְמָה אֵת
יַעֲקֹב אִישׁ וּבֵיתוֹ בָּאוּ: (שמות א:א)

And these are the names of Bnei Yisrael who
came to Egypt, with Yaakov; each man with his
household. (Shemot 1:1)

The Midrash HaGadol makes the following observation – On
the verse אִישׁ וּבֵיתוֹ בָּאוּ – "Each man and his family came (to Egypt)
. . . ."

> Said Rabbi Hama: Because Yaakov Avinu knew that the Egyptians
> were immersed in sexual immorality, he therefore arose (i.e., he
> was proactive) and married off his sons and grandsons prior to
> them arriving in Egypt.   (Midrash HaGadol)

מדרש הגדול

אמר ר' חמא לפי שידע יעקב אבינו שהמצרים שטופים בזמה, לכך עמד והשיא
את בניו ובני בניו נשים קודם שיבואו למצרים.

Recognizing the pragmatic challenges of living in an immoral
or amoral society is a prerequisite for a moral family to survive.
Suggesting superior discipline of the average person is naive and
perhaps irresponsible. One must not present the average person
with a morally polluted environment without the tools to transcend and survive the pollution.

Yaakov understands that his family has had little experience
with the pagan Egyptian social mores. To protect his family
structure from Egyptian sexual immorality he seeks a "family

structure," marriage, to insulate his children from the pollution of Egypt.

In our world we have no simplistic solutions to the moral ambivalence in which our youth mature. Our society seems to have created an environment of "moral relativity" or "situation ethics." There are no clear "ethical" or "unethical," "moral" or "immoral" rules! It is "situational." "It all depends."

Men and women of all ages, live together without benefit of marriage vows, and their relationship is acknowledged, by family and community. At times it seems that "formal sanction" is neither sought nor required by family or community.

Yaakov understood that he must protect his family from the consequences of entering the Egyptian amoral environment. Yaakov leaves us with the challenge of what do we do to protect our children from the contemporary social moral ambivalence or amorality which permeates Western civilization.

Respect for Parents / כבוד הורים

וַיָּמָת יוֹסֵף וְכָל־אֶחָיו וְכֹל הַדּוֹר הַהוּא:
(שמות א:ו)

And Yosef died, and all his brothers, and all that generation. (Shemot 1:6)

On ten occasions the sons of Yaakov said to Yosef: "your servant our father" – and [on each occasion] Yosef heard this matter and remained silent. [However], remaining silent is considered to be consenting to what has been said. Therefore, the years of his life were shortened by ten years, as it says, "and Yosef died, and all his brothers" (Shemot 1:6).　　　　(Pirkei D'Rabbi Eliezer Ch. 39)

פרקי דרבי אליעזר פ' ל"ט

י' פעמים אמרו בני יעקב ליוסף "עַבְדְּךָ אָבִינוּ" – ושמע יוסף את הדבר הזה ושתק, ושתיקה כהודאה. לפיכך נתקצרו משני חייו י' שנים שנאמר "וַיָּמָת יוֹסֵף וְכָל־אֶחָיו" (שמות א:ו).

The text questions the apparent premature death of יוסף, who was next to the youngest of the 12 sons of Yaakov. Nonetheless we are told of יוסף's death together with his brothers. The Rabbis of the interpretive school of Rabbinic literature sought every possible opportunity to pose a question which would result in a moral imperative.

How one speaks to, or of, a parent is the question the Rabbis choose to intersect into this otherwise benign verse. When Yosef's brothers first approach him as the Egyptian official in charge of the land's food supply – they speak of their father Yaakov as "your servant." Ten times they call Yaakov "your servant" and ten times Yosef hears his father being called "your servant" and ten times Yosef says nothing to prevent such a demeaning term being applied to Yaakov, his father. The text considers this inexcusable, indeed a profound breach of moral conduct. Though Yosef was still unknown as Yaakov's son, nonetheless, Yosef should have found a good reason to prevent his brothers from the repetitious reference to their father as "your servant." The respect due a parent is never abrogated.

Torah places the highest priority upon the mitzvah of respecting parents. The Talmud (Jerusalem Talmud, Peah 1:1) states:

> Rabbi Shimon Bar Yochai says: Great is the mitzvah of respecting parents for it appears that G-d prefers that we respect our parents even more than we respect Him, as it is written – "Respect G-d with your wealth," (Mishlei 3:9) [that is to say] if you have [wealth with which to serve G-d] then you must do so, should you not [possess wealth], you have no obligations to G-d. On the other hand [regarding] respecting parents, [should economic support be required to support parents] it is written: "Honor your father and your mother" (Shemot 20:12), you are obligated to do so, even if you must beg from door to door, [to acquire the means to support your parents]. (Jerusalem Talmud Peah 1:1, Torah Shelemah on Shemot Ch. 20, source 288).

ירושלמי פאה א:א, תורה שלמה שמות פרק כ' רפח

רשב"י אומר גדול כבוד אב ואם שהעדיפן הקב"ה יותר מכבודו, שבכבוד הקב"ה נאמר "כַּבֵּד אֶת־ה' מֵהוֹנֶךָ" (משלי ג:ט) אם יש לך אתה חייב ואם לאו אתה פטור, אבל בכבוד אב ואם נאמר "כַּבֵּד אֶת־אָבִיךָ וְאֶת־אִמֶּךָ" (שמות כ:יב) ואפילו אתה מחזר על הפתחים.

Honor your father and your mother.   (Shemot 20:12)

שמות כ:יב

כַּבֵּד אֶת־אָבִיךָ וְאֶת־אִמֶּךָ.

This pasuk is stated numerous times in the Torah, an unusual redundant demonstration of the centrality of this mitzvah.

Contemporary society needs to take a serious lesson from this

Torah value and obligation. We have noted this particular mitzvah previously, yet it needs continued focus and emphasis for it is a critical foundation block of Torah and Jewish civilization in our times, as it has been throughout Jewish history.

Gratitude / הכרת הטוב

וַיָּקָם מֶלֶךְ־חָדָשׁ עַל־מִצְרָיִם אֲשֶׁר לֹא־יָדַע אֶת־
יוֹסֵף: (שמות א:ח)

*And there arose a new king over Egypt, who did
not know Yosef.* (Shemot 1:8)

Why does scripture so severely punish someone who lacks gratitude [literally, "who denies good"]? Because this is a form of
heresy towards the Holy One, blessed is He because a heretic of
the Holy One, blessed is He also denies the good done [to him].
In fact, this type of person denies the good that a friend does for
him, and the next day he then denies the good of his Maker. So too
[Scripture] says about Pharaoh "who did not know Yosef" (Shemot
1:8). Surely until this moment [literally, "day"], Egypt knew about
the kindnesses of Yosef, but even though it was known, it was not
considered and there was a lack of gratitude for all he had done.
This is why, at the end, they denied the good of the Holy One,
blessed is He, by saying "I do not know the Lord" (Shemot 5:2).
This comes to teach us that a lack of gratitude is associated with
the essence of heresy.   (Mishnat Rabbi Eliezer, Parsha 7, p. 137)

משנת רבי אליעזר פרשה ז דף קלז

מפני מה ענש הכתוב ביותר לכפויי טובה? מפני שהוא כעניין כפירה בהקב"ה.
אף הכופר בהקב"ה כופה טובה הוא. האדם הזה הוא כופה טובתו של חבירו
למחר הוא כופה טובתו של קונו. וכן הוא אומר בפרעה, "אֲשֶׁר לֹא־יָדַע אֶת־
יוֹסֵף" (שמות א:ח) והלא עד היום הזה מצרים יודעין חסדו של יוסף, אלא שהיה
יודע ולא השגיח עליו, וכפה טובתו, ולבסוף כפה טובתו של הקב"ה, שאמר "לֹא
יָדַעְתִּי אֶת־ה'" (שמות ה:ב) הא למדת שכפיית הטובה הוקשה לכפירה בעיקר.

This text demonstrates how חז"ל view the individual who fails to
acknowledge kindness extended by another. One who does not

304

manifest gratitude toward a human benefactor will eventually fail to acknowledge the "Universal Benefactor," the Almighty. חז"ל wonder why is Pharaoh's failure to recognize Yosef's role in predicting and preparing for the impending Egyptian famine so cataclysmic in its consequences. "Why?" asks the text was Egypt so severely stricken for not recognizing Yosef's service to the Egyptian people? One who fails to acknowledge kindness to a human benefactor will eventually fail to acknowledge the "Eternal Benefactor." Gratitude, according to the Torah, is an ethical imperative which needs to be manifest in all of human experience, be it to one's fellow or to the Almighty. Failing one is to fail all.

Torah and Wisdom / תורה וחכמה

הָבָה נִתְחַכְּמָה לוֹ פֶּן־יִרְבֶּה וְהָיָה כִּי־תִקְרֶאנָה
מִלְחָמָה וְנוֹסַף גַּם־הוּא עַל־שֹׂנְאֵינוּ וְנִלְחַם־בָּנוּ
וְעָלָה מִן־הָאָרֶץ: (שמות א:י)

Come, let us deal wisely with them; in case they
multiply, and it may happen that when there will
be a war they may join our enemies and fight
against us and depart from the land. (Shemot 1:10)

"Come , let us deal wisely" (Shemot 1:10) – There is a good type
of wisdom, and there is a bad type of wisdom. The wisdom of
Torah and *Musar* is the good type of wisdom, and the wisdom relating to deception is the bad type of wisdom. (Rabbeinu Bachya)

רבינו בחיי

"הָבָה נִתְחַכְּמָה לוֹ" (שמות א:י) יש חכמה טובה ויש חכמה רעה, החכמה בתורה
ובמוסר הינו חכמה טובה והחכמה בעניני ערמומיות היא חכמה רעה.

חכמה that is "wisdom" is not inherently moral, ethical, or good.
"Wisdom" may be and often has been a tool to accomplish an evil
agenda. The tyrants of history, as well as the acts of the simple
citizen, have often been guided with evil wisdom. To succeed in
one's agenda, wisdom is helpful, perhaps even an imperative.

The Talmud suggests that חכמה is both self acquired and G-d's
blessing. The Talmud states:

The Holy One, blessed is He, gives wisdom only to one who already has wisdom (Brachot 55a).

ברכות נה.

אין הקב"ה נותן חכמה אלא למי שיש בו חכמה.

306

The Midrash in קהלת רבה פ"א relates the following dialog:

A matron asked Rabbi Yossi bar Chalafta: She said, "What is the meaning of 'He gives wisdom to the wise' (Daniel 2:21)? There is no need for a verse simply to state that 'He gives wisdom to the wise'. Instead, it should have said, 'He gives wisdom to those who are not wise and knowledge to those without understanding.'" He answered her, "I will explain with a parable. If two people came to borrow money from you, one rich and the other poor, to whom would you lend, the rich man or the poor?" She replied, "To the rich man." He said to her, "Why?" to which she answered, "Because if the rich man loses my money he can repay me, but if the poor man loses my money, how will he repay me?" He said to her, "Have not your ears heard what you have said with your mouth? If the Holy One, blessed is He, gave wisdom to fools, they would sit and meditate upon it in privies, theatres, and bath houses; but the Holy One, blessed is He, gave wisdom to the wise who sit and meditate upon it in synagogues and houses of study." (Kohelet Rabbah 1:17)

קהלת רבה פ"א-יז

מטרונה אחת שאלה את רבי יוסי בר חלפתא, אמרה ליה מהו דין שנאמר "יָהֵב חָכְמְתָא לְחַכִּימִין" (דניאל ב:כא), לא הוה צריך קרא למימר אלא "יהב חכמתא לחכימין" לא הוה צריך קרא למימר אלא יהב חכמתא ללא אלא יהב חכמתא ללא חכימין ומדע ללא ידעי ביהב? אמר לה מ של אם יבאו אצלך שני בני אדם ללות ממך ממון, אחד מהן עשיר ואחד מהן עני, לאיזה אתה מלוה, לעשיר או לעני? אמרה לו לעשיר, אמר לה, ולמה? א"ל שאם אבד העשיר ממוני יש לו מהיכן יפרוע, אבל אם אבד העני ממוני מאין יפרע לי? אמר לה ולא ישמעו אזניך מה שאתה מוציאה מפיך? אילו נתן הקב"ה חכמה לטפשים היו יושבים והוגין בה בבתי קרקסאות ובבתי תיאטריאות ובבתי מרחצאות, אלא נתן חכמה לחכימין והם יושבים והוגים בה בבתי כנסיות ובבתי מדרשות.

The Midrash suggests that חכמה – wisdom is bestowed upon, or acquired only by those who have (perhaps inherently) the ability to understand and utilize wisdom.

It is possible that the author of this Midrash understood what contemporary science has determined; we are born with a given potential "IQ" and then may choose how, and if, we utilize this innate capacity for learning and developing intellectually. The premise of this Midrash is that wisdom is given to those who have the innate capacity to utilize this wisdom.

Competition among scholars increases wisdom, teaches the Talmud:

Envy among scholars increases wisdom. (Bava Batra 22)

בבא בתרא כב.
קנאת סופרים תרבה חכמה.

Thus חכמה is a human quality cherished by תורה, for only with wisdom can one fully comprehend the essence of תורה.

Futile Labor / בפרך

וַיַּעֲבִדוּ מִצְרַיִם אֶת־בְּנֵי יִשְׂרָאֵל בְּפָרֶךְ:
(שמות א:יג)

And the Egyptians made Bnei Yisrael work with
rigor. (Shemot 1:13)

What [type of labor] is "work with rigor"? – This is work that has
no limit, or work that is unnecessary.

(Yalkut Or HaAfeila manuscript, Torah Shelemah on Shemot Ch. 1,
source 137)

ילקוט אור האפלה כת"י, תורה שלמה שמות פרק א' קלז
איזו היא "עבודת פרך?" זה עבודה שאין לה קצבה, או עבודה שאינו צריך לה.

What does the תורה mean when it describes the Children of Israel working in Egypt בְּפָרֶךְ? Rabbi Menachem Kasher, the editor
of תורה שלמה, cites a manuscript in which בְּפָרֶךְ is translated as labor
which obviously has "no purpose," i.e., spinning a wheel which
connects to nothing.

It is daily labor with no fruition. Total futility.

How demoralizing. Daily brutal slave labor which lacks the
basic inherent human need to achieve. Denied even the most fundamental human aspiration "to accomplish" was the daily life of
the Jewish slave in Egypt. How sophisticated were the Egyptians
in their management of the Hebrew slaves. Deny the individual
any sense of purpose in daily life and you eventually break his
personality. Thus you have a mindless slave, a human machine.

How instructive is this understanding of Egyptian slavery. A
life without an agenda, without a transcending purpose, with-

309

out a sense of self and other, is a life devoid of any meaning and consequence. This insight helps us to understand the nature of the multitude of the Children of Israel who left Egypt. It was a generation which no longer understood human initiative, choice, and purpose. Having no need to depend upon self or of action depending upon free choice, this generation had no experience of assuming personal responsibility.

The various Midrashic commentaries and Talmudic sources make the point that most of the Jewish slaves in Egypt at the time of the Shemot did in fact not leave Egypt. They preferred the harsh Egyptian slavery rather than perils of freedom. Freedom requires choice and accepting consequences.

The Egyptians are Compared to Bitter Herbs / נמשלו מצרים כמרור

וַיְמָרְרוּ אֶת־חַיֵּיהֶם בַּעֲבֹדָה קָשָׁה . . . . :

(שמות א:יד)

And they made their lives bitter with hard slavery . . . .
(Shemot 1:14)

Rabbi Shmuel bar Nachmani said in Rabbi Yonatan's name: Why were the Egyptians compared to maror (as it is written, "and they made their lives bitter" – Rashi)? To teach you that just as maror is soft at the start [of eating] and hard by the end [of eating], so too were the Egyptians: Their beginning was soft, but their end was hard! (Talmud Bavli, Pesachim 39a).

פסחים לט.

אמר ר' שמואל ב"ר נחמני א"ר יונתן למה נמשלו מצרים כמרור (דכתיב "וַיְמָרְרוּ אֶת־חַיֵּיהֶם" – רש"י) לומר לך מה מרור זה שתחלתו רך וסופו קשה אף מצרים תחלתן רכה וסופן קשה.

The Egyptian enslavement was developed over time. At first Yosef invited his father, Yaakov, and all of his brothers to settle in Egypt as royal guests. Yosef's brothers were all shepherds, a profession unacceptable in ancient Egypt. Pagan Egypt worshipped animals; thus the family settled in Goshen. The Children of Israel were free to pursue their lives as they chose, free citizens of the land.

Then slowly Egypt became a cruel master rather than a gracious host, a critical lesson to be remembered. Throughout our history, we have served societies of every faith, of every form of social structure, of every culture.

The most cataclysmic and catastrophic event occurred in the

second half of the 20th century in a land and society whose assimilation was most popular and successful. We were integrated in the economic, academic, and even social structure of the land. Nonetheless, Germany was "the" venue and vehicle for the most cataclysmic period in all of Jewish history.

Germany was the story of Egypt in our time. Welcomed, successful, integrated and then enslaved and viciously destroyed.

The lesson of Egypt, Spain, Germany, and all of Jewish history is to be ever vigilant. The slightest compromise of our freedom may potentially compromise all of our freedom.

עצת מרים / Miriam's Advice

וַיֵּלֶךְ אִישׁ מִבֵּית לֵוִי וַיִּקַּח אֶת־בַּת־לֵוִי:
(שמות ב:א)

And there went a man from the house of Levi and took [for his wife] a daughter of Levi. (Shemot 2:1)

Where did he go? Said Rabbi Yehuda bar Zevina, "he went to follow the counsel of his daughter." A Tanna taught: Amram was the greatest man of his generation; when he saw that the wicked Pharaoh had decreed "Every son that is born shall be cast by you into the river" (Shemot 1:22) he said "our efforts are worthless!" He arose and divorced his wife, after which everyone arose and divorced their wives. His daughter said to him, "Father, your decree is worse than Pharaoh's, because Pharaoh decreed only against the males while you have decreed against both the males and females. Pharaoh only decreed concerning this world, whereas you have decreed concerning this world and the World to Come. In the case of the wicked Pharaoh it is doubtful whether his decree will or will not be fulfilled, whereas in your case, because you are righteous it is certain that your decree will be fulfilled," as it is said: "You shall also decree a thing, and it shall be established to you" (Iyov 22:28). He arose and took his wife back, and they all arose and took their wives back. (Sotah 12a)

סוטה יב.

להיכן הלך? אמר רב יהודה בר זבינא: שהלך בעצת בתו. תנא: עמרם גדול הדור היה, כיון שאמר פרעה הרשע "כָּל־הַבֵּן הַיִּלּוֹד הַיְאֹרָה תַּשְׁלִיכֻהוּ" (שמות א:כב) אמר: לשוא אנו עמלין עמד וגירש את אשתו, עמדו כולן וגירשו את נשותיהן. אמרה לו בתו: אבא, קשה גזירתך יותר משל פרעה, שפרעה לא גזר אלא על הזכרים, ואתה גזרת על הזכרים ועל הנקבות, פרעה לא גזר אלא בעוה"ז, ואתה בעוה"ז ולעוה"ב פרעה הרשע, ספק מתקיימת גזירתו ספק אינה

313

מתקיימת, אתה צדיק בודאי שגזירתך מתקיימת שנאמר: "וַתִגְזַר־אֹמֶר וְיָקָם לָךְ"
(איוב כב:כח) עמד והחזיר את אשתו, עמדו כולן והחזירו את נשותיהן.

The Talmud introduces the classic debate between the pragmatist and the idealist. Amram (the future father of Moshe) in response to Pharaoh's decree to kill all male infants born to Jewish mothers, separates from his wife, Yocheved. All the Jewish men do likewise.

Along comes Miriam, Amram's daughter, and challenges her father. "Pharaoh decreed that all Jewish male infants shall be drowned. You, having separated from your wife, have in effect, precluded the possible birth of female babies as well, thus the end of our people."

Amram recognizes the wisdom of Miriam and returns to his wife to resume their marital relationship and indeed Moshe is born.

A number of significant lessons may be gleaned from this Talmudic insight.

Miriam insists that all is not lost, in spite of Pharaoh's decree. True, argues Miriam, you may lose a male child, but why not consider the possibility of a baby girl? Why surrender to the tyrant so completely?

Now this event occurs at a time when a child, no less a daughter, does not so boldly challenge a parent. Yet Miriam does exactly that. Amram accepts the admonition, as does his wife Yocheved, and they resume their marital relationship, thus the birth of משה. Optimism, heeding the wisdom of a child (no matter the age of the child or parent), and willing to engage in acts which may lead to grave consequences are all part of אמונה - בטחון – "faith and trust," which is the attitude that motivates Amram and Yocheved to continue a normal relationship of marriage.

During the period of the Holocaust this very debate occupied the minds of Jewish families. The "final solution," that is, the destruction of the Jewish people, was being organized, and a sophisticated process was employed by the evil powers who ruled most of the European continent. "Why have children," was the cry of many Jews, "if this is our destiny?"

A sophisticated, civilized, and cultured nation employed scientific and efficient methods to destroy our people. The civilized world, before it was threatened, was silent and did little to help a threatened nation. It was the story of Egypt except with a far more sophisticated enemy and method of destruction.

Many a Jew began to question the future of the Jewish people. "Why have children?" Jews in the free world pondered. It was the story of the generation of the parents of Moshe.

Yet reason, courage, and faith prevailed and the results are obvious. Miriam, who challenged her father and mother in the first encounter with a threatened Jewish future, served as an inspiration and role model for Jewish wives and husbands throughout Jewish history, and indeed during the period of the Holocaust.

Courage and faith in G-d and in the future have indeed been the hallmark of the Jewish people. The modern State of Israel, as well as the contemporary Shemot from the former Soviet Union, are manifestations of this faith in G-d and the destiny of the Jewish people. The survivors of the Holocaust who now live in Israel and throughout the world demonstrate that Jews always affirm their faith in G-d and in themselves with courage and fortitude, and ultimately, "with G-d's help," prevail.

עין טוב / A Good Eye

וַיִּגְדַּל הַיֶּלֶד וַתְּבִאֵהוּ לְבַת־פַּרְעֹה וַיְהִי־לָהּ
לְבֵן וַתִּקְרָא שְׁמוֹ מֹשֶׁה וַתֹּאמֶר כִּי מִן־הַמַּיִם
מְשִׁיתִהוּ: (שמות ב:י)

And the child grew, and she brought him to
Pharaoh's daughter, and he became her son. And
she called his name Moshe and she said "for I
drew him from the water." (Shemot 2:10)

Rabbi Joshua of Siknin, quoting Rabbi Levi, said: The Holy
One, blessed is He, said to Bityah Pharaoh's daughter, "Moshe
was not your son, yet you called him your son: So will I call you
My daughter, although you are not" as it says, "And these are the
sons of Bityah" (Divrei Hayamim I 4:8) [which reads] *bat yah* [the
daughter of G-d]. (Vayikra Rabbah 1:3)

ויקרא רבה פ"א:ג

ר' יהושע דסכנין בשם ר' לוי: אמר לה הקב"ה לבתיה בת פרעה, משה לא היה
בנך וקראתו בנך, אף את לא את בתי ואני קורא אותך בתי, שנאמר "וְאֵלֶּה בְּנֵי
בִתְיָה" (דברי הימים א ד:ח), בת י"ה.

Two most astonishing comments of the Midrash concerning the
name of משה.

The first, G-d speaks to Batya (בתיה), the daughter of Pharaoh,
acknowledging that she saved משה from the basket in the water
into which his mother יוכבד placed him. Batya then raised Moshe
in Pharaoh's palace, and she referred to משה as her son. "And the
boy grew up and they brought him to Pharaoh's daughter and he
was to her as a son." And she called him משה and she said – כִּי מִן
הַמַּיִם מְשִׁיתִהוּ (שמות ב:י), "for I drew him from the water."

One may ask, did not עמרם or יוכבד, the father and mother of משה, bestow a name upon the infant when he was born? Are we to understand the מדרש, that השם allowed, and indeed chose, a pagan to name the most important person in all of תורה, indeed of Jewish history.

No doubt this is the case with משה. The תורה teaches that acknowledging a kindness, הכרת הטוב is a fundamental value of Jewish tradition. The Torah also establishes an appreciation of עין טוב the value of "seeing good in every opportunity." The daughter of Pharaoh sees an infant adrift in "the water." She does not turn away. She is the Princess of Egypt, the daughter of Pharaoh, of what concern is this child to her? Yet she had what is called an עין טוב, literally "a good eye." She saw a positive opportunity to save a child and regardless of the implications that this was a Jewish child, she did not hesitate. The text in Mishlei (משלי כב:ט) is most appropriate: עין טוב הוא יברך. A person with a "good eye," that is, a positive attitude seeking the best in all situations, "is to be blessed."

Take advantage of what is at hand, the consequences may be extraordinary. Faith, vision, courage, and determination are the lessons of Pharaoh's daughter and her place in the תורה.

ששת ימים תעבוד / Six Day Work Week

וַיְהִי בַּיָּמִים הָהֵם וַיִּגְדַּל מֹשֶׁה וַיֵּצֵא אֶל־אֶחָיו
וַיַּרְא בְּסִבְלֹתָם וַיַּרְא אִישׁ מִצְרִי מַכֶּה אִישׁ־
עִבְרִי מֵאֶחָיו: (שמות ב:יא)

And it came to pass in those days, when Moshe
was grown, that he went out to his brothers, and
looked on their burdens; and he saw an Egyptian
beating a Hebrew, one of his brothers. (Shemot 2:11)

Another interpretation of "and he looked on their burdens" (Shemot 2:11): He saw that they had no rest. He [therefore] went and
said to Pharaoh: 'If someone has a slave and does not let him rest
one day during the week, he dies. Similarly, if you will not let your
slaves rest one day in the week, they will die!' [Pharaoh] replied,
'Go and do for them as you say.' Moshe therefore went and established for them the Shabbat day for rest.

(Shemot Rabba 1:28)

שמות רבה א:כח

דבר אחר "וַיַּרְא בְּסִבְלֹתָם" (שמות ב:יא) ראה שאין להם מנוחה. הלך ואמר
לפרעה מי שיש לו עבד אם אינו נח יום אחד בשבוע הוא מת, ואלו עבדיך
אם אין אתה מניח להם יום אחד בשבוע הם מתים. אמר לו לך ועשה להן כמו
שתאמר, הלך משה ותקן להם את יום השבת לנוח.

Perhaps this is the first mention in human history of a "six-day
work week" for slaves or any laborer. The תורה views human activity as limited, guided by תורה, the observance of שבת, manda-
tory for all.

כלל ישראל introduced this concept prior to society's acceptance
of the concept of one day of rest. How radical was this idea in the

non-Jewish community throughout history?! For in fact it was manifest largely amongst nobility, the wealthy, the powerful. The rest of society continued to work seven days a week.

It was not until the 20th century when the labor unions introduced the 40-hour five day week norm for "every man." It took society many centuries to adopt this human value.

Faith in G-d /
כלום אתה יכול להחיות כמוני

... וַיַּרְא אִישׁ מִצְרִי מַכֶּה אִישׁ־עִבְרִי מֵאֶחָיו:
וַיִּפֶן כֹּה וָכֹה וַיַּרְא כִּי אֵין אִישׁ וַיַּךְ אֶת־הַמִּצְרִי
וַיִּטְמְנֵהוּ בַּחוֹל: (שמות ב:יא-יב)

And he saw an Egyptian beating a Hebrew, one
of his brothers. And he looked this way and
that, and when he saw that there was no man,
he smote the Egyptian and hid him in the sand.
(Shemot 2:11–12)

The text describes the attack of an Egyptian upon an אִישׁ עִבְרִי "a
Jewish man." משה witnesses the attack, after determining that אֵין
אִישׁ there is no one to save the victim, i.e., אֵין אִישׁ – "there is no
man" willing to interfere, and משה kills the Egyptian to save the
innocent person. In a remarkable text we disover a unique view of
the relationship, between משה and G-d.

'He smote the Egyptian' – [Moshe said] 'You have already written
of me "My servant Moshe . . . is trusted in all My House"' (Bamidbar 12:7). The Holy One, blessed is He, replied, "I never told you
to kill the Egyptian!" He [Moshe] replied, "You killed all the firstborn of Egypt, yet I am to die because of a single Egyptian?" The
Holy One, blessed is He, replied "Are you like Me? [Can you] kill
and give back life? You cannot give back life like Me!" (Midrash
Petirat Moshe, Torah Shelemah on Shemot Ch. 2, source 105).

מדרש פטירת משה - תורה שלמה שמות פרק ב' קה
"וַיַּךְ אֶת־הַמִּצְרִי", כבר כתבתי עלי, "עַבְדִּי מֹשֶׁה בְּכָל־בֵּיתִי נֶאֱמָן הוּא" (במדבר
יב:ז), אמר לו הקב"ה כלום אמרתי לך שתהרוג את המצרי, א"ל ואתה הרגת כל

320

בכורי מצרים ואני אמות בשביל מצרי אחד, א"ל הקב"ה ואתה דומה אלי ממית
ומחיה כלום אתה יכול להחיות כמוני.

A text which demonstrates the quintessence of the Jewish understanding of man's relations with G-d. You argue with and challenge the Almighty. The more profound one's faith, the more
intimate and accountable are both G-d and the human. Moshe is
challenged by G-d for having killed the Egyptian (this by itself is
noteworthy – G-d cares about an Egyptian, an oppressor of G-d's
people.)

Moshe in response is not the humble supplicant. Quite the
contrary, he responds to G-d's criticism with a confrontation.
G-d, did you not kill all the firstborn of Egypt, and you criticize
my killing of one Egyptian?

To which G-d asserts His authority, i.e., His all knowing of
human events. You משה, says the Almighty, compare yourself to
Me. You are indeed My trusted servant, yet you are human, thus
inherently limited in knowledge and understanding.

A classic illustration of a confrontation between the Jewish person of "faith" in G-d and "G-d." When faith is clear and absolute
then challenging the Almighty is, in a sense, challenging a good
friend. Anything is acceptable so long as the relationship remains
true and absolute. Obviously משה's faith was the quintessence of
faith, in a sense "knowing" G-d. Thus, he did not hesitate to challenge and question G-d.

In our time many a person of faith angrily and bitterly questioned G-d concerning the Holocaust. Yet for many, the confrontation did not diminish the quality of their faith in G-d.

A mourner standing at the internment of a loved one, with
clenched teeth and anger, says "Blessed be the righteous Judge"
(ברוך דיין אמת) and then in the words of *Kaddish*, the mourner pro-
ceeds to praise the greatness of the Almighty, "Sanctified be the
name of G-d." The authenticity of faith is at times most demonstrated in the midst of anger, pain, and loss. This faith then rec-
onciles the mourner with G-d and in a sense with self.

Judging the Wicked One / מִי הוּא רָשָׁע

וַיֵּצֵא בַּיּוֹם הַשֵּׁנִי וְהִנֵּה שְׁנֵי־אֲנָשִׁים עִבְרִים
נִצִּים וַיֹּאמֶר לָרָשָׁע לָמָּה תַכֶּה רֵעֶךָ: (שמות ב:יג)

And when he went out the second day, behold!
Two men of the Hebrews were fighting together,
and he said to the wicked one, "Why would you
strike your fellow?" (Shemot 2:13)

(A) Said Rabbi Yitzchak: From here you learn that whoever hits his friend is called a wicked person as it says, "and he said to the wicked one" (Shemot 2:13). (Schechter Genizah manuscripts)

(B) "And he said to the wicked one 'Why would you strike your fellow?'" (Shemot 2:13). Said Resh Lakish: Whoever lifts his hand against his neighbor, even if he did not hit him, is called a wicked man as it is written, "and he said to the wicked one, 'Why would you strike your fellow?'" It does not say 'Why have you struck your fellow', but 'why would you strike your fellow,' showing that even though he had not struck him yet, he was termed a wicked man. (Sanhedrin 58b)

מגנזי שכטר ח"א מכת"י עמוד קיד

(A) א"ר יצחק מיכן את למד שכל מי שהוא מכה לחבירו נקרא רשע, שנאמר
"וַיֹּאמֶר לָרָשָׁע" (שמות ב:יג).

סנהדרין נח:

(B) ועוד, "וַיֹּאמֶר לָרָשָׁע לָמָּה תַכֶּה רֵעֶךָ" (שמות ב:יג). אמר ריש לקיש: המגביה ידו
על חבירו, אף על פי שלא הכהו נקרא רשע, שנאמר "וַיֹּאמֶר לָרָשָׁע לָמָּה תַכֶּה רֵעֶךָ"
(שם). "למה הכית" לא נאמר, אלא "לָמָּה תַכֶּה", אף על פי שלא הכהו נקרא רשע.

The תורה does not teach, nor sanction, pacifism, when the individual, the group or the nation are threatened. Nonetheless,

322

violence within a peaceful society is harshly condemned. משה sees two members of the community engaged in a dispute, when one of the protagonists raises his hand, he is considered a רשע, an "evil person." The Talmud derives two lessons from this text.

From the Midrash (A) we learn from this single act of violence that one who "lifts his hand" and "strikes" another is called a רשע – an "evil person." To commit one act of violence is inherently evil. (B) To raise an arm in a "gesture" of violence is according to the Talmud (Sanhedrin 58b) "an act of violence," though an attack did not in fact occur. Even the "potential" aggressor is judged a רשע – an evil person.

As we search classic Rabbinic texts for the criterion of רשע, we discover the field is rather eclectic.

Nonetheless the Rabbis chose to define a רשע primarily in the genre of בין אדם לחבירו in the realm of interpersonal relationships.

To illustrate:

> Four types of people are called wicked: One who stretches out his hand against his fellow to strike him . . . one who borrows and does not repay . . . one who is arrogant and is not ashamed in the presence of someone greater than himself . . . and one who is argumentative. (Bamibar Rabbah, Parshat Korach 18)

במדבר רבה פרשה קרח פ' יח

ארבעה נקראו רשעים הפושט ידו לחבירו להכותו . . . והלוה ואינו משלם . . . ומי שיש בו עזות פנים ואינו מתבייש לפני מי שגדול הימנו . . . ומי שהוא בעל מחלוקת.

One who does not give [charity] and discourages others to give [charity] is wicked. (Avot 5:13)

אבות ה:יג

לא יתן ולא יתנו אחרים, רשע.

The wicked promise much and do not even do little.

(Bava Metziah 87a)

ב"מ פז.

רשעים אומרים הרבה ואפילו מעט אינם עושים.

Cursed be the wicked, for even the good that they do is intended to do evil. (Tanchuma, Mikeitz 3)

תנחומא פ' מקץ סי' ג

ארורים הרשעים שאפילו הטובה שעושים מתכוונים לרעה.

These citations defining a רשע are exclusively in the realm of ethics and interpersonal relationships, not at all concerning rituals.

The sources are careful to reject "self condemnation" thus אין אדם משים עצמו רשע (כתובות יח:) "One may not self incriminate." To believe oneself to be a רשע, an "evil" person, one loses all sense of self-worth. Considering oneself to be worthless allows for actions wherein right or wrong – ethical or unethical have no meaning.

There are yet other considerations concerning a רשע (best defined as an evil person).

What should be the attitude of the community concerning the רשע? Obviously should the רשע, the "evil person" present a threat to an individual or the community, he must be stopped; we have already addressed that. Nonetheless, is the רשע to be condemned forever? Obviously the ultimate nonredeemable רשע, i.e., those who initiated the Holocaust or other historic evils, are not considered in this inquiry. The designation רשע is for the individual who does evil to community, family, friends, or strangers. The world is populated with all too many individuals who would qualify for the designation רשע, though not having committed murder, rape, robbery, arson, etc., for which there are designated consequences stated between תורה and civil codes.

He is the רשע who pollutes the social structure without necessarily breaking the law. The daily events which are perpetrated by individuals who commit acts which are "evil." What of the average individual who fails the test of יושר justice, in speech and deed. Yet the תורה asks for "patience," though, as a result of evil deeds, one may qualify for the designation רשע, an "evil person."

The זוהר introduces a rather novel and perhaps a contemporary attitude and judgment of a רשע (excluding those who have committed historic evils or capital crimes).

It is forbidden to pray that the wicked be removed from this world, for had the Holy One, blessed is He, taken Terach from the world when he was an idol-worshipper, Avraham would not have come into the world and there would have been no tribes of Israel. (Zohar, Vayera 105; Midrash HaNe'elam)

זהר, וירא קה, מדרש הנעלם

אסור לו לאדם להתפלל על הרשעים שיסתלקו מן העולם שאלמלא סלקו
קודשא בריך הוא לתרח מן העולם כשהיה עובד ע"ז לא בא אברהם אבינו
לעולם ושבטי ישראל לא היו.

Be careful of what you pray for, cautions this text. Certainly the text does not suggest that we cannot or should not pray for the demise of the historic tyrants or רשעים of כלל ישראל, the Jewish people, and society at large. The text teaches two critical values, first be careful whom you consider a רשע, an "evil person." Secondly, view even the רשע, "the evil person" in the larger context of society.

Many a felon has, after incarceration, become a productive citizen. Praying for his death is problematic on two levels, first by what authority are you judge and jury; secondly, why not pray for positive consequences of this "evil person" (obviously, as previously mentioned, this excludes the quintessential tyrants of history).

Who indeed can or may pass ultimate judgment, is left either to the Almighty or when appropriate, the Jewish or legal civil authorities.

Our challenge is, what may or must we do to allow and encourage the person (apparently) of evil to become a productive citizen or who may give birth to those who may be a blessing to humankind. Be prudent when you judge others, you may not know all the facts.

Lashon Hara / לשון הרע

וַיֹּאמֶר מִי שָׂמְךָ לְאִישׁ שַׂר וְשֹׁפֵט עָלֵינוּ הַלְהָרְגֵנִי
אַתָּה אֹמֵר כַּאֲשֶׁר הָרַגְתָּ אֶת־הַמִּצְרִי וַיִּירָא
מֹשֶׁה וַיֹּאמַר אָכֵן נוֹדַע הַדָּבָר: (שמות ב:יד)

And he said, "Who made you a prince and a judge over us? Do you intend to kill me, as you killed the Egyptian?" And Moshe feared, and said, "Certainly this matter is known." (Shemot 2:14)

Rabbi Yehuda son of Rabbi Shalom, said in the name of Rabbi Hanina the Great, and our sages quoted it in the name of Rabbi Alexandri saying: Moshe was thinking in his heart and saying [to himself]: 'In what way have Israel sinned that they should be enslaved more than all the nations?' When he heard these words ["who made you a prince and a judge over us? . . ."] he said [to himself] 'They speak *lashon hara* (talebearing) about one another, so how can they be worthy of salvation?' Therefore he said, "certainly this matter is known" (Shemot 2:14), meaning that now I know the cause of their enslavement. (Shemot Rabbah 1:30)

שמות רבה, פ'א - ל
רבי יהודה בר רבי שלום בשם ר' חנינא הגדול ורבותינו בשם רבי אלכסנדרי
אמרו, היה משה, מהרהר בלבו ואומר מה חטאו ישראל שנשתעבדו מכל
האומות, כיון ששמע דבריו אמר לשון הרע יש ביניהן היאך יהיו ראויין לגאולה
לכך אמר "אָכֵן נוֹדַע הַדָּבָר" (שמות ב:יד) עתה ידעתי באיזה דבר הם משתעבדים.

Consider all the possible faults or sins משה may have attributed to cause the enslavement of the Children of Israel. It is not idolatry, murder, theft, or any other of the classic human failures and sins. Rather Moshe judges the people as "gossips." They spoke ill of each other. When משה says אָכֵן נוֹדַע הַדָּבָר (Shemot 2:14), "Now I know why they were enslaved." They malign one another, they denigrate each other, they are guilty of לשון הרע, "speaking ill of another person," and of the often violated moral imperative לֹא־ תֵלֵךְ רָכִיל בְּעַמֶּיךָ (ויקרא יט:טז) "Do not go about as a talebearer among your people" (Vayikra 19:16). These acts undermine the quality and nature of the communities, personal relationships and trust. לשון הרע "speaking ill of another," be it true or false, is a violation of the תורה, transcending all other ritual or interpersonal mitzvot. While it may seem trivial, in the judgment of the תורה and Rabbinic sources, לשון הרע is considered the quintessence of evil and moral bankruptcy. When a people are morally and ethically compromised, their enemies are dominant and victorious.

The lesson of this Midrash is self evident. לֹא־תֵלֵךְ רָכִיל בְּעַמֶּיךָ (ויקרא יט:טז) "Do not go about as a talebearer, a gossip," (Vayikra 19:16) the Torah admonishes us, be it true or false, gossip is an affliction which may destroy even those far removed from the venue of the gossip.

Indeed, רש"י comments on the text:

'Certainly this matter is known' – [This phrase should be interpreted] according to its basic meaning [that it was now public knowledge that he had slain the Egyptian]. Its midrashic interpretation explains that [it was at this point that Moshe said to himself that] 'the matter I was wondering about, [i.e.] why the Israelites are considered more sinful than all the seventy nations [of the world], to be subjugated with back-breaking labor, has become known to me, because now I see that they are deserving of it'.

רש"י

אָכֵן נוֹדַע הַדָּבָר. כמשמעו. ומדרשו, נודע לי הדבר שהייתי תמה עליו, מה חטאו ישראל מכל שבעים אמות להיות נרדים בעבודת פרך, אבל רואה אני שהם ראויים לכך.

Once again, the focus is not upon the spiritual relationship of the children of Avraham, Yitzchak, and Yaakov with G-d, rather רש"י focuses upon the מדרש which attributes the enslavement to their interpersonal relationships which lacked ethical qualities.

We Do Not Rely On a Miracle / אין סומכין על הנס

... וַיִּבְרַח מֹשֶׁה מִפְּנֵי פַרְעֹה ... : (שמות ב:טו)

... And Moshe fled from before Pharaoh ...
(Shemot 2:15)

When you see a fateful moment, do not stand against it but give way to it ... And whoever gives way to the moment will have the moment fall into his hand ... Moshe gave way to the moment, as stated "and Moshe fled from before Pharaoh" (Shemot 2:15), so the moment returned and fell into his hand, as stated "and the man Moshe was very great in the eyes of Pharaoh and in the eyes of his people" (Shemot 11:3).　　(Midrash Tanhuma Vayetze 5)

מדרש תנחומא ויצא ה

בשעה שאתה רואה השעה חצופה לא תעמוד כנגדה אלא תן לה מקום ... וכל מי שנותן מקום לשעה, השעה נופלת בידו ... משה נתן מקום לשעה, שנאמר "וַיִּבְרַח מֹשֶׁה מִפְּנֵי פַרְעֹה" (שמות ב:טו), וחזרה השעה ונפלה בידו, שנאמר "גַּם הָאִישׁ מֹשֶׁה גָּדוֹל מְאֹד בְּאֶרֶץ מִצְרַיִם בְּעֵינֵי עַבְדֵי־פַרְעֹה וּבְעֵינֵי הָעָם" (שמות יא:ג).

Allow circumstances (within the parameters of תורה) to guide your judgment and then act accordingly. When משה was in danger, Pharaoh was seeking to kill him (Pharaoh having heard of Moshe's attack upon the Egyptian), משה fled, וַיִּבְרַח מֹשֶׁה, says the תורה. משה did not assume that G-d would protect him from his Egyptian assailants without initially acting on his own.

This reflects a fundamental axiom of Judaism, אין סומכין על הנס (פסחים סד:), one may not make choices and decisions based upon the certainty of a miracle altering the natural consequences of events.

Moreover the Talmud teaches לעולם אל יעמוד אדם במקום סכנה ויאמר

עושין לי נם, שמא אין עושין לו נם (תענית כ:). One may not act precipitously and assume that a miracle will occur to be saved from the consequences of a rash or dangerous act. While no doubt miracles and unexplained events have occurred both in history and in the lives of individuals, indeed this is all part of our tradition, nonetheless one may not a priori choose to act in a manner which only a miracle may ensure safety and success.

Yishar Koach For Saving Us / יישר כחך שהצלתנו

וַתֹּאמַרְןָ, אִישׁ מִצְרִי הִצִּילָנוּ מִיַּד הָרֹעִים...:
(שמות ב:יט)

And they said, "An Egyptian man delivered us from the hand of the shepherds" . . . (Shemot 2:19)

This is what the daughters of Yitro said to Moshe: 'Ye'asher Kochacha (literally, may your strength be firm) for saving us from the hand of the shepherds.' Moshe replied: 'The Egyptian that I killed, he saved you.' This is why they said to their father, 'an Egyptian man' (Shemot 2:19), meaning 'who caused that this Egyptian man who had killed would come to us.' (Shemot Rabbah 1:32)

שמות רבה פ"א:לב
כך אמרו בנות יתרו למשה יישר כחך שהצלתנו מיד הרועים, אמר להם משה
אותו מצרי שהרגתי הוא הציל אתכם, ולכך אמרו לאביהן "אִישׁ מִצְרִי" (שמות
ב:יט), כלומר מי גרם לזה שיבא אצלנו איש מצרי שהרג.

This extraordinary מדרש raises the historic conundrum, positive consequences of negative, radical and even devastating events, caused by evil powers and their followers.

One may (with great sensitivity) raise the question, were it not for the Holocaust would the world's powers have agreed at a session of the United Nations Security Council to establish the modern State of Israel. How extraordinary that the United States and the Soviet Union voted in favor of this action.

The Talmud (שבת קנא.) observes גלגל הוא שחוזר בעולם, "The wheel always comes full circle in the world," which suggests that life and its events are in some inexplicable way connected.

To appreciate this link one needs a sensitive and attentive eye.

When we use the phrase אם ירצה השם, i.e., "G-d willing," we express our אמונה ובטחון – our faith and trust that our plans and efforts will "G-d willing" come to fruition. In the final analysis, we can never determine with certainty which of our plans and efforts will succeed. Yet we dare not be impeded in our action due to the uncertainty of the possible consequences of our deeds, so long as we act in keeping with our legal and religious standards and laws.

To be a Man of G-d / לִהְיוֹת אִישׁ אֱ־לֹוהִים

וַתֹּאמַרְן אִישׁ מִצְרִי הִצִּילָנוּ מִיַּד הָרֹעִים וְגַם־
דָּלֹה דָלָה לָנוּ וַיַּשְׁקְ אֶת־הַצֹּאן: (שמות ב:יט)

And they said, "An Egyptian delivered us from
the hand of the shepherds, and also drew enough
water for us, and watered the flock". (Shemot 2:19)

Rabbi Berachiah said: Moshe was more beloved than Noach.
Noach, after having been called "a righteous man" (Bereishit 6:9),
is called "a man of the ground" (Bereishit 9:20), but Moshe, after
having been called "an Egyptian man" (Shemot 2:19) was then
called "the man of G-d" (Devarim 33:1). (Bereishit Rabbah 36:3)

בראשית רבה פ' לו:ג

אמר רבי ברכיה חביב משה מנח, נח משנקרא "אִישׁ צַדִּיק" (בראשית ו:ט) נקרא
"אִישׁ הָאֲדָמָה" (בראשית ט:כ), אבל משה משנקרא "אִישׁ מִצְרִי" (שמות ב:יט) נקרא
"אִישׁ הָאֱ־לֹהִים" (דברים לג:א).

This מדרש helps us understand the characteristics of a צדיק, a righteous person. Noach was called a צדיק, a "righteous man", then he
was called a "man of the earth," אִישׁ הָאֲדָמָה.

Moshe, on the other hand, was called אִישׁ מִצְרִי, an "Egyptian
man" (Shemot 2:19) and was then called אִישׁ הָאֱ־לֹהִים, "a man of
G-d" (Devarim 33:1).

What were the qualitative differences between משה and נח?

Noach was told by G-d (that) the world and all its inhabitants
are about to be destroyed. What was Noach's reaction? וַיַּעַשׂ נֹחַ כְּכֹל
אֲשֶׁר צִוָּה אֹתוֹ אֱ־לֹהִים כֵּן עָשָׂה (Bereishit 6:22). Without hesitation, נח
did what he was told and built an ark for himself and his family.
Noach asked no questions, no confrontation with G-d. Perhaps

He should spare the world. On the other hand, Moshe ascends Mt. Sinai, is given the "Ten Commandments," the ultimate historic moment (when) G-d reveals himself to משה and speaks to the Children of Israel (Shemot 19:21). At that moment all Jewish, indeed all human values are established, to remain unchallenged and relevant throughout history. Yet it is then that the Children of Israel build a golden calf to worship. Moshe, first called אִישׁ מִצְרִי (Shemot 2:19), an "Egyptian" man, now becomes אִישׁ הָאֱ-לֹהִים "a man of G-d" (Devarim 33:1) only when he responds to the sin of the golden calf.

The distinction between Moshe and Noach is the designation of Noach, אִישׁ צַדִּיק, "a righteous man," and Moshe, אִישׁ הָאֱ-לֹהִים, "a man of G-d." "Righteous" may be relative to the social, moral and spiritual environment in which the term is introduced. In an unjust society, be it an ancient pagan civilization or a contemporary society of "relative" righteousness, the term often has been employed to describe what appears to be "righteous" when compared to the norm of contemporary values.

The contrast between Moshe and Noach is radical. Noach is acquiescent to G-d's judgment to destroy the world and humankind. Moshe argues with G-d when G-d threatens to destroy the Jewish People as a result of the sin of the "Golden Calf." Moshe becomes the quintessential leader who confronts all, even the Almighty, on behalf of even a sinful people. That indeed is the role model of Jewish leadership – a "person of G-d," אִישׁ הָאֱ-לֹהִים. Yet when evil is to befall the Jewish people, though deserved, a "Moshe" Jewish leader argues even with G-d so that the People of Israel may be spared.

Leadership demands loyalty to one's people. While it is required of leadership to admonish when appropriate, nonetheless, when harm is to befall the people, perhaps even when deserved, the leader must always seek to admonish while also seeking to defend his people, endeavoring to protect them to the greatest extent possible.

The Uniqueness of Tzipporah / צפורה

וַיּוֹאֶל מֹשֶׁה לָשֶׁבֶת אֶת־הָאִישׁ וַיִּתֵּן אֶת־צִפֹּרָה
בִּתּוֹ לְמֹשֶׁה: (שמות ב:כא)

And Moshe was content to dwell with the man;
and he gave Moshe his daughter Tzipporah.
(Shemot 2:21)

She is Tzipporah and she is the Cushite woman (see Bamidbar 12:1). And why is she called a Cushite? Just as a Cushite's skin is out of the ordinary, so too Tzipporah was outstanding in good deeds. (Midrash Hagadol)

מדרש הגדול

היא צפורה היא כושית ולמה נקראת כושית אלא מה כושי משונה בעורו כך
היתה צפורה משונה במעשיה הטובים.

And also in Moed Katan 16b it is written "Tzipporah was outstanding in good deeds" (Rashi previously explained the term "outstanding in good deeds" to mean "completely righteous.")
(Torah Shelemah on Shemot Ch. 2, notes on source 173)

תורה שלמה, שמות ב בהערה קעג

וגם במועד קטן טז: כתוב: צפורה משונה במעשיה." (רש"י מקודם לזה מפרש
משונה במעשיו - צדיק גמור)

Implication – משונה – described "spiritual – moral – ethical" משונה – difference, i.e., of a "higher" and "purer" quality. A rather extraordinary semantic interpretation of משונה.

In Hebrew the word שנה means "to change," the root of משונה. Yet we are familiar with perhaps the most well known phrase of Jewish tradition מה "נשתנה" הלילה הזה. Why is this night "different"

נשתנה – from all other nights of the year? Once again "different" is the critical "idea" introduced in the opening phrase of the "inquiry" – אלא מה כושי משונה בעורו. Just as a כושי is different in the color black of her skin, so was צפורה "different" in her "good deeds," משונה במעשיה הטובים. The מדרש makes a remarkably contemporary distinction – the "qualitative" difference is the critical "difference" not the "involuntary difference," i.e., the color of one's skin does not determine the quality of one's life. What we do or fail to do with our days, weeks, and years determines who and what we are.

Praying in Plural / לשון רבים

וַיְהִי בַיָּמִים הָרַבִּים הָהֵם וַיָּמָת מֶלֶךְ מִצְרַיִם
וַיֵּאָנְחוּ בְנֵי־יִשְׂרָאֵל מִן־הָעֲבֹדָה וַיִּזְעָקוּ וַתַּעַל
שַׁוְעָתָם אֶל־הָאֱלֹהִים מִן־הָעֲבֹדָה: (שמות ב:כג)

And it came to pass in the course of those many
days that the king of Egypt died; and the People
of Israel sighed because of their bondage, and
they cried, and their cry came up to G-d because
of their bondage. (Shemot 2:23)

What is the meaning of 'out of my straights' (Tehillim 118:5)?
[It means that] whatever way that Israel called to the Holy One,
blessed is He, He answers them. . . . When they call to Him as
G-d [such as] 'and their cry came up to G-d' (Shemot 2:23), He
answered them as G-d: 'And G-d heard their groaning' (Shemot
2:24). (Midrash Tehillim 118, Torah Shelemah on Shemot Ch. 2,
source 190)

מדרש תהלים מזמור קיח, תורה שלמה שמות פרק ב' קץ

מהו "מִן־הַמֵּצַר" (תהלים קיח:ה) בכל לשון שישראל קוראין להקב"ה עונה להם
וכו' קראוהו בה', "וַתַּעַל שַׁוְעָתָם אֶל־הָאֱלֹהִים" (שמות ב:כג), ועֲנה אותם בה',
"וַיִּשְׁמַע אֱלֹהִים אֶת־נַאֲקָתָם" (שמות ב:כד).

This מדרש gives insight into the most mystical of religious-spiri-
tual experiences. Prayer, a human being of flesh and blood, faith
and doubt, inexperienced and spiritually inarticulate, endeavors
to communicate with "Hashem," the Divine.

The Midrash specifically states בכל לשון, in "every language"
our prayers reach the Almighty. The door opens wide to personal
prayers, offered by the "inexperienced worshipper." Though

336

public prayer needs a universal language and structure, so that the
Jew may enter any synagogue in the world and recognize certain
universal prayer texts in Hebrew, e.g., the *Shema*. Nonetheless,
the individual may express in words of petition or gratitude in any
language, a prayer to the Almighty.

Moreover, everyone qualifies to pray; we need no one to pray
for us, each person may reach out to Hashem, the Almighty.
There are a number of classic Rabbinic texts which give insight
and help us understand Judaism's approach to prayer.

First, all are equally qualified to pray. The Midrash articulates
this view very clearly:

> Everyone is equal before the Holy One, blessed is He . . . Know
> that concerning Moshe, the greatest of all the prophets, the same
> is said [about Moshe, as is said,] of a poor man. Of Moshe it is
> written 'a prayer of Moshe the man of G-d' (Tehillim 90:1), and
> of a poor man it says 'a prayer of the afflicted, when he faints and
> pours out his complaint before the Lord' (ibid. 102:1). In both
> cases, the word 'prayer' is used to teach you that before G-d all are
> equal in prayer. (Shemot Rabbah 21:4)

שמות רבה פ' כ"א-ד

הכל שוין לפני הקב"ה ... תדע שהרי משה רבן של כל הנביאים כתוב בו מה
שכתוב בעני, במשה כתיב "תְּפִלָּה לְמֹשֶׁה אִישׁ־הָאֱ־לֹהִים" (תהלים צ:א) בעני
כתיב "תְּפִלָּה לְעָנִי כִי־יַעֲטֹף וְלִפְנֵי ה' יִשְׁפֹּךְ שִׂיחוֹ" (שם קב:א), זו תפלה וזו תפלה.

This מדרש compares the prayer of משה רבנו with the prayer of an
anonymous "poor person," and concludes "this is prayer and this
is prayer." Thus no *a priori* qualitative distinction exists between
the sincere prayer of משה רבנו and that of the universal "poor person," הֶעָנִי or the "simple" person, the universal "Human." While
משה may be more articulate, the "poor person" who is hungry
and desperate, is perhaps as effective as משה. It is the sincerity and
intensity of the prayer which determines its efficacy.

One need consider the text:

> Said Rabbi Hiyya bar Abba in the name of Rabbi Yochanan: A
> person should always pray in a house that has windows, as it says

"Now his windows were open in his upper chamber towards Jerusalem" (Daniel 6:11). (Brachot 34b)

ברכות לד:

אמר רבי חייא בר אבא אמר רבי יוחנן: לעולם יתפלל אדם בבית שיש בו חלונות, שנאמר: "וְכַוִּין פְּתִיחָן לֵהּ בְּעִלִּיתֵהּ נֶגֶד יְרוּשְׁלֶם" (דניאל ו:יא).

Why the need for "windows" in a בית הכנסת, in a place where one worships?

Windows compel recognition of the world and the humanity in which the בית הכנסת, the synagogue exists. Do not pray while ignoring the world.

Jewish prayers found in the formal Jewish prayer book are (with few exceptions) formulated in the plural. "Help us," "Grant us," "Forgive us," "Heal us." Thus the admonition that a Jewish place of worship have windows suggests that we recognize the community outside of the four walls of the sanctuary of prayer. The efficacy of prayer depends upon the worshiper's concern not only for "self," but also for the "other," the "community."

Assimilation / התבוללות

וַיְהִי בַיָּמִים הָרַבִּים הָהֵם וַיָּמָת מֶלֶךְ מִצְרַיִם
וַיֵּאָנְחוּ בְנֵי־יִשְׂרָאֵל מִן־הָעֲבֹדָה וַיִּזְעָקוּ וַתַּעַל
שַׁוְעָתָם אֶל־הָאֱ־לֹהִים מִן־הָעֲבֹדָה: (שמות ב:כג)

And it came to pass in the process of time, that
the king of Egypt died; and the Children of Israel
groaned from the labor, and they cried, and
their cry came up to G-d because of the slavery.
(Shemot 2:23)

There is a remarkable מדרש which states:

"The Children of Israel groaned" – because [the Egyptians] began
to compel them to idolatry.
(Midrash, Torah Shelemah on Shemot Ch. 2, source 181).

מדרש תורה שלמה שמות פרק ב קפא
"וַיֵּאָנְחוּ בְנֵי־יִשְׂרָאֵל," שהתחילו להעבירם לעבודת אלילים.

The תורה שלמה then identifies the source of this מדרש:

It is cited in the Ritva's commentary on the Haggadah: 'The
Children of Israel groaned,' which was explained by our Rabbis
of blessed memory. They also explained that they began to turn
them towards idolatry. And this idea is also explained in the commentary on the Haggadah attributed to Rashi – 'The Children of
Israel groaned from the labor,' meaning that they were turning
them to idol worship. This is because the first king did not turn
them so much to idolatry because of his love of Yosef, but this new
king decreed upon them decrees and forced them to serve idols.

מובא בפירוש הריטב"א להגדה של פסח: ויאנחו בני ישראל דרשו רבותינו
ז"ל כו' עוד דרשו שהתחילו להעבירם לע"ז. ועניין זה מבואר גם בפירוש הגדה
של פסח המיוחס לרש"י ויאנחו בני ישראל מן העבודה: שהיו מעבירין אותם
לעבודה זרה לפי שהמלך הראשון לא היה מעבירין כל כך לע"ז מפני חיבת יוסף
אבל זה המלך החדש גזר עליהם גזירות והכריחם לעבוד ע"א.

What an extraordinary text attributed to classic sources. Perhaps
under the yoke and pain of Egyptian enslavement בני ישראל did
indeed sink to "idol worship," עבודה זרה. Perhaps this source suggests that there was (is) a limit to human endurance. Enslavement, deprivation of basic human needs, loss of all dignity and
choice, all products of enslavement may in fact corrupt even the
grandchildren of Avraham, Yitzchak, and Yaakov.

Yet there are classic sources which take issue with this extraordinary view. We find the following:

> The Egyptians said to them, 'Why are you worshipping Him?
> If you serve the gods of Egypt your workload will be lightened!'
> Israel replied saying, 'Perhaps Avraham, Yitzchak and Yaakov for-
> got our Father in heaven so that their children could follow their
> example?' They (the Egyptians) replied, 'No'. They (Israel) said,
> 'Just as they did not leave Him, so too we will not leave Him.'
> (Seder Eliyahu Rabbah, Torah Shelemah on Shemot Ch. 2, in
> notes on source 181).

> סדר אליהו רבה פכ"א מובא בתורה שלמה פרק ב' בהערה קפא
> היו המצרים אומרים להם, למה אתם עובדים אותו, אם תעבדו אלהי מצרים
> יקל עבודתו מכם, משיבין ישראל ואומרים להם, שמא עזבו אברהם יצחק ויעקב
> את א-לוהנו שבשמים שיעזבו בניהן אחריהן. אמרו להן, לאו. אמרו, כשם שהם
> לא עזבו אותו כך אנו לא נעזבנו.

These classic sources suggest our ancestors in Egypt did at one
point worship idols.

Yet an equally significant source (סדר אליהו רבה פכ"א) insists that
the enslaved descendant of Avraham, Yitzchak, and Yaakov did
not assimilate into the Egyptian pagan culture.

Perhaps both views are correct. There were those who

remained true and faithful while other descendants of the Jewish matriarchs and patriarchs did defect and join the pagan world.

This diverse response to the pagan environment of Egypt is in no small measure replicable in our American society. There are those who are seduced by American culture, dominant Christian society and the amalgam and assimilation of all cultures, religions, and moral perspectives.

Freedom encourages this respect of the "other" be it religion, race, or economic and political orientation. The message of brotherhood, "has not one G-d created us all," has led to an environment which rejects both cultural exclusivity and religious "social" limitations and barriers.

In fact, Judaism respects all racial barriers. Jewish law and tradition is "color blind." While there has not been significant "racial" intermarriage in the American Jewish community, this does not reflect a judgment based upon any religious doctrine or tradition.

Our "assimilation" concerns are clearly and exclusively religious. A family with a mixed religious orientation is by its very nature limited in transmitting a clear and positive message of Jewish faith, history, tradition, and values.

Indeed, to demonstrate that there is no "racial" or "social" implication in the "intermarriage objection," converts of all faiths, of all races and social strata are welcome and are equal in every sense as a "born" Jew. Obviously, in the ultimate, the convert must be self-motivated.

Prayer and Action / תפילה

וַיְהִי בַיָּמִים הָרַבִּים הָהֵם וַיָּמָת מֶלֶךְ מִצְרַיִם
וַיֵּאָנְחוּ בְנֵי־יִשְׂרָאֵל מִן־הָעֲבֹדָה וַיִּזְעָקוּ וַתַּעַל
שַׁוְעָתָם אֶל־הָאֱ־לֹהִים מִן־הָעֲבֹדָה: (שמות ב:כג)

And it came to pass in the process of time, that
the king of Egypt died; and the People of Israel
sighed because of the slavery, and they cried, and
their cry came up to G-d because of the slavery.
(Shemot 2:23)

"And their cry came up to G-d" (Shemot 2:23). "Out of my
straights I called out to G-d" (Tehillim 118:5). What is the
meaning of 'out of my straights' (Tehillim 118:5)? [It means that]
whatever way that Israel called to the Holy One, blessed is He,
He answers them. . . . (Midrash Tehillim 118, Torah Shelemah on
Shemot Ch. 2, source 190)

מדרש תהלים מזמור קיח, תורה שלמה שמות פרק ב' קצ

"וַתַּעַל שַׁוְעָתָם אֶל־הָאֱ־לֹהִים" (שמות ב:כג). "מִן־הַמֵּצַר קָרָאתִי יָּ־הּ" וגו' (תהלים
קיח:ה). מהו "מִן־הַמֵּצַר" (תהלים קיח:ה) בכל לשון שישראל קוראין להקב"ה עונה
להם וכו'.

The מדרש affirms the belief that תפילה (prayer) when recited sin-
cerely, in any language, is accepted by הקב"ה (the Almighty). It is
not language that matters, it is the sincerity and integrity of the
prayer that matters.

It is concentration of thought and focus upon the personal experience of prayer. "What am I saying," "to whom am I speaking,"
(i.e., praying), "in addition to my personal needs and requests –
do I include others in my prayers?" Most traditional prayers in

the סדור (prayer book) are written in "plural" – we/our/us. While there is an authentic and historic tradition of personal prayer, nonetheless, as we have mentioned elsewhere, the all-inclusive language of the סדור (prayer book) is consistent.

The Talmud (ברכות לד.) raises the issue of the proper "length" of prayer.

> Our Rabbis taught: Once a certain student went down [to lead the prayer service] before the Ark in the presence of Rabbi Eliezer, and he prolonged [the prayers] excessively. His students said to him: Master, how longwinded is this fellow! He replied to them: Is he drawing it out any more than our teacher Moshe, of whom it is written: "The forty days and the forty nights etc." (Devarim 9:25). Another time it happened that a certain student went down [to lead the prayer service] before the Ark in the presence of Rabbi Eliezer, and he shortened the prayer excessively. His students said to him: How brief is this fellow! He replied to them: Is he any more brief than our teacher Moshe, who prayed as it is written: "Heal her now, O G-d, I beg of You." (Bamidbar 12:13)

תנו רבנן: מעשה בתלמיד אחד שירד לפני התיבה בפני רבי אליעזר והיה מאריך יותר מדאי. אמרו לו תלמידיו: רבינו, כמה ארכן הוא זה – אמר להם: כלום מאריך יותר ממשה רבינו? דכתיב ביה: "אֶת־אַרְבָּעִים הַיּוֹם וְאֶת־אַרְבָּעִים הַלַּיְלָה" וגו' (דברים ט:כה). שוב מעשה בתלמיד אחד שירד לפני התיבה בפני רבי אליעזר והיה מקצר יותר מדאי. אמרו לו תלמידיו: כמה קצרן הוא זה אמר להם: כלום מקצר יותר ממשה רבינו? דכתיב: "אֵ-ל נָא רְפָא נָא לָהּ". (במדבר יב:יג)

It is obvious the Talmud considers quality over quantity as the "determinate" factor of prayer. משה רבנו is the דוגמה – the "role model" of תפילה when he prayed (was מתפלל) for his sister מרים. משה prayed, אֵ-ל נָא רְפָא נָא לָהּ – "G-d please heal her." This is the quintessence of תפילה – "quality and brevity." We also find משה מתפלל (praying) excessively. There is a pragmatism which enters the experience of תפילה – prayer. The Rabbis (מדרש רבה שמות כא') describe ה' addressing משה רבנו when משה was מתפלל as כלל ישראל (the People of Israel) was trapped between the sea and the Egyptians.

The Holy One, blessed is He, said to Moshe: "There is a time to pray extensively and there is a time to pray briefly. My children are in pain. The sea is closing in on them. The enemy is pursuing them and you are standing engaged in extensive prayer. 'Speak to the Children of Israel and tell them to move on'" (Shemot Rabbah 21:8).

שמות רבה פ' כא:ח

אמר לו הקב"ה למשה עת לקצר ועת להאריך בני שרווים בצער והים סוגר והאויב רודף ואתה עומד ומרבה בתפלה דבר אל בני ישראל ויסעו.

This is a lesson of faith and courage. The sea would not respond until the first foot is into the water. Even the most faithful, the most devout, must respond to a difficult seemingly impossible situation with a practical act, to engage in every manner to discover a possible solution. Thus the sea does not allow passage until נחשון בן עמינדב steps into the water to demonstrate his faith with a positive response to an obviously difficult situation. Only then does the sea respond.

Rabbi Yitzchok also said: If someone says to you 'I have laboured and not found [what I am looking for]', do not believe him. If he says, 'I have not laboured but still have found [what I am looking for]', do not believe him [either]. [But] if he says, 'I have laboured and found [what I am looking for],' you may believe him. This is true with words of Torah, but with business, it all depends on the assistance of heaven. (Megillah 6b)

מגילה ו:

ואמר רבי יצחק, אם יאמר לך אדם: יגעתי ולא מצאתי - אל תאמן, לא יגעתי ומצאתי - אל תאמן, יגעתי ומצאתי - תאמן. הני מילי - בדברי תורה. אבל במשא ומתן - סייעתא הוא מן שמיא.

The point of Rabbi Yitzchok is the need to "strive." Yet in this context Rabbi Yitzchok is focused upon the intellectual, the study of תורה. To understand, to ponder a difficult text or concept, necessitates careful thought and analytical insight.

Yet the practical dilemma of solving the daily complexity of life, ר' יצחק says, one needs "the help of heaven," i.e., "G-d's help." Rabbi Yitzchok implies that we are in a sense helpless, save סייעתא דשמיא in effect "G-d's help." Solutions to the pragmatic – materialistic challenges are in the hands of ה'. Yet man needs to strive to respond in practical ways. One may not sit back expecting ה' to replace the human role in the daily practical challenges of life. Obviously ה' is ever present and we are commanded to choose the values of תורה, which command the quintessence of moral and ethical values.

The quality of life has changed radically. Medicine, education, science, transportation, communication, technology, and economic expectations have improved in many parts of the world.

Though much needs yet to be done, considerable progress has been demonstrated, giving faith and hope for the future בעה"ת.

Compassion Towards One Another / ראה שהיו מרחמים זה על זה

וַיַּרְא אֱ-לֹהִים אֶת־בְּנֵי יִשְׂרָאֵל וַיֵּדַע אֱ-לֹהִים:
(שמות ב:כה)

And G-d saw the Children of Israel, and G-d took notice of them. (Shemot 2:25)

"G-d saw the Children of Israel" – what did He see? He saw how they had compassion towards one another. When one of them completed their quota of bricks before their friend, he would come and help his friend. When the Holy One, blessed is He, saw how they had compassion towards one another He said "They deserve compassion, for he who shows compassion has compassion shown to him, as it says: 'He will show you compassion, and have compassion on you'" (Devarim 13:18).

(Midrash, Torah Shelemah on Shemot Ch. 2, source 208).

מדרש תורה שלמה שמות פרק ב רח

וַיַּרְא אֱ-לֹהִים, מה ראה, ראה שהיו מרחמים זה על זה כשהיה אחד מהם משלים סכום הלבנים קודם חבירו היה בא ומסייע עם חבירו, כשראה הקב"ה שהיו מרחמים זה על זה אמר ראויים אלו לרחם עליהם, כל המרחם מרחמים עליו שנאמר "וְנָתַן לְךָ רַחֲמִים וְרִחַמְךָ" (דברים יג:יח).

The מדרש suggests הקב"ה (the Almighty) views and judges us as we view, judge, and behave toward one another.

This מדרש would like to understand what it is that motivated G-d to redeem Israel at this moment of their long enslavement. The text (Shemot 2:25) states "G-d saw" and "G-d knew." What did G-d "know" and what did G-d "see"?

The מדרש suggests that it was the compassion one Jewish slave demonstrated toward another Jewish slave.

346

When a Jewish slave completed the task assigned to him/her, he/she would turn to a slave who had as yet not completed the assigned task and would help complete the task.

Note there was no "religious" act in the classic sense, yet the most profound of religious acts, assisting another person, is here described as the prime motivator of Jewish redemption.

Again, the Midrash wants us to understand that the transcending value of human kindness, is a fundamental value of Judaism.

Compassion / רחמים

וַיַּרְא אֱ-לֹהִים אֶת־בְּנֵי יִשְׂרָאֵל וַיֵּדַע אֱ-לֹהִים:
(שמות ב:כה)

And G-d saw the Children of Israel, and G-d
took notice of them. (Shemot 2:25)

"G-d saw the Children of Israel." What did He see? He saw how
they had compassion towards one another. When one of them
completed their quota of bricks before their friend, he would
come and help his friend. When the Holy One, blessed is He, saw
how they had compassion towards one another He said "They deserve compassion, for he who shows compassion has compassion
shown to him, as it says: 'He will show you compassion, and have
compassion on you'" (Devarim 13:18).

(Midrash, Torah Shelemah on Shemot Ch. 2, source 208)

מדרש תורה שלמה שמות פרק ב רח

מה ראה, ראה שהיו מרחמים זה על זה כשהיה אחד מהם משלים סכום הלבנים
קודם חבירו היה בא ומסייע עם חבירו, כשראה הקב"ה שהיו מרחמים זה על
זה אמר ראויים אלו לרחם עליהם, כל המרחם מרחמים עליו שנאמר "וְנָתַן־לְךָ
רַחֲמִים וְרִחַמְךָ" (דברים יג:יח).

רחמים is a quality of compassion which is "G-d like." There is a
fascinating statement in the Talmud אפילו בשעת כעסו של הקדוש ברוך
הוא (even when ה' is angry) – זוכר את הרחמים (He remembers His
compassion) (פסחים פז:).

The מדרש tells us that even when the Jewish People were enslaved in Egypt they demonstrated a moral relationship with one
another.

It is not common nor is it recorded in history that any slave

348

populations ever manifested a clear moral and ethical quality of life. Yet here the rabbis of the מדרש go out of their way to record the moral/ethical quality of the Jewish slaves.

> And Moshe was shepherding the flock of Yisro his father-in-law, the priest of Midian; and he led the flock far away into the desert, and came to the mountain of G-d, to Horeb. (Shemot 3:1)

שמות ג:א

וּמֹשֶׁה הָיָה רֹעֶה אֶת־צֹאן יִתְרוֹ חֹתְנוֹ כֹּהֵן מִדְיָן וַיִּנְהַג אֶת־הַצֹּאן אַחַר הַמִּדְבָּר וַיָּבֹא אֶל־הַר הָאֱ־לֹהִים חֹרֵבָה:

> Greater is the enjoyment of his own toil than he who fears Heaven. . . . The Divine Presence only rested on Moshe when he was working, as it says: "and Moshe was shepherding the flock" (Shemot 3:1) and it then says, "and the angel of the Lord appeared to him" (ibid v.2). (Midrash Gadol V'Gedolah Ch. 14, Torah Shelemah on Shemot Ch. 3, source 6)

מדרש גדול וגדולה פי"ד תורה שלמה שמות פרק ג ו

גדול הנהנה מיגיעו יותר מירא שמים כו' . . . ולא שרתה שכינה על משה אלא מתוך מלאכה, שנאמר "וּמֹשֶׁה הָיָה רֹעֶה" (שמות ג:א) וכתיב "וַיֵּרָא מַלְאַךְ ה'" (שמות ג:ב).

How remarkable is this מדרש – the שכינה, the "presence of ה'," did not rest upon משה רבנו except within the context "of work." The verse states משה was a רועה צאן, a "shepherd." Only then does the (verse) פסוק state וַיֵּרָא מַלְאַךְ ה' אֵלָיו. The implication of this text is clear. The greatest of all נבאים achieved נבואה only after וּמֹשֶׁה הָיָה רֹעֶה אֶת־צֹאן being a רועה צאן, entering the practical world of labor.

This מדרש leaves little doubt that a נביא (prophet) must also be part of the practical world, so that his experience allows for an understanding of the world of those to whom he prophesizes and endeavors to influence.

Anguish For an Animal / צַעַר בַּעֲלֵי חַיִּים

וּמֹשֶׁה הָיָה רֹעֶה אֶת־צֹאן יִתְרוֹ חֹתְנוֹ כֹּהֵן מִדְיָן
וַיִּנְהַג אֶת־הַצֹּאן אַחַר הַמִּדְבָּר וַיָּבֹא אֶל־הַר
הָאֱ־לֹהִים חֹרֵבָה: (שמות ג:א)

And Moshe was shepherding the flock of Yisro
his father-in-law, the priest of Midian; and he
led the flock far away into the desert, and came
to the mountain of G-d, to Horeb. (Shemot 3:1)

Our Rabbis teach us: Once when our teacher Moshe, peace be
upon him, was shepherding Yisro's flocks in the wilderness, a kid
ran away from him and he ran after it until it reached a shady spot.
When it came to the shady spot there was a water hole and the kid
stopped to drink. When Moshe reached the kid, he said, "I did
not know that you ran away because you were tired and thirsty."
So he put it on his shoulder and walked back. Said the Holy One,
blessed is He: "You have compassion in the way that you tend to
the flock. So too with [the rest of] your life, you will tend to My
flock of Israel." This is the meaning of the words "and Moshe was
shepherding the flock" (Shemot 3:1).

(Midrash Shemot Rabbah 2:2)

מדרש שמות רבה ב:ב

אמרו רבותינו כשהיה משה רבינו ע"ה רועה צאנו של יתרו במדבר ברח ממנו גדי
ורץ אחריו עד שהגיע לחסית כיון שהגיע לחסית נזדמנה לו בריכה של מים ועמד
הגדי לשתות, כיון שהגיע משה אצלו אמר אני לא הייתי יודע שרץ היית מפני צמא
עיף אתה הרכיבו על כתיפו והיה מהלך, אמר הקב"ה יש לך רחמים לנהוג צאנו
של בשר ודם כך חייך, אתה תרעה צאני ישראל, הוי "וּמֹשֶׁה הָיָה רֹעֶה" (שמות ג:א).

This מדרש demonstrates the תורה's ethical and spiritual values concerning animals. משה is considered worthy of becoming the מנהיג

350

ישראל, the emancipator and leader of כלל ישראל, the Jewish nation, not due to brilliance, wisdom, or charismatic personality. Rather he is chosen by ה' because משה cared about the needs of sheep though they were the possessions of a stranger. אמר הקב"ה the מדרש attributes the statement to ה', "If you demonstrate compassion towards an animal, the possession of a human being, you are worthy of leading and being the shepherd of My Children of Israel."

This order of priorities which ה' has demonstrated in His choice of the ultimate of Jewish leaders manifests Judaism's transcending values in all human activity. Yes, even an animal is worthy of our concern and sensitivity.

The Talmud demands that the owner of an animal feed the animal first, and only then may the owner eat.

> It is forbidden for someone to taste anything until he has given food to his animals, as it says, "And I will give grass in your field for your cattle" (Devarim 11:15), and it then says, "And you shall eat and be satisfied" (ibid.). (Gittin 62a)

גיטין סב.

אסור לו לאדם שיטעום כלום עד שיתן מאכל לבהמתו, שנאמר: (דברים יא:טו) "וְנָתַתִּי עֵשֶׂב בְּשָׂדְךָ לִבְהֶמְתֶּךָ", והדר "וְאָכַלְתָּ וְשָׂבָעְתָּ" (שם).

> One may not acquire an animal unless food has been prepared for them. (Jerusalem Talmud Yevamot 15:3)

ירושלמי יבמות פ' ט"ו:ג

אין אדם רשאי ליקח לו בהמה חיה ועוף אלא אם כן התקין להן מזונות.

The Jerusalem Talmud continues: One may not possess an animal or poultry unless a sufficient amount of food has been prepared for sustenance.

Only in modern times (20th century) has even civilized society demonstrated any ethical sensitivity toward animals. So long as the animal served the master, its needs were provided to maintain its health and strength. The animal of no value to its owner had no inherent rights for food and drink.

In fact, the American society for the Prevention of Cruelty to

Animals is a relatively recent development. Moreover, there are few countries throughout the world who protect an animal beyond the point necessary to serve its intended purpose. However, Judaism's standards demand a serious concern for the well-being of one's animals as a religious imperative equal to all other standards of human behavior.

The treatment of an animal is viewed as a Torah commandment. The prohibition against inflicting pain upon an animal is a תורה commandment, states the Talmud.

The suffering of living creatures is a Biblical law. (Bava Metzia 32:)

בבא מציעא לב:
צער בעלי חיים דאורייתא.

Moreover, כשם שרחמיו של הקדוש ברוך הוא על האדם כך רחמיו על הבהמה – Just as the Holy One, blessed is He, shows mercy on humanity, so too He shows mercy on animals (see Midrash Devarim Rabbah, Ki Tetzeh 6).

Great is Labor / גדול המלאכה

וּמֹשֶׁה הָיָה רֹעֶה אֶת־צֹאן יִתְרוֹ חֹתְנוֹ כֹּהֵן מִדְיָן
וַיִּנְהַג אֶת־הַצֹּאן אַחַר הַמִּדְבָּר וַיָּבֹא אֶל־הַר
הָאֱ־לֹהִים חֹרֵבָה: (שמות ג:א)

And Moshe was shepherding the flock of Yisro his father-in-law, the priest of Midian; and he led the flock far away into the desert, and came to the mountain of G-d, to Horeb. (Shemot 3:1)

The text (שמות ג:א) וּמֹשֶׁה הָיָה רֹעֶה is the source of Judaism's respect for labor. To earn the income necessary to sustain oneself and ultimately one's family and society is an ethical imperative. A מדרש comments on the verse:

> Greater is the enjoyment of his own toil than he who fears Heaven. . . . The Divine Presence only rested on Moshe when he was working, as it says: "And Moshe was shepherding the flock" (Shemot 3:1), and it then says, "And the angel of the Lord appeared to him" (ibid v.2). (Midrash Gadol V'Gedolah Ch. 14, Torah Shelemah on Shemot Ch. 3, source 6)

מדרש גדול וגדולה פי"ד תורה שלמה שמות פרק ג ו

גדול הנהנה מיגיעו יותר מירא שמים כו' . . . ולא שרתה שכינה על משה אלא
מתוך מלאכה, שנאמר "וּמֹשֶׁה הָיָה רֹעֶה" (שמות ג:א) וכתיב "וַיֵּרָא מַלְאַךְ ה'"
(שמות ג:ב).

A remarkable view of חז"ל concerning "labor:" The מדרש lauds the value of "labor" in that it exceeds "fear of" or "reverence for" "heaven" – i.e., G-d. The שכינה did not manifest itself to משה רבנו, until וּמֹשֶׁה הָיָה רֹעֶה "and Moshe was a shepherd." משה had to first engage in "labor," as do most people, only then, did G-d engage משה.

יראת שמים – "fear or awe of heaven" (a spiritual state) a metaphor for "fear or awe of the Almighty" is a lesser spiritual achievement than earning one's income from one's labor. משה רבנו was not granted his unique spiritual development, says this מדרש, until he became a shepherd and earned his livelihood through his labor.

How radical is this prerequisite for spiritual greatness. Earning a living "by one's labor," says this מדרש, must be accomplished prior to spiritual maturity. Meditation, prayer, withdrawal from the "work-a-day world" as the path to the ultimate in spirituality is not correct, says this מדרש. Moshe became the משה רבנו only after he was רועה צאן, a shepherd.

The מדרש suggests that in order to grow and attain spirituality, one must understand the practical experience of human existence.

How does one live a productive life? Face reality, says the מדרש. Only then can you respond in a moral, ethical, spiritual manner. Judaism is of this world. Labor, social life, family life, academic and political life, are all components of life, and all are lived either productively or destructively.

Once again we face the absence of neutrality in Judaism's view of the human experience. Nothing, if in harmony with the Torah's imperative of "mitzvah," is "unholy" or "irrelevant."

The greatest Jewish personality in history is introduced as a shepherd, not one who withdraws from or rejects life. Quite the contrary, he earns his livelihood in a manner quite common in his day. It is this "man" born of woman and man, experiencing the vicissitudes of life, to whom G-d speaks from the "burning bush." In fact, משה is conducting his business as a shepherd, a laborer of his day, when השם appears in the "burning bush."

Right and Proper / כדין וכשורה

וּמֹשֶׁה הָיָה רֹעֶה אֶת־צֹאן יִתְרוֹ חֹתְנוֹ כֹּהֵן מִדְיָן
... : (שמות ג:א)

*And Moshe was shepherding the flock of Yisro his
father-in-law, the priest of Midian . . . (Shemot 3:1)*

"The flock of Yisro his father-in-law" – but not his own. For Rabbi
Yossi said: Just as he gave Tzipporah his daughter to Moshe, would
he not have also given him flocks? Surely, Yisro was wealthy [and
therefore we would have expected that Moshe would have been
given his own flock]. However, Moshe kept only Yisro's flock to
avoid the possibility of people saying that he gave them his best
care only because his own flock was there too. Therefore it says,
"the flock of Yisro his father-in-law" (Shemot 3:1) but not his
own. Rabbi Tanchum said: Even though (Yisro) was an idolater,
he (Yisro) had shown him kindness, he (Moshe) kept his flock as
was right and proper, in good, rich and luxuriant pasture.

(Zohar Vol. 2 21a)

זהר ח"ב כא.

ולא שלו דאמר רבי יוסי וכי מה שנתן את צפורה בתו למשה לא נתן לו צאן
ובקר והלא יתרו עשיר היה אלא משה לא היה רועה את צאנו כדי שלא יאמרו
בשביל שהיה צאנו עמו היה רועה אותן בטוב ולכן כתיב "אֶת־צֹאן יִתְרוֹ חֹתְנוֹ"
(שמות ג:א), ולא את שלו. רבי תנחום אמר אף על גב שהיה עובד כוכבים ומזלות
בשביל שעשה עמו חסד היה רועה צאנו כדין וכשורה במרעה טוב שמן ודשן.

The Zohar ponders the specificity of the ownership of the sheep.
Did not Yisro give Moshe some sheep when Moshe married his
daughter?

Nonetheless, the זוהר seeks to focus upon the lesson of משה רבנו's teaching of "honesty of labor." משה sought to demonstrate the integrity of his labor, he was careful in his task as a shepherd not because the sheep were his – the פסוק makes clear it was צֹאן יִתְרוֹ חֹתְנוֹ – his father-in-law, יתרו's sheep. Nonetheless, משה was very careful in his task as a shepherd.

Moreover, says Rabbi Tanchum, though Yisro was a pagan, "he worshipped the stars and the signs of the Zodiac," nonetheless, Yisro displayed kindness to משה. Thus Moshe entered into a relationship of reciprocal responsibility and cared for Yisro's flock as though they were his own.

This מדרש teaches the absolute value of a mutually responsible relationship regardless of the faith, station, or wealth of the other.

It is the integrity of those involved, not their faith. While Judaism does insist that familial relationships and matters of faith be exclusively within the family of the Jewish people, nonetheless our secular, economic, academic and professional lives need not be exclusively with the greater Jewish family and community. Moreover, there are no rules and standards of the economic and professional world which suggest or require Jewish exclusivity.

In fact, Halacha, Jewish law, demands an even more exacting standard of ethical conduct of economic integrity when dealing with someone not Jewish.

The Talmud maintains stealing an item from someone constitutes theft only if the stolen item is worth at least a "Prutah" which was the lowest coinage in Talmudic times.

This law pertains to "theft" committed by a Jew towards a Jew. In our time we might say theft of something worth less than one cent is not theft. Thus stealing a single tissue is not theft.

However taking anything without permission from a non-Jew, i.e., taking a single tissue, constitutes theft. Our behavior towards people not of the Jewish community is more exacting than within the family.

And Moshe Was a Shepherd /
ומשה היה רועה

וּמֹשֶׁה הָיָה רֹעֶה אֶת־צֹאן יִתְרוֹ חֹתְנוֹ ... :
(שמות ג:א)

*And Moshe was shepherding the flock of Yisro
his father-in-law . . . (Shemot 3:1)*

Our Rabbis teach us: Once when our teacher Moshe, peace be
upon him, was shepherding Yisro's flocks in the wilderness, a kid
ran away from him and he ran after it until it reached a shady spot.
When it came to the shady spot there was a water hole and the kid
stopped to drink. When Moshe reached the kid, he said, "I did
not know that you ran away because you were tired and thirsty."
So he put it on his shoulder and walked back. Said the Holy One,
blessed is He: "You have compassion in the way that you tend to
the flock. So too with [the rest of] your life, you will tend to My
flock of Israel." This is the meaning of the words "And Moshe was
shepherding [the flock]" (Shemot 3:1).

(Midrash Shemot Rabbah 2:2)

מדרש שמות רבה ב:ב

אמרו רבותינו כשהיה משה רבינו ע"ה רועה צאנו של יתרו במדבר ברח ממנו
גדי ורץ אחריו עד שהגיע לחסית כיון שהגיע לחסית נזדמנה לו בריכה של מים
ועמד הגדי לשתות, כיון שהגיע משה אצלו אמר אני לא הייתי יודע שרץ היית
מפני צמא עיף אתה הרכיבו על כתיפו והיה מהלך, אמר הקב"ה יש לך רחמים
לנהוג צאנו של בשר ודם כך חייך, אתה תרעה צאני ישראל, הוי "וּמֹשֶׁה הָיָה
רֹעֶה" (שמות ג:א).

This מדרש demonstrates what qualifications are required for
"Jewish leadership." משה רבנו had compassion upon a sheep when

its need for water became obvious. The מדרש suggests that משה רבנו apologized to this animal for failing to recognize its needs sooner and corrected the situation at once.

No miracle, nothing metaphysical, no heavenly voice until human sensitivity is manifest by משה רבנו to a sheep. Once the human act of חסד, of kindness, by משה רבנו is manifest then ה' selects משה רבנו to be "the" Jewish leader to bring בני ישראל out of Egypt. Nothing spectacular, only (perhaps "only" is the wrong word) a simple act of חסד – kindness – is the catalyst to select משה as the leader of the Jewish people.

The kindness of משה רבנו demonstrated an inner quality which would enable him to confront and defeat Pharaoh of Egypt and then lead the Jewish People on a four-decade journey to what was to become the Jewish homeland.

The Wonder of the Simple in Life / מתוך הסנה

וַיֵּרָא מַלְאַךְ ה' אֵלָיו בְּלַבַּת־אֵשׁ מִתּוֹךְ הַסְּנֶה
וַיַּרְא וְהִנֵּה הַסְּנֶה בֹּעֵר בָּאֵשׁ וְהַסְּנֶה אֵינֶנּוּ אֻכָּל:
(שמות ג:ב)

And the angel of the Lord appeared to him in
a flame of fire from within the bush; and he
looked, and behold, the bush burned with fire,
yet the bush was not being consumed. (Shemot 3:2)

"From within the bush" (Shemot 3:2). Rabbi Yehoshua said:
Why did the Holy One, blessed is He, reveal Himself from the
highest heavens to speak with Moshe from within the bush? ...
Because whenever Israel is suffering, it is as though there is suffering before Him, "In all their suffering He was suffering" (Isaiah
63:9). (Mechilta D'Rabbi Shimon Bar Yochai, Torah Shelemah on
Shemot Ch. 3, source 38)

מכדרשב"י תורה שלמה שמות פרק ג לח

"מִתּוֹךְ הַסְּנֶה" (שמות ג:ב) – ר' יהושע אומר מפני מה נגלה הקב"ה משמי מרום
והיה מדבר עם משה מתוך הסנה... שכל זמן שישראל שרויין בצרה כאלו צרה
לפניו שנאמר "בְּכָל־צָרָתָם לוֹ צָר" (ישעיה סג:ט).

"From within the bush" (Shemot 3:2). A non-Jew asked Rabbi
Yehoshua Ben Korcha: "Why did the Holy One, blessed is He,
choose to speak to Moshe from within the bush?" He said to
him, "Had he spoken from within a carob or sycamore [tree] you
would have asked me the same question! Yet I will not leave your
question unanswered. So why from within the bush? To teach that
there is no place devoid of the Divine Presence, not even a bush."
(Shemot Rabbah 1:9)

שמות רבה פרק א:ט

"מִתּוֹךְ הַסְּנֶה" (שמות ג:ב), שאל גוי אחד את ר' יהושע בן קרחה, מה ראה
הקב"ה לדבר עם משה מתוך הסנה, א"ל אלו מתוך חרוב או מתוך שקמה כך
היית שואלני. אלא להוציאך חלק אי אפשר, אלא למה מתוך הסנה, ללמדך
שאין מקום פנוי בלא שכינה אפילו הסנה.

The מדרש introduces the radical idea, radical in ancient times and
perhaps for some, radical in our time as well.

The Almighty is manifest not only in the grandeur of nature,
i.e., birth of the human, the grandeur of the great mountain
ranges, the setting or rising of the sun, and the world's seeming
natural wonders. Not at all; rather, it is in the lowly unnoticed
"burning bush," the least dramatic of nature's wonders. G-d
chooses this "bush" to be "ignited," attracting attention to itself.
Perhaps someone else would not have been impressed even with
the fire within the bush, attributing it to some natural phenom-
ena. It necessitates eyes which see and a mind which responds.

Many events occur (in life) which are often ignored, failing to
see unique opportunities which, once passed, may never occur
again.

Moshe stopped and said, "How awesome is this place." That
is, let me ask why and how this is happening. It was at that very
moment when Moshe stopped and asked "why" that G-d spoke
to him.

Though "the bush was not consumed," Moshe could have
moved on with a "shrug of the shoulder." Particularly in ancient
times, inquisitiveness was not in vogue. This text teaches that
G-d is indeed everywhere at all times. In the most radical and significant moments and in the daily routine of our lives. We need
but "stop" and ask as did Moshe "what is happening," מה נורא המקום
הזה – "How awesome is this place."

In our society much of life passes quickly, unnoticed. "How
awesome is this place" is not a common response. "How awesome is this moment" is rarely said or heard. Life passes by, we
grow older, children become adults, man lands on the moon, we
cross oceans and continents, we cure fatal illness, yet we do not
acknowledge "how awesome is this place."

When the extraordinary becomes ordinary, when the awesome becomes common, when discovery ceases to be acknowledged with awe, we lose the "presence of wonder." This is true of the awesome power of words. When unique words are degraded, we are impoverished. "Love," I love my child, my spouse, my parents, my social friend, and then I love my steak, my dress/suit, my car, etc. "How awesome" is the word "love," yet it loses its value and meaning when hyphenated with the common car, ball game, clothing, etc.

As Moshe stops and responds to the wonder of the "burning bush," he is told, "Moshe, Moshe," that is to say, stop, pay attention, listen – do not ignore what is before you. Indeed Moshe responds, "I am here," and it is then that the Almighty speaks to him.

Life is often a "wonder" which is diminished or even ignored. We need to become aware of the "how awesome" in everyday life.

Thorns / קוצים

וַיֵּרָא מַלְאַךְ ה' אֵלָיו בְּלַבַּת־אֵשׁ מִתּוֹךְ הַסְּנֶה
וַיַּרְא וְהִנֵּה הַסְּנֶה בֹּעֵר בָּאֵשׁ וְהַסְּנֶה אֵינֶנּוּ אֻכָּל:
(שמות ג:ב)

And the angel of the Lord appeared to him in
a flame of fire from within the bush; and he
looked, and behold, the bush burned with fire,
yet the bush was not being consumed. (Shemot 3:2)

Said Rabbi Pinchas the Priest the son of Rav Hama: What is the
significance of this bush? Just as when a person puts their hand into it
(ie. into a thorn-bush) he does not feel [the thorns], but when he takes
it out it scratches, so too when Israel descended to Egypt they did not
pay attention to them, but when they went out, they departed "with
signs and wonders and battle" (Devarim 4:34). (Shemot Rabbah 2:5)

שמות רבה ב:ה

א"ר פנחס הכהן ב"ר חמא מה הסנה הזה כשאדם מכניס ידו לתוכו אינו מרגיש
וכשהוא מוציאה מסתרטת כך כשירדו ישראל למצרים לא הכיר בהן בריה
כשיצאו יצאו "בְּאֹתֹת וּבְמוֹפְתִים וּבְמִלְחָמָה" (דברים ד:לד).

In a sense, this מדרש foretells the historic Jewish experience of the
exile. Jews arrive in a country, a new society, and are eventually
welcomed. Time passes, Jews become part of the economic and
at times even the social society. Spain, the Fertile Crescent countries, then Western Europe, Germany, England, France, etc. We
enter the society believing we are, in fact, respected and welcome.
We serve as physicians, attorneys, business people, craftsmen.
Then the tide turns, a tyrant arises and we are denied who we
were, what we contributed to society, and in denying our past, we
are denied the present and future.

והסנה איננו אכל / Fire Power

וַיֵּרָא מַלְאַךְ ה' אֵלָיו בְּלַבַּת־אֵשׁ מִתּוֹךְ הַסְּנֶה
וַיַּרְא וְהִנֵּה הַסְּנֶה בֹּעֵר בָּאֵשׁ וְהַסְּנֶה אֵינֶנּוּ אֻכָּל:

(שמות ג:ב)

And the angel of the Lord appeared to him in a
flame of fire from within the bush; and he looked,
and behold, the bush burned with fire, yet the
bush was not being consumed. (Shemot 3:2)

"The bush burned with fire, but the bush was not being consumed" (Shemot 3:2).Great is peace! For the first time the Holy
One, blessed is He, revealed Himself to Moshe, [He did so] not
out of the midst of the [Holy] Creatures, or the Cherubim, or
the Ophanim, but out of that which was emblematic of peace, as
it says "And the angel of the Lord appeared to him in a flame of
fire" (ibid.). He showed him the fire burning the vegetation, yet it
did not consume it or extinguish it. (Mishnat Rabbi Eliezer Ch. 4,
Torah Shelemah on Shemot Ch. 3, source 61)

משנת רבי אליעזר פ' ד תורה שלמה שמות פרק ג סא
"וְהִנֵּה הַסְּנֶה בֹּעֵר בָּאֵשׁ וְהַסְּנֶה אֵינֶנּוּ אֻכָּל" (שמות ג:ב). גדול הוא השלום שלא
נגלה הקב"ה על משה רבינו תחלה לא בחיות ולא בכרובים ולא באופנים אלא
מתוך דבר שהוא שלום, שנאמר "וַיֵּרָא מַלְאַךְ ה' אֵלָיו בְּלַבַּת־אֵשׁ" (שם), הראהו
האש בוערת בירקות ואינה אוכלתן ואינם מכבים אותה.

"Opposites can live in peace and harmony" is the lesson of this
classic text of Rabbinic literature. The very coexistence of that
which is to be consumed by its natural enemy is the lesson of the
"burning bush."

Moshe is taught in his very first encounter with Hashem that
under the proper circumstances we may, and at times we must,

transcend and indeed conquer what appears to be the "absolute law of nature."

Fire and wood are incompatible. The bush is to be consumed by fire, or the fire is to be extinguished by water.

Yet the burning bush revealed to משה that:

(A) Nature can be controlled and even at times conquered.

(B) G-d is not subservient to nature, i.e., miracles.

(c) That which seems impossible may in fact be possible.

There are a number of principles we may derive from this text.

* G-d is not subservient to nature, yet G-d allows nature to function by its rules.
* People of different racial, religious, cultural, political, and national background can and should live in harmony. "Fire and water" can be compatible; it depends upon how one applies the inherent qualities of these natural powers. Fire enables us to cook our food, heat our homes, indeed, heal, travel, invent, etc.

Yet fire can consume all we cherish in life and civilization. Weapons are a form of fire. All are measured by "firepower," be it a pistol or an H-bomb, it is "fire power" in its most destructive manifestation.

Water gives life in many ways, yet it may also destroy life and property. Thus the "burning bush" which is "not consumed" is the metaphor of this conflict in nature – "to consume" or "not consume," bring blessing or destruction. Let nature have its way or learn to control and harness natural power for good.

Powers which are inherently good though potentially destructive are the challenge which our society confronts.

Atomic energy, space travel, communication, computer technology, the potential of science to heal, and discover, etc., all represent unprecedented opportunities, resulting from firepower. All are potentially dangerous, as they are potentially valuable to human society.

Will the fire of our time consume or will it enhance, will it destroy or build?

Never in all of human history was the opportunity and choice as fundamental to civilization as it is in our day.

Peace / שלום

וַיֵּרָא מַלְאַךְ ה' אֵלָיו בְּלַבַּת־אֵשׁ מִתּוֹךְ הַסְּנֶה
וַיַּרְא וְהִנֵּה הַסְּנֶה בֹּעֵר בָּאֵשׁ וְהַסְּנֶה אֵינֶנּוּ אֻכָּל:
(שמות ג:ב)

And the angel of the Lord appeared to him in
a flame of fire from within the bush; and he
looked, and behold, the bush burned with fire,
yet the bush was not being consumed. (Shemot 3:2)

Great is peace! For the first time the Holy One, blessed is He,
revealed Himself to Moshe, [He did so] not out of the midst of
the [Holy] Creatures, or the Cherubim, or the Ophanim, but out
of that which was emblematic of peace, as it says "And the angel
of the Lord appeared to him in a flame of fire" (ibid.). He showed
him the fire burning the vegetation, yet it did not consume it or
extinguish it. (Mishnat Rabbi Eliezer Ch. 4, Torah Shelemah on
Shemot Ch. 3, source 61)

משנת רבי אליעזר פ' ד תורה שלמה שמות פרק ג סא
גדול הוא השלום שלא נגלה הקב"ה על משה רבינו תחלה לא בחיות ולא
בכרובים ולא באופנים אלא מתוך דבר שהוא שלום, שנאמר " וַיֵּרָא מַלְאַךְ
ה' אֵלָיו בְּלַבַּת־אֵשׁ" (שם), הראהו האש בוערת בירקות ואינה אוכלתן ואינם
מכבים אותה.

The inherent value of שלום – "peace" is the focus of this חז"ל text.
The first encounter of 'ה with משה רבנו was fire-burning vegetation and the vegetation is "not consumed" nor is the fire "extinguished" – it seems a remarkable or perhaps a "miraculous"
"peace" within the forces of nature. Fire does not destroy and
wood is not consumed by fire. This is the "burning bush" event
early in משה רבנו's encounter with 'ה.

The משנת רבי אליעזר chooses an unnatural event, i.e., "the burning bush" to demonstrate a possible "peace" within the "forces of nature" in this event. Fire does not "destroy" or "consume." It's a source of energy. Is this peace within "the natural forces"? The result would be a lack of heat-light-energy, etc. Yet must it be so?

Fire is a natural phenomenon which can be a power of ultimate good and constructiveness, yet it is easily a power of destruction and evil. The manner in which this natural power is directed and applied by the individual or society determines its destiny, for good or evil.

The Sorrow of Israel / צַעַרָן שֶׁל יִשְׂרָאֵל

וַיַּרְא ה' כִּי סָר לִרְאוֹת וַיִּקְרָא אֵלָיו אֱ-לֹהִים
מִתּוֹךְ הַסְּנֶה וַיֹּאמֶר מֹשֶׁה מֹשֶׁה וַיֹּאמֶר הִנֵּנִי:
(שמות ג:ד)

And when the Lord saw that he turned aside
to see, G-d called to him out of the midst of the
bush, and said, "Moshe, Moshe." And he said,
"Here I am." (Shemot 3:4)

The Holy One, blessed is He, said to him: 'You have put aside
your work and have gone to share the sorrow of Israel, behaving
towards them like a brother. I will also leave those on high and
below and I will speak with you.' Hence it is written 'and when
the Lord saw that he turned aside to see' (Shemot 3:4); because
G-d saw that Moshe turned aside from his duties to look upon
their burdens, 'He called to him out of the midst of the bush'
(Shemot 3:4).   (Shemot Rabbah 1:27)

שמות רבה פרק א:כז
אמר הקב"ה (למשה) אתה הנחת עסקיך והלכת לראות בצערן של ישראל,
ונהגת בהן מנהג אחים, אני מניח את העליונים ואת התחתונים ואדבר עמך
הה"ד "וַיַּרְא ה' כִּי סָר לִרְאוֹת" (שמות ג:ד), ראה הקב"ה במשה שסר מעסקיו
לראות בסבלותם לפיכך "וַיִּקְרָא אֵלָיו אֱ-לֹהִים מִתּוֹךְ הַסְּנֶה" (שם).

The מדרש suggests that משה רבנו demonstrated a concern for the
suffering of the Children of Israel. משה felt Israel's plight, though
at the time this was not משה's responsibility.

Thus הקב"ה saw in משה the qualities necessary for leadership of
כלל ישראל.

Justice is the Most Precious /
חביב הוא המשפט

וְעַתָּה לְכָה וְאֶשְׁלָחֲךָ אֶל־פַּרְעֹה וְהוֹצֵא אֶת־
עַמִּי בְנֵי־יִשְׂרָאֵל מִמִּצְרָיִם: (שמות ג:י)

And now, go and I will send you to Pharaoh so
you may bring out My people, the Children of
Israel, from Egypt. (Shemot 3:10)

"And now, go and I will send you" (Shemot 3:10). Rabbi Yehudah
said: Justice is the most precious of all the commandments . . . .
For even if someone has numerous good deeds, he is only praised
in the world by virtue of justice and righteousness. And from
whom do you learn this? From Moshe the man of G-d, who out of
all his good deeds was praised only for his justice and righteousness . . . Rabbi Zeira said . . . Whoever performs acts of justice
and righteousness ensures that he will become an instrument of
salvation. Moshe, the greatest man of the world, commenced [his
public life] with an act of justice, as it says: "he went out on the
second day . . ." (Shemot 2:13) and it is written "Who made you
a ruler and a judge over us?" (Shemot 2:14). Said the Holy One,
blessed is He, to him, "Through the acts of justice that you have
performed, you have made yourself an instrument of salvation:
Come now therefore, and I will send you" as it says, "And now, go
and I will send you" (Shemot 3:10).

(Midrash, Torah Shelemah on Shemot Ch. 3, source 147)

מדרש תורה שלמה שמות פרק ג קמז

"וְעַתָּה לְכָה וְאֶשְׁלָחֲךָ" (שמות ג:י). אמר ר' יהודה חביב הוא המשפט מכל המצות
כו' ואפילו ביד אדם כמה מעשים טובים אינו משובח בעולם אלא בצדק ומשפט
וממי את למד ממשה איש הא־לוהים שמכל מעשים טובים שהיו בידו לא

נשתבח אלא בצדקה ומשפט כו' א"ר זעירה כו' וכל שהוא עושה משפט וצדקה
גורם לישועה שתבא על ידו, משה גדול שבעולם התחיל במשפט שנאמר "וַיֵּצֵא
בַּיּוֹם הַשֵּׁנִי וגו'" (שמות ב:יג) וכתיב "מִי שָׂמְךָ וגו'" (שמות ב:יד) א"ל הקב"ה התחלת
לעשות משפט גרמת לישועה שתבוא על ידך שנא' "וְעַתָּה לְכָה וְאֶשְׁלָחֲךָ"
(שמות ג:י).

Beyond any doubt משה רבנו is considered by all, the greatest Jewish leader, lawgiver, emancipator, and religious personality. Yet
the greatest attribute this מדרש accords to משה is his unwillingness
to stand by as one rises to strike an innocent man. Moshe first
interferes when he sees an Egyptian killing one of the Children
of Israel, and he slays the Egyptian. Then when he witnesses a
Jew strike a Jew he attempts to interfere and is challenged by the
assailant, "Will you slay me as you slew the Egyptian? (Shemot
2:14) Who appointed you as Lord and Judge over us (the Jewish
People)?"

It is this quality of "concern," of "caring," of willingness to
endanger self to protect the innocent stranger that qualifies משה
to be the leader of the Children of Israel and indeed the recipient
of the Ten Commandments from the Almighty on Mount Sinai.

My People and Your People / עַמִּי וְעַמֶּךְ

וְעַתָּה לְכָה וְאֶשְׁלָחֲךָ אֶל־פַּרְעֹה וְהוֹצֵא אֶת־
עַמִּי בְנֵי־יִשְׂרָאֵל מִמִּצְרָיִם: (שמות ג:י)

And now, go and I will send you to Pharaoh so
you may bring out My people, the Children of
Israel, from Egypt. (Shemot 3:10)

A Midrash suggests yet an additional unique quality of Moshe as
the leader of the Children of Israel as they are emancipated, given
the Ten Commandments, and become a nation.

"So you may bring out My people" (Shemot 3:10). Initially, the
Holy One, blessed is He, said to Moshe, "And now, go and I will
send you to Pharaoh so you may bring out My people, the Children of Israel, from Egypt" (Shemot 3:10). But once he did that
deed, what did He say? "Go, descend, for your people have become corrupt" (Shemot 32:7). Said Moshe before the Holy One,
blessed is He: "Master of the Universe, when they sin, they are
called mine; and when they are worthy, they are called Yours.
Yet, whether they sin or are worthy, they are Yours, as it is written 'they are Your people, and Your inheritance'" (Devarim 9:29).
(Pesikta D'Rav Kahana Ch. 16, Torah Shelemah on Shemot Ch. 3,
source 150)

פסיקתא דרב כהנא פ' טז תורה שלמה שמות ג קנ

"וְהוֹצֵא אֶת־עַמִּי" (שמות ג:י), בתחלה אמר הקב"ה למשה "וְעַתָּה לְכָה וְאֶשְׁלָחֲךָ
אֶל־פַּרְעֹה וְהוֹצֵא אֶת־עַמִּי בְנֵי־יִשְׂרָאֵל מִמִּצְרָיִם", וכיון שעשו אותו מעשה, מה
כתיב תמן, "לֶךְ־רֵד כִּי שִׁחֵת עַמְּךָ" (שמות לב:ז), אמר משה לפני הקב"ה רבונו
של עולם, כד אינון חטאין דידי אינון, וכד אינון זכאין דידך אינון, בין חטאין בין
זכאין דידך אינון, דכתיב "וְהֵם עַמְּךָ וְנַחֲלָתֶךָ" (דברים ט:כט).

370

How astonishing – משה seems to challenge G-d when he is commanded to go to Pharaoh and take "My people, the Children of Israel, from Egypt" (שמות ג:י). Yet when this same people build a Golden Calf, they are considered by G-d "your [Moshe's] people."

Where does such a demanding and challenging dialogue take place in any religious-theological text? Moshe, as it were, considers G-d to be accountable to the principles of "consistency." Moshe says to G-d, either this people (Israel) is mine or Yours. You cannot claim the People of Israel as Yours when they seem to be to Your liking and then cast them away and say they are mine due to their sinfulness.

In fact, Moshe demonstrates the authentic Jewish view of our relationship with G-d. If our faith is personal – "I and Thou" – then it is intimacy which allows for accountability of both G-d and the people. If my G-d is a reality to me with attributes of "justice," then, teaches Moshe, I may challenge my G-d to demonstrate this justice consistently.

Healing / רפואה

... בְּהוֹצִיאֲךָ אֶת־הָעָם מִמִּצְרַיִם תַּעַבְדוּן אֶת־
הָאֱ־לֹהִים עַל הָהָר הַזֶּה: (שמות ג:יב)

*... When you take the people out of Egypt, you
will worship G-d on this mountain.* (Shemot 3:12)

And why was the Torah not given to them when they left Egypt?
Did He not say to Moshe "When you have brought the people
out of Egypt, you will serve G-d upon this mountain"? Said Rabbi
Yehudah Bar Shalom: You may compare this to a prince who recovered from sickness. His father said "let us wait three months
for his complete recovery" [before he takes up his duties]. Similarly, when they left Egypt, some were still suffering from their
enslavement. Said the Holy One, blessed is He, "Let us wait for
them until they are completely healed, and then I will give them
the Torah." (Tanchuma Yitro 10, Torah Shelemah on Shemot Ch.
3, source 166)

תנחומא יתרו י, תורה שלמה שמות ג קסו

ולמה לא נתנה התורה כשיצאו ממצרים, לא כך אמר למשה "בְּהוֹצִיאֲךָ אֶת־
הָעָם מִמִּצְרַיִם תַּעַבְדוּן אֶת־הָאֱ־לֹהִים עַל הָהָר הַזֶּה", אר"י בר שלום משל לבן
מלכים שעמד מחליו אמר אביו נמתין לו ג' חדשים עד שתשוב נפשו מן החולי,
אף כך כשיצאו ישראל ממצרים היו בהן בעלי מומין מן השעבוד, אמר הקב"ה
נמתין להם עד שיתרפאו ואח"כ אתן להם את התורה.

This מדרש introduces the idea that "pain" of "disfigurement" may
affect the attitude and judgment of the victim. Thus הקב"ה suggested that מתן תורה the "giving" and "receiving" of the תורה be
delayed until there has been sufficient time for בני ישראל to have
somewhat recuperated from their ordeal in Egypt.

A remarkable sensitivity to the impact of enslavement. No doubt the laws and traditions of the American South contributed to the upheaval which occurred when "civil rights" laws were ruled by the United States Supreme Court, to be Federal laws not subject to local or state legislation. In fact there was a significant reaction even in the North, though not supported by legal, political or social bodies, as was the case in the South.

נמתין להם / We Will Wait For Them

וַיֹּאמֶר כִּי־אֶהְיֶה עִמָּךְ וְזֶה־לְּךָ הָאוֹת כִּי אָנֹכִי
שְׁלַחְתִּיךָ בְּהוֹצִיאֲךָ אֶת־הָעָם מִמִּצְרַיִם תַּעַבְדוּן
אֶת־הָאֱ־לֹהִים עַל הָהָר הַזֶּה: (שמות ג:יב)

And He said, 'For I will be with you; and this shall
be a sign to you, that I have sent you; When you
take the people out of Egypt, you will serve G-d
upon this mountain.' (Shemot 3:12)

"When you take the people out of Egypt, you will serve G-d upon
this mountain" (Shemot 3:12). And why was the Torah not given
to them when they left Egypt? Did He not say to Moshe "When
you have brought the people out of Egypt, you will serve G-d
upon this mountain"? Said Rabbi Yehudah Bar Shalom: You may
compare this to a prince who recovered from sickness. His father
said "let us wait three months for his complete recovery" [before
he takes up his duties]. Similarly, when they left Egypt, some were
still suffering from their enslavement. Said the Holy One, blessed
is He, "Let us wait for them until they are completely healed,
and then I will give them the Torah." (Tanchuma Yitro 10, Torah
Shelemah on Shemot Ch. 3, source 166)

תנחומא יתרו י, תורה שלמה שמות ג קסו

"בְּהוֹצִיאֲךָ אֶת־הָעָם מִמִּצְרַיִם תַּעַבְדוּן אֶת־הָאֱ־לֹהִים" (שמות ג:יב). ולמה לא נתנה
התורה כשיצאו ממצרים, לא כך אמר למשה "בְּהוֹצִיאֲךָ אֶת־הָעָם מִמִּצְרַיִם
תַּעַבְדוּן אֶת־הָאֱ־לֹהִים עַל הָהָר הַזֶּה", אר"י בר שלום משל לבן מלכים שעמד
מחליו אמר אביו נמתין לו ג' חדשים עד שתשוב נפשו מן החולי, אף כך כשיצאו
ישראל ממצרים היו בהן בעלי מומין מן השעבוד, אמר הקב"ה נמתין להם עד
שיתרפאו ואח"כ אתן להם את התורה.

Neither a people nor an individual can, without pause, pass from

374

slavery to freedom. This Midrash, centuries prior to any scientific understanding of the psychological-emotional workings of the human being, gives reason for the delay of the giving of the תורה and the establishment of a Jewish State.

In the above parable of a king's son who rises from his illness, he is told by his father "wait three months until you are fully restored to health." Thus suggests the מדרש, the Children of Israel having just been emancipated from centuries of enslavement in Egypt could not overnight, as it were, receive the תורה. Wait three months until you have recovered from your illness of enslavement and only then may you be prepared to receive the תורה. (In fact, they were not prepared, thus the Golden Calf.) This מדרש suggests a people can not easily transition from centuries of enslavement to become a free and responsible people. Indeed after the sin of the עגל (Golden Calf), it took 40 years for the Children of Israel to enter "the Promised Land," a journey which should have not taken even one year. Any emancipated Jewish slave over the age of 20 did not enter what was to become "the Land of Israel." It was the sin of the "Golden Calf" which caused G-d to decree the death of those emancipated Jewish slaves who were over 20 at the time of the Shemot.

We have in our time witnessed the emancipation of many a people and nations which have resulted in anarchy and oppression. Very few of the nations created post World War II, when the great colonial powers were forced to emancipate their vast colonial empire, developed into responsible, lawful democracies. With some notable exceptions, Israel and India being of the most prominent, newly emancipated states did not form free and democratic states. Be it Asia or Africa the vast majority of the newly formed nations are dictatorships of one form or another.

Furthermore, one must with great respect, love, and sensitivity, consider the complexity of the Holocaust survivor who endeavors to resume a normal life, rejoin society, earn a living, seek companionship, marry, have a family, raise children, all after having been reduced to a "nonperson," numbered and selected for extermination in a gas chamber.

How, one may wonder, does a survivor transcend all this incomprehensible trauma and then endeavor to have faith in G-d and man?

Perhaps the greatest miracle of our time was the Jewish People's response to "man's inhumanity to the Jewish People." Building a sovereign Jewish State in which Holocaust survivors played a catalytic role, Holocaust survivors formed a democracy in which all people, all races, and all religions are guaranteed their absolute human rights.

Indeed the ultimate task of the Jewish people is תקון עולם – "fix the world," cure it from its evils of war, unjustified hatred, and oppression of the weak. Hopefully, in time, Israel, the historic Jewish nation situated in a hostile environment of Arab lands, will be able to demonstrate the Messianic promise of peace and freedom for all of humanity.

אהיה / I will be

וַיֹּאמֶר אֱ־לֹהִים אֶל־מֹשֶׁה אֶהְיֶה אֲשֶׁר אֶהְיֶה
וַיֹּאמֶר כֹּה תֹאמַר לִבְנֵי יִשְׂרָאֵל אֶהְיֶה שְׁלָחַנִי
אֲלֵיכֶם: (שמות ג:יד)

And G-d said to Moshe, "I will be as I will be."
And He said, "So shall you say to the Children of
Israel, 'I will be' has sent me to you." (Shemot 3:14)

"I will be as I will be" (Shemot 3:14). The Holy One, blessed is
He, said to Moshe: "Go and say to Israel 'I was with you in this
enslavement (i.e., Egypt) as I will be with you in your future en-
slavements' (i.e., the future exiles of the Jewish people)." He said
to Him: "Master of the Universe: Please do not speak of future
troubles, suffice when the difficulty arises!" to which the Holy
One, blessed is He replied: "Go and tell them: 'I will be with you'
has sent me to you" (ibid.). (Brachot 9b)

ברכות ט:

"אֶהְיֶה אֲשֶׁר אֶהְיֶה" (שמות ג:יד). אמר לו הקדוש ברוך הוא למשה: לך אמור להם
לישראל: אני הייתי עמכם בשעבוד זה ואני אהיה עמכם בשעבוד מלכיות. אמר
לפניו: רבונו של עולם דיה לצרה בשעתה. אמר לו הקדוש ברוך הוא: לך אמור
להם "אֶהְיֶה שְׁלָחַנִי אֲלֵיכֶם" (שם).

One of the Talmudic interpretive texts of this difficult verse implies the question, why the redundant use of the word אֶהְיֶה as G-d
introduces Himself to מֹשֶׁה, G-d states אֶהְיֶה אֲשֶׁר אֶהְיֶה. The Talmud
then introduces a dialog between ה' and His trusted servant מֹשֶׁה.
אֶהְיֶה I will be with you in this enslavement, i.e., Egypt. אֲשֶׁר אֶהְיֶה as
I will be with you in your future enslavement (the future exiles of
the Jewish people). To which מֹשֶׁה responds to G-d: "Please do not

377

speak of future troubles, suffice when the difficulty arises." That is to say, do not prematurely introduce difficulties, though they may be destined to occur.

This Talmudic text reveals Judaism's extraordinary understanding of G-d's history. משה demonstrates that one who has an authentic relationship with the Almighty may argue with the Almighty. Moreover the Talmud suggests one ought not prematurely anticipate difficulty in life, perhaps conditions may change, new opportunities may arise; what seems today an insurmountable trauma may tomorrow be resolved, with G-d's help.

We are told that Jews in the death camps of World War II adopted a Yiddish song "זאָג ניט קיין מאָל אַז דו גייסט דעם לעצטן וועג". "Do not ever say that you are now going on your last journey." Do not give up hope though the situation is desperate. In fact we know that there were and are survivors of the worst camps – Auschwitz, Treblinka, etc.

This is a profound lesson we need to consider. One may not ignore the difficulties which occur in one's life. Nonetheless one must develop an understanding of priorities and allow the most crucial immediate problems to receive attention and effort, and not allow future possibilities to encroach upon the immediate. A limited response even by משה, "the most trusted servant of G-d," is considered proper in this text.

The Uniqueness of / אברהם יצחק ויעקב
Avraham, Yitzchak and Yaakov

וַיֹּאמֶר עוֹד אֱ-לֹהִים אֶל-מֹשֶׁה כֹּה תֹאמַר אֶל-
בְּנֵי יִשְׂרָאֵל ה' אֱ-לֹהֵי אֲבֹתֵיכֶם אֱ-לֹהֵי אַבְרָהָם
אֱ-לֹהֵי יִצְחָק וֵא-לֹהֵי יַעֲקֹב שְׁלָחַנִי אֲלֵיכֶם זֶה-
שְׁמִי לְעֹלָם וְזֶה זִכְרִי לְדֹר דֹּר: (שמות ג:טו)

And G-d said further to Moshe: "So shall you say
to the Children of Israel, The Lord G-d of your
fathers, the G-d of Avraham, the G-d of Yitzchak,
and the G-d of Yaakov, has sent me to you. This is
My name forever, and this is My remembrance to
all generations." (Shemot 3:15)

"The Lord G-d of your fathers, the G-d of Avraham, the G-d
of Yitzchak, and the G-d of Yaakov" (Shemot 3:15). From where
do we know that we should say [in our prayers the formula of]
"Blessed are you, O Lord our G-d and the G-d of our fathers: The
G-d of Avraham, the G-d of Yitzchak, and the G-d of Yaakov," as
it says "And G-d said moreover to Moshe, 'Thus shall you say to
the People of Israel, The Lord G-d of your fathers, the G-d of
Avraham, the G-d of Yitzchak, and the G-d of Yaakov.'" (Mechilta
Bo Masechta D'Pischa Ch. 16, Torah Shelemah on Shemot Ch.
3, source 196)

מכילתא בא מסכתא דפסחא פט"ז, תורה שלמה שמות ג קצו

"אֱ-לֹהֵי אֲבֹתֵיכֶם אֱ-לֹהֵי אַבְרָהָם אֱ-לֹהֵי יִצְחָק וֵא-לֹהֵי יַעֲקֹב" (שמות ג:טו). מנין
שאומרים ברוך אתה ה' א-לֹהינו וא-לֹהי אבותינו א-לֹהי אברהם א-לֹהי יצחק
וא-לֹהי יעקב, שנאמר "עוֹד אֱ-לֹהִים אֶל-מֹשֶׁה 'כֹּה תֹאמַר אֶל-בְּנֵי יִשְׂרָאֵל ה'
אֱ-לֹהֵי אֲבֹתֵיכֶם אֱ-לֹהֵי אַבְרָהָם אֱ-לֹהֵי יִצְחָק וֵא-לֹהֵי יַעֲקֹב.'"

379

It is said in the name of the בעל שם טוב זצ"ל (Baal Shem Tov), "Why does the text repeat the word אֱ-לֹהֵי (the G-d of) before the mention of each of the אבות (Patriarchs)?" He suggests each had a unique and personal relationship with ה'. Unlike the other Patriarchs, אברהם – Avraham – was the first and perhaps only monotheist of his time. He entered into a ברית – a covenant with ה'. Coming from a pagan family and society it was אברהם whose personal quest and rejection of the pagan world led him to have faith in and a relationship with G-d the creator of the universe and of all life. It was Avraham with whom ה' made the covenant and it was Avraham who faced the test of absolute faith as G-d told him to sacrifice his son Yitzchak. Thus Avraham not only found his creator and Divine Being in a world of idolatry, but he was also willing to demonstrate that faith in the ultimate test with which he was confronted.

Then we have the faith of יצחק – Yitzchak – son of the monotheist Avraham, brother of a hostile Ishmael. As an adult, Yitzchak, 37 years old, was freely willing to allow himself to be sacrificed by his aged father Avraham to a G-d he could not see, hear, or understand. Avraham could not have faced the trial of the Akedah, the potential sacrifice of his beloved Yitzchak, without the approval and cooperation of 37-year-old Yitzchak. This experience no doubt impacted upon Yitzchak and his relationship with his faith in G-d.

Then we have the third and most complex of the Patriarchs, יעקב – Yaakov. As his life develops, four wives, the mothers of his 12 sons and one daughter. A Patriarch of an eclectic group of children, how daunting a task of continuous traumas.

Thus teaches the בעל שם טוב, each Jew – whether by birth or by choice a descendant of the Patriarchs and Matriarchs – needs to develop, as did they, a very unique and personal relationship with ה'. Only then can one experience the intensity and profundity of faith which informs and affects every aspect of life.

In our time may we compare the faith of a Jew who experienced Auschwitz and all that implies, with a Jew who was born and raised in the United States?

May we compare a Sabra (Israeli native) with someone born in the Soviet Union who then came to Israel? May we compare one born to an observant family to one who discovered the treasure of Torah and mitzvot as a result of a personal journey and quest?

What of the "returning Jew," the בעל תשובה, raised in an observant home, experienced an education of Jewish content, observed Jewish law and tradition, who then abandoned this heritage and commitment, then, regardless of reason, finds his or her way back to Jewish learning, observance, community, and commitment? A בעל תשובה, "a master of returning" to tradition and observance. The Talmud states:

> In the place where penitents stand, even the full-fledged righteous do not stand (Brachot 34b).

ברכות לד:

מקום שבעלי תשובה עומדין צדיקים גמורים אינם עומדין.

The lesson is clear. Each Jew needs to find a path to authentic Jewish study, observance, and faith. Each path and each individual may be unique in this process.

In essence, the vehicle of discovery is and in fact needs to be suitable to the individual, so long as the ultimate destination is a clear knowledge of Jewish thought, history, and Torah. This knowledge should then enable the individual to develop a serious personal commitment to, and an understanding of, Judaism.

Respect For In-Laws / כבוד חותנו

וַיֵּלֶךְ מֹשֶׁה וַיָּשָׁב אֶל־יֶתֶר חֹתְנוֹ וַיֹּאמֶר לוֹ
אֵלְכָה־נָּא וְאָשׁוּבָה אֶל־אַחַי אֲשֶׁר־בְּמִצְרַיִם
וְאֶרְאֶה הַעוֹדָם חַיִּים וַיֹּאמֶר יִתְרוֹ לְמֹשֶׁה לֵךְ
לְשָׁלוֹם: (שמות ד:יח)

And Moshe went and returned to Jeter (ie. Yisro)
his father-in-law, and said to him: 'Please let me
go and return to my brothers who are in Egypt,
so I can see whether they are still alive'. And Yisro
said to Moshe, 'Go in peace.' (Shemot 4:18)

The son of Rabbi Hiyya the Great said: He did not go to Pharaoh
until Yisro had released him of his vow. Then why does it say "And
Moshe went" (Shemot 4:18)? Where did he go? He went to fetch
his wife and sons. Yisro said to him "Where are you taking them?"
and he (Moshe) answered "To Egypt." [Yisro] said [in protest],
"Those who are already in Egypt want to get out, and you are
taking them there?!" He (Moshe) replied, "They will soon be
leaving to stand at Mount Sinai to hear the mouth of the Holy
One, blessed is He, proclaim, 'I am the Lord our G-d'; should my
own sons not hear this just like the others?" Immediately, Yisro
said to Moshe, "Go in peace" (ibid.), saying to him, 'Go in peace,
enter in peace, and come back in peace.' (Shemot Rabbah 4:4,
Torah Shelemah on Shemot Ch. 4, source 90)

שמו"ר פ"ד — ד, תורה שלמה שמות פרק ד צ

בנו של רבי חייא הגדול אמר, לא הלך אצל פרעה עד שהתיר לו יתרו את נדרו,
וא"ת למה נאמר "וַיֵּלֶךְ מֹשֶׁה" (שמות ד:יח) להיכן הלך? שהלך ליטול אשתו ובניו.
א"ל יתרו להיכן אתה מוליכן. א"ל למצרים. א"ל אותם שהם במצרים מבקשין
לצאת ואת מוליכן. א"ל למחר הן עתידין לצאת ולעמוד על הר סיני לשמוע מפי

382

הקב"ה 'אנכי ה' אלהיך' ובני לא ישמעו כמו הם. מיד ויאמר יתרו למשה "לֵךְ
לְשָׁלוֹם" (שם). א"ל לך לשלום ותכנס לשלום ותבא לשלום.

This מדרש teaches the importance of a respectful relationship of a
father-in-law and son-in-law.

משה advises his father-in-law יתרו of his planned visit to Egypt.
Lesson one, there is a sense of communication between משה and
his father-in-law. Lesson two, the father-in-law, without rancor,
challenges the wisdom of משה by querying why he wishes to go
to Egypt when those in Egypt are anxious to leave. Third, משה
responds to יתרו in a respectful and logical (in context) answer.

A dialogue ensued. What could have been a confrontation,
perhaps even with justification, is described as an intelligent and
reasoned conversation, with mutual respect and understanding.

A renowned ethics scholar in the early 20th century of the
famed Lithuanian Yeshiva of Slabodka, Lithuania, known as "Der
Alter" (which means "the elder") asked, "If משה was instructed by
G-d to go to Egypt, challenge Pharaoh and bring the Children
of Israel out of Egyptian bondage, why was it necessary for משה
to ask permission from his father-in-law to leave and proceed to
Egypt?"

Says the Elder of Slabodka, "Had משה not, out of a sense of
gratitude, asked his father-in-law permission to leave and proceed
to Egypt and respond to G-d's mandate to free the Children of Israel from bondage, משה would not have been worthy of being the
leader of the Jewish people." Thus teaches this profound teacher
of Jewish ethics, only one with a serious commitment to ethics
may be a Jewish leader.

My Child / בני

וְאָמַרְתָּ אֶל־פַּרְעֹה כֹּה אָמַר ה' בְּנִי בְכֹרִי
יִשְׂרָאֵל: (שמות ד:כב)

And you shall say to Pharaoh, "So said the Lord:
'My son, My firstborn Israel.'" (Shemot 4:22)

"My son, My firstborn Israel" (Shemot 4:22). "Is Ephrayim my
dear son?" (Jeremiah 31:19). This is the meaning of the verse, "For
I was a son to My Father" (Mishlei 4:3). Come and see how even
when Israel numbers countless thousands and myriads, they are
simply regarded by G-d as an only son. . . . And every single one is
considered as if he is the only son, as it says "My son, My firstborn
Israel" (Shemot 4:22), and it is written "Let My son go, that he may
serve Me" (Shemot 4:23). Therefore he says, "For I was a son to My
Father" (Mishlei 4:3) meaning that when a man has an infant son,
if he sins, his father does not drive him away because he is only an
infant . . . So too with Israel. Even they unwittingly sin, He regards
them as but an infant son; as it says, 'For Israel was a child and I
loved him' (Hoshea 11:1), "My dear son" (Jeremiah 31:19). (Agga-
dat Bereishit 5:1, Torah Shelemah on Shemot Ch. 4, source 123)

אגדת בראשית פ"ה:א, תורה שלמה שמות פרק ד קכג

"בְּנִי בְכֹרִי יִשְׂרָאֵל" (שמות ד:כב). "הֲבֵן יַקִּיר לִי אֶפְרַיִם" (ירמיהו לא:יט), זש"ה "כִּי־בֵן
הָיִיתִי לְאָבִי וגו'" (משלי ד:ג), בא וראה אפילו הן ישראל אלף אלפים ורבו ריבוון,
אינם חשובים לפני המקום אלא כבן יחיד כו'. הרי כל אלו ואלו לא היו לפניו
אלא כאחד יחידי שנאמר "בְּנִי בְכֹרִי יִשְׂרָאֵל" (שמות ד:כב), וכתיב "שַׁלַּח אֶת־בְּנִי
וְיַעַבְדֵנִי" (שמות ד:כג). לפיכך הוא אומר "כִּי־בֵן הָיִיתִי לְאָבִי" (משלי ד:ג), כשם
שבנו של אדם כשהוא תינוק קטן, אם יחטא אין אביו מסלק עליו מפני שהוא
תינוק קטן וכו' כך ישראל אפילו חוטאין בשגגה מעלה עליהן שהן כתינוק קטן,
שנאמר "כִּי נַעַר יִשְׂרָאֵל וָאֹהֲבֵהוּ וגו'" (הושע יא:א), "הֲבֵן יַקִּיר לִי" (ירמיהו לא:יט).

The text ponders the question why does 'ה refer to the Children of Israel enslaved in Egypt in the singular – i.e., "My son, My eldest," Israel. Three times the text emphasizes the theme of the singularity of the multitude of slaves in Egypt. Moreover, the status of תינוק קטן – "young child," in contemporary terms a "minor," is the metaphor for בני ישראל, "the Children of Israel."

Indeed does not a parent endeavor to judge a child – particularly a young child – with special compassion and empathy?

The Almighty judged the Children of Israel as individuals and as children. Though countless women, men, and children were to be emancipated from Egyptian bondage, the text insists upon the singularity of each slave to be emancipated; each an individual, a woman, a man, a boy, a girl. The Torah teaches respect for the individual, who only when multiplied became a multitude, a nation, a people.

Moreover, the text suggests that the "children"of Israel who had been slaves in Egypt and who are now to be emancipated, are to be judged as "children."

We are required to understand the individual, each within the context of his/her social – intellectual – political, spiritual, and psychological environment. Yesterday's slave cannot overnight, as it were, be expected to become a responsible citizen, a free, independent, and choosing citizen.

In fact the events of Israel's journey after emancipation demonstrate the complexity of transition from slave to free man and woman. A journey of perhaps weeks becomes a 40-year odyssey, before a nation of slaves becomes a sovereign state and people.

And He Kissed Him / וישק לו

וַיֹּאמֶר ה' אֶל־אַהֲרֹן לֵךְ לִקְרַאת מֹשֶׁה הַמִּדְבָּרָה
וַיֵּלֶךְ וַיִּפְגְּשֵׁהוּ בְּהַר הָאֱ־לֹהִים וַיִּשַּׁק־לֹו:
(שמות ד:כז)

*And the Lord said to Aharon: "Go to greet Moshe
in the wilderness." And he went, and met him in
the mount of G-d, and kissed him.* (Shemot 4:27)

"And kissed him" (Shemot 4:27). We do not know to whom the
Holy One, blessed is He, showed honor – to Aharon or to Moshe.
Some say to Aharon who was in Egypt and who prophesied to
Israel that the Holy One, blessed is He, would one day redeem
them so that Moshe would come and confirm that this is what
Aharon had said so that Israel would say: 'Aharon had prophesied
truthfully.' Others say that it was to Moshe, so that Moshe should
come and they should believe his words.   (Shemot Rabbah 5:10)

שמו"ר פ"ה:י

"וַיִּשַּׁק־לֹו" (שמות ד:כז). אין אנו יודעין למי חלק הקב"ה כבוד אם לאהרן אם
למשה. י"א לאהרן שהיה במצרים ומתנבא להם לישראל שעתיד הקב"ה לגאול
אותם, כדי שיבא משה ויעיד על דבריו של אהרן ויהיו ישראל אומרים: אמת
היה מתנבא אהרן. וי"א למשה, כדי שיבא משה ויאמינו לדבריו.

The תורה speaks of (וַיִּשַּׁק־לֹו) "and he kissed him." Who kissed
whom asks the מדרש? There is no indication in the text who is
"he" and who is "him." That is, who is the more catalytic personality during the enslavement and during the emancipation of
the Children of Israel. Who was the more honored by the Almighty, Moshe or Aharon? The מדרש suggests both Aharon and
Moshe played a distinct role in Israel's survival while in Egyptian

bondage and then in Israel's emancipation, thus both are equally honored.

While yet enslaved, Aharon conveyed faith in G-d to the Children of Israel that ultimately redemption will come and they will be emancipated from bondage, while משה brought a renewed faith in 'ה and in the ultimate emancipation and redemption of Israel.

משה and אהרן were critical to the survival and then emancipation of Israel. Aharon helped the people maintain their identity and faith, while משה was the great emancipator who forced the people to choose between continued enslavement or the perilous journey leading to Sinai and their encounter with 'ה as a free people.

Aharon kept the enslaved Children of Israel confident and faithful while in Egyptian slavery. משה compelled confrontation, choice, and faith radically different than the tranquility of Egyptian enslavement.

Life does indeed offer two paths, one safe, comfortable, and tranquil; the other, perilous, unpredictable, and at times traumatic – yet potentially dynamic, creative, and rewarding.

There is an original insight presented in the Talmud (Avodah Zarah 54b) which describes the nature and implications of freedom of choice.

Our Rabbis taught: Philosophers asked the elders in Rome: "If your G-d has no desire for idolatry, why does He not abolish it?" They replied, "Were it to be something that the world does not need, He would have abolished it. But these people worship the sun, moon, stars and planets. [Does this mean that] He should destroy the Universe on account of fools? Instead, the world follows its natural course, and as for the fools who act wrongly, they will have to give a reckoning." (Avodah Zarah 54b)

ע"ז נד:

ת"ר, שאלו פלוסופין את הזקנים ברומי: אם א-להיכם אין רצונו בעבודת כוכבים, מפני מה אינו מבטלה? אמרו להם: אילו לדבר שאין העולם צורך לו היו עובדין הרי הוא מבטלה, הרי הן עובדין לחמה וללבנה ולכוכבים ולמזלות, יאבד עולם מפני השוטים? אלא עולם כמנהגו נוהג, ושוטים שקלקלו עתידין ליתן את הדין.

Should evil be immediately self-destructive, that is, a stolen seed planted in the ground should never bloom, a spoken lie would not be heard, an act of violence would be of no consequence. Human choice and experience would cease to have any meaning.

In fact, it was human initiative and determination which led to every advance or catastrophe in human experience. The advances in science, technology, law, human rights, government and its powers, were all the consequence of human initiative. The horrors of war, the historic events of persecution and oppression, the Holocaust, were all the result of the decisions of individuals and groups who acted in defiance of all that is moral and ethical. All of human history is the consequence of human choice and the acts which followed. Man's action is not absolved by G-d's ultimate design of world history.

The Talmud teaches the historic and self-evident truth that in the ultimate, "evil" creates its own consequences, as does "good." Human action is never in a vacuum. The choices of the individual or the collective, i.e., government and organized groups, result in forming the individual's or the collective's quality of life and destiny.

Derech Eretz / דֶּרֶךְ אֶרֶץ

וַיֵּלֶךְ מֹשֶׁה וְאַהֲרֹן וַיַּאַסְפוּ אֶת־כָּל־זִקְנֵי בְּנֵי
יִשְׂרָאֵל: וַיְדַבֵּר אַהֲרֹן אֵת כָּל־הַדְּבָרִים אֲשֶׁר־
דִּבֶּר ה' אֶל־מֹשֶׁה וַיַּעַשׂ הָאֹתֹת לְעֵינֵי הָעָם:
(שמות ד:כט-ל)

And Moshe and Aharon went and gathered
together all the elders of the People of Israel. And
Aharon spoke all the words which the Lord had
told Moshe, and [he] performed the signs in the
sight of the people. (Shemot 4:29–30)

The wise man does not speak before him that is greater than he
in wisdom or in age. This refers to Moshe, as it says "And Aharon
spoke all the words which the Lord had told Moshe, and [he] performed the signs in the sight of the people." (Shemot 4:30). And
who was most fitting to speak, Moshe or Aharon? Surely Moshe!
For Moshe heard [the words] from the mouth of the Almighty,
while Aharon heard them [only] from the mouth of Moshe. But
thus said Moshe [to himself]: Shall I then speak while my older
brother is standing by? He therefore told Aharon to speak, and it
is for this reason that it is said "Aharon spoke all the words which
the Lord had told Moshe."   (Avot D'Rabbi Natan Ch. 37)

אבות ד"ר נתן פרק ל"ז

חכם אינו מדבר לפני מי שגדול ממנו בחכמה ובמנין זה משה שנאמר "וַיְדַבֵּר
אַהֲרֹן אֵת כָּל־הַדְּבָרִים אֲשֶׁר־דִּבֶּר ה' אֶל־מֹשֶׁה וַיַּעַשׂ הָאֹתֹת לְעֵינֵי הָעָם" (שמות
ד:ל). וכי מי ראוי לדבר משה או אהרן. הוי אומר משה שמשה שמע מפי הגבורה
ואהרן שמע מפי משה. אלא כך אמר משה אפשר שאדבר במקום שאחי גדול
ממני עומד שם לפיכך אמר לו לאהרן דבר. לכך נאמר "וַיְדַבֵּר אַהֲרֹן אֵת כָּל־
הַדְּבָרִים אֲשֶׁר־דִּבֶּר ה' אֶל־מֹשֶׁה."

A lesson in the principle of דרך ארץ, "respect." אהרן was the older brother. The Midrash teaches, a wise person does not speak prior to that of an elder.

ה' speaks to משה repeatedly: ויאמר ה' אל משה, וידבר ה' אל משה.

Up to this point ה' has spoken to משה at least a dozen times. Nonetheless אהרן the older brother is given the honor to address the elders of Israel.

The text clearly states וילך משה ואהרן – both assemble the "elders of Israel." Nonetheless, it is אהרן who speaks to them.

A lesson in "respect for elders." Jewish tradition requires an elder or parent or teacher (Rabbi and lay) be assigned a special seat at the table or synagogue, or assembly hall, which is then maintained as the Rabbi's (or elder's) place of honor which no other person is to occupy.

Elsewhere we have referred to the place of honor assigned to father and mother at the head of the dining table, be it humble or elaborate. Thus, a designation of exclusive place or space is the Torah's way of helping us remember the respect due a parent, teacher, Rabbi, etc. Values need symbols to aid us in our pursuit of living a value-laden life.

Joint Mission / שְׁלִיחוּת

וַיֹּאמֶר פַּרְעֹה מִי ה' אֲשֶׁר אֶשְׁמַע בְּקֹלוֹ לְשַׁלַּח
אֶת־יִשְׂרָאֵל לֹא יָדַעְתִּי אֶת־ה' וְגַם אֶת־יִשְׂרָאֵל
לֹא אֲשַׁלֵּחַ: (שמות ה:ב)

And Pharaoh said, "Who is the Lord, that I
should obey His voice to let Israel go? I do not
know the Lord, and I will not let Israel go."
(Shemot 5:2)

"Who is the Lord that I should obey His voice" (Shemot 5:2).
Rabbi Levi said: For seven days the Holy One, blessed is He,
urged Moshe at the bush to send him [on the mission to liberate the Children of Israel], and he replied, "send whomever you
choose" (Shemot 4:13). The Holy One, blessed is He, said to
Moshe, "By your life! You will eventually go!" When he did go,
and demanded "Thus said the Lord, the G-d of Israel" (Shemot
5:1), that wicked man replied, "Who is the Lord, that I should
obey His voice?" (Shemot 5:2), Moshe began to say, "I have now
fulfilled my mission." (Tanchuma Yashan Vayikra Ch. 4, Torah
Shelemah on Shemot Ch. 5, source 13)

תנחומא ישן ויקרא ד', תורה שלמה שמות ה יג

"מִי ה' אֲשֶׁר אֶשְׁמַע בְּקֹלוֹ" (שמות ה:ב). אמר ר' לוי שבעת ימים היה הקב"ה
מפתה את משה בסנה לשלחו, והוא משיבו "שְׁלַח־נָא בְּיַד־תִּשְׁלָח" וכו' (שמות
ד:יג), א"ל הקב"ה למשה חייך סופך לילך, כיון שהלך ואמר " כֹּה־אָמַר ה' אֱ־לֹהֵי
יִשְׂרָאֵל" (שמות ה:א), אמר אותו רשע "מִי ה' אֲשֶׁר אֶשְׁמַע בְּקֹלוֹ" (שמות ה:ב),
התחיל משה אומר אני כבר עשיתי שליחותי.

משה was the reluctant emancipator, G-d's reluctant emissary to
the enslaved Children of Israel – "send someone else," משה pleads
with ה'.

מֹשֶׁה is the humble servant of ה', as the תורה states "וְהָאִישׁ מֹשֶׁה עָנָו (במדבר יב:ג) "מְאֹד, "מֹשֶׁה was the humblest of all" (Bamidbar 12:3). Nonetheless מֹשֶׁה was selected by ה' to be the "great emancipator" of the Children of Israel. מֹשֶׁה pleads with ה', שְׁלַח־נָא בְּיַד־תִּשְׁלָח "send whomever you choose" (Shemot 4:13), so long as you allow me to be at peace.

The תורה has מֹשֶׁה argue with ה' and give ה' advice – "send whomever you choose." ה' in Verse 14 demonstrates anger and argues with מֹשֶׁה – there is continued dialog, ה' unwilling to accept מֹשֶׁה's rejection offers yet another manner in which מֹשֶׁה may accept the role of "Emancipator" and leadership. ה' says to מֹשֶׁה – Let אהרן your brother speak for you הֲלֹא אַהֲרֹן אָחִיךָ הַלֵּוִי יָדַעְתִּי כִּי־דַבֵּר יְדַבֵּר הוּא (שמות ד:יד). Your task is to go to פרעה and demand the release of בני ישראל – you are to confront פרעה, your spokesman in the confrontation will be your brother אהרן.

A profound lesson of shared responsibilities. No one need have all the skills and all the talents necessary to complete a mission. Seek others who may help. ה' assures מֹשֶׁה that his brother אהרן will be at his side and if needed can speak to פרעה for him.

Greatness, the text suggests, is often accomplished as we seek the assistance of others who share our values and our goals. To recognize one's limitations is part of successful striving for growth and achievement.

Three Day Strategic Plan / שלשת ימים

...נֵלְכָה־נָּא דֶרֶךְ שְׁלֹשֶׁת יָמִים... :(שמות ה:ג)

...Let us go for a three day journey... (Shemot 5:3)

The ספר עטרת חכמים asks an original and challenging question:[1]

What is the reason he didn't tell him to send them forever? And why were the plagues sent upon Pharaoh, because surely G-d brought the Israelites to his hand? The answer is that had Moshe our teacher, peace be upon him, come to him [to ask] that he send them permanently and had Pharaoh refused, then the plagues would not have come upon him because what king would want to send away 600,000 slaves with good will. But when Moshe our teacher, peace be upon him, requested in the name of G-d for him to let them go for three days and to serve G-d, then in this instance he did not send them and therefore it was correct that he was afflicted with the plagues. (Sefer Ateret Chachamim)

ספר עטרת חכמים

הטעם מה שלא אמר לו שישלחם לעולמים? גם מדוע מגיע לפרעה המכות, הלא ה' מסר את ישראל בידו? אמנם התשובה היא: כי באם היה בא אליו משה רבינו ע"ה שישלח אותם לחלוטין, ופרעה היה ממאן, אז לא היה מגיע לו באות המכות, כי איזה מלך רוצה לשלוח ששים רבוא עבדים ברצון הטוב, אבל כאשר בקש משר"עה בשם ה', וכי יתנם ללכת על ג' ימים, לעבוד את ה', ועל כן זה לא שלחם, לכן מגיע לו מכות על פי דין.

An original and challenging view of the confrontation between פרעה and משה רבנו. Why does משה רבנו not demand of פרעה to allow

---

1.   Nb. The author has summarized this source in his own words.

393

כלל ישראל to be freed from their enslavement? Obviously it was the plan of 'ה to free כלל ישראל from Egyptian slavery.

Nonetheless, a demand for a three-day journey to worship their G-d was a more practical proposal.

The view of the עטרת חכמים is one of practical negotiations. The objective was the ultimate freedom for the Children of Israel with Egyptian consent. At first Egypt did not only allow Israel to leave, then Egypt demanded of Moshe and Aharon to rise in the middle of the night and get all of Israel out of Egypt.

Self-Sacrifice / מסירת נפש

וַיֻּכּוּ שֹׁטְרֵי בְּנֵי יִשְׂרָאֵל אֲשֶׁר־שָׂמוּ עֲלֵהֶם נֹגְשֵׂי
פַרְעֹה לֵאמֹר מַדּוּעַ לֹא כִלִּיתֶם חָקְכֶם לִלְבֹּן
כִּתְמוֹל שִׁלְשֹׁם גַּם־תְּמוֹל גַּם־הַיּוֹם: (שמות ה:יד)

And the officials of the People of Israel whom
Pharaoh's task masters had appointed over them
were beaten, saying "Why have you not fulfilled
your task in making bricks as previously, neither
yesterday nor today?" (Shemot 5:14)

From here you learn that there were worthy men who risked their
lives for Israel and who bore blows so that their task might be
lighter. For this they merited the Holy Spirit, as it says, "And G-d
said to Moshe: 'Gather to Me seventy men of the elders of Israel
whom you know to be the elders of the people and its officers, take
them to the Tent of Meeting and have them stand there with you'
(Bamidbar 11:16). Said the Holy One, blessed is He, 'Since they
were hit for their sake, therefore they will merit the Holy Spirit
and be appointed as prophets over them.'"

(Shemot Rabbah 5:23)

שמו"ר פ"ה:כג

מכאן אתה למד שהיו כשרים ומסרו עצמם על ישראל וסבלו מכות כדי להקל
מעליהם ולפיכך זכו לרוח"ק שנא' "וַיֹּאמֶר ה' אֶל־מֹשֶׁה אֶסְפָה־לִּי שִׁבְעִים אִישׁ
מִזִּקְנֵי יִשְׂרָאֵל אֲשֶׁר יָדַעְתָּ כִּי־הֵם זִקְנֵי הָעָם וְשֹׁטְרָיו וְלָקַחְתָּ אֹתָם אֶל־אֹהֶל מוֹעֵד
וְהִתְיַצְּבוּ שָׁם עִמָּךְ" (במדבר יא:טז), אמר הקב"ה הם לקו עליהם לפיכך יזכו
לרוח"ק ויתמנו נביאים עליהם.

What are the qualifications for Jewish leadership? What are the
criterion by which to judge Jewish leaders?

The Midrash clearly defines leadership as, "they endured pain and suffering" in order to alleviate the suffering of the Jewish slaves of Egypt. Thus they earned the privilege to acquire רוח הקודש – "divine inspiration," which qualified them to be of the "70 elders." G-d says they will "stand there with you" [with משה]. "And I will come down and talk with you there, and I will take the spirit which is upon you and will put it upon them and they will bear the burden of the people with you, that you bear it not by yourself alone." (Bamidbar 11:17).

The Almighty advises or indeed commands His "trusted servant" Moshe – You cannot and should not serve as the sole leader of the Children of Israel. Yes, you are the great emancipator. Nonetheless, you need qualified individuals who will share your leadership responsibilities and burdens. Those who have demonstrated a sense of compassion and empathy for כלל ישראל – they are qualified to lead.

Anger / כעם

וַיִּפְגְּעוּ אֶת־מֹשֶׁה וְאֶת־אַהֲרֹן נִצָּבִים לִקְרָאתָם
בְּצֵאתָם מֵאֵת פַּרְעֹה. וַיֹּאמְרוּ אֲלֵהֶם יֵרֶא ה' עֲלֵיכֶם
וְיִשְׁפֹּט אֲשֶׁר הִבְאַשְׁתֶּם אֶת־רֵיחֵנוּ בְּעֵינֵי פַרְעֹה
וּבְעֵינֵי עֲבָדָיו לָתֶת־חֶרֶב בְּיָדָם לְהָרְגֵנוּ: (שמות ה:כ-כא)

And they [the leaders of the Jewish people in
Egypt] met Moshe and Aharon standing before
them as they left Pharaoh. And they said to them,
"May the Lord look upon you and judge, for you
have made us abhorrent in the eyes of Pharaoh
and in the eyes of his servants, to put a sword in
their hand to slay us." (Shemot 5: 20—21)

"And they said to them, 'May the Lord look upon you and judge'"
(Shemot 5:21) – From this we see that a man is not held responsible [for what he says] in his moment of anger, for [what he says]
is not considered to be a sin in such a situation. (Midrash Lekach
Tov, Torah Shelemah on Shemot Ch. 5, source 78)

מדרש לקח טוב, תורה שלמה שמות פרק ה עח
"וַיֹּאמְרוּ אֲלֵהֶם יֵרֶא ה' עֲלֵיכֶם וְיִשְׁפֹּט" (שמות ה:כא), מיכן שאין אדם נתפס בשעת
כעסו, שלא נחשב להם עון בדבר הזה.

Thus we learn that a person cannot objectively "perceive" (comprehend) what is being said or what is happening when anger
prevails. The angry person no longer has the capacity for objective thinking.

Torah ethics do not equivocate in response to "anger." To cite
but a few classic Rabbinic judgments:

1. *Babylonian Talmud Pesachim 66b*

Resh Lakish said: Anyone who gets angry – if he is a scholar, his wisdom departs from him; if he is a prophet, his prophecy departs from him.

ר״ל אמר כל אדם שכועס אם חכם הוא חכמתו מסתלקת ממנו אם נביא הוא נבואתו מסתלקת ממנו.

The Talmud teaches: Be it "wisdom" or "prophecy," anger vacates the positive powers of those gifts. Prophecy and wisdom demand an objective and just perspective. Anger, the Rabbis teach, distorts judgment. In a more radical view the Talmud compares the individual in anger to an idolator.

2. *Babylonian Talmud Shabbat 105b*

Tearing one's clothing, breaking one's utensils, or throwing about one's money in anger, is comparable to worshipping idols, so states the Talmud:

תניא רבי שמעון בן אלעזר אומר משום חילפא בר אגרא, שאמר משום רבי יוחנן בן נורי: המקרע בגדיו בחמתו, והמשבר כליו בחמתו, והמפזר מעותיו בחמתו – יהא בעיניך כעובד עכו״ם.

Perhaps a bit of hyperbole, nonetheless the Talmud seeks to radicalize its judgment of "anger" so as to make its message clear and emphatic.

3. *Babylonian Talmud Nedarim 22b*

Even the Divine Presence is unimportant to an angry person.

כל הכועם אפילו שכינה אינה חשובה כנגדו.

An individual who otherwise recognizes the presence of the Almighty in his life, in a state of anger even the Divine is dismissed and irrelevant.

4. *Babylonian Talmud Nedarim 22b*

The irate person forgets his studies and (increases or) makes himself foolish.

כל הכועס . . . משכח תלמודו ומוסיף טיפשות.

Judaism is intolerant of a person losing control over actions or emotions. Though there are occasions when anger is in order, perhaps obligatory. Witnessing injustice, cruelty, brutality, one must respond with anger and condemnation. Yet even in such circumstances one must consider with objective judgment, how best to respond, to achieve the most positive results.

It is interesting to note the statement in פרקי אבות ב:י (Ethics of the Fathers 2:10) "Do not easily become angry," ואל תהי נוח לכעוס. The term "easily" suggests that "hasty" anger is improper, yet after careful and objective judgment "anger" may, or perhaps, must be in order. To be calm and placid in response to all situations may well suggest approval or at least acquiescence, which may have unanticipated negative consequences. Anger from a Torah perspective is necessary and at times obligatory in response to immoral, unethical, and destructive words, acts, and attitudes.

Send Whomever You Choose — Personal
Relationship with G-d / שלח נא ביד תשלח

וַיְדַבֵּר אֱ-לֹהִים אֶל-מֹשֶׁה וַיֹּאמֶר אֵלָיו אֲנִי ה':
(שמות ו:ב)

*And G-d spoke to Moshe, and said to him, I am
the Lord. (Shemot 6:2)*

"And G-d spoke to Moshe" (Shemot 6:2). Rabbi Nechemiah said:
"The Holy One, blessed is He, said to Moshe, 'I am fully aware of
the suffering of My children in Egypt,' as it says, "And G-d saw
the Children of Israel, and G-d knew" (Shemot 2:25). "My children are in agony, while you are at ease. I wish to liberate them
from Egypt, yet you tell Me, 'send whomever you choose' (Shemot
4:13)."

(Mechilta Vaera, Torah Shelemah on Shemot Ch. 6, source 8)

מכילתא וארא, תורה שלמה שמות פרק ו ח

"וַיְדַבֵּר אֱ-לֹהִים אֶל-מֹשֶׁה" (שמות ו:ב), רבי נחמיה אומר, אמר לו הקב"ה למשה
גלוי וידוע לפני צער של בני במצרים שנאמר "וַיַּרְא אֱ-לֹהִים אֶת-בְּנֵי יִשְׂרָאֵל וַיֵּדַע
אֱ-לֹהִים" (שמות ב:כה) - בני שרויין בצרה ואתה שרוי ברויח אני מבקש להוציאן
ממצרים ואתה אומר לי "שְׁלַח-נָא בְּיַד-תִּשְׁלָח" (שמות ד:יג).

Rabbi Yehoshua Ben Karha said: The Holy One, blessed is He,
said to Moshe, 'The Israelites were not worthy for Me to give
them the manna in the wilderness. Instead, they should have suffered hunger, thirst and nakedness. But what could I do seeing
that I desired to repay them with the reward due to My beloved
Avraham for his hospitality to the angels?' as it says: "He stood
by them under the tree, and they ate" (Bereishit 18:8). "Behold, I

wish to liberate them from Egypt, yet you tell Me 'send whomever You choose'" (Shemot 4:13). (Mechilta Vaera)

מכילתא וארא
רבי יהושע בן קרחה אומר, אמר לו הקב"ה למשה לא היו ישראל ראויין לתת
להם מן במדבר אלא רעב וצמא וערום ועריה, אבל מה אעשה שמשלם אני
להם שכר אוהבי אברהם שעשה לפני מלאכי השרת, שנאמר "וְהוּא עֹמֵד
עֲלֵיהֶם תַּחַת הָעֵץ וַיֹּאכֵלוּ" (בראשית יח:ח), והריני מבקש להוציאן ממצרים, ואתה
אומר לי "שְׁלַח־נָא בְּיַד־תִּשְׁלָח" (שמות ד:יג).

It seems הקב"ה is angry with משה רבנו for משה's response, שְׁלַח־נָא
בְּיַד־תִּשְׁלָח – "send whomever you choose" to lead בני ישראל out of Egyptian enslavement. It seems as if משה has no desire to lead כלל ישראל from their oppressive enslavement. It is an incredibly dismissive response of משה רבנו to הקב"ה. Moshe says, "This is not my concern, nor is it my task; go find someone else;" שְׁלַח־נָא בְּיַד־ תִּשְׁלָח – "send anyone you choose [just not me.]"

According to this מכילתא even the most outstanding of all leaders of כלל ישראל, משה רבנו, has his moments of ultimate frustration and says to הקב"ה send whomever you want, just not me. Moshe says, "Please," נא – "send anyone, not me" – שלח-נא ביד-תשלח.

When there is a profound relationship between הקב"ה (G-d) and the individual, not only משה רבנו, but any person of profound faith may express frustration and respectful confrontation with הקב"ה. משה רבנו gave us the gift of this quality of faith, אמונה. One who believes in ה' (G-d), faces all of life's vicissitudes with the faith – אמונה - that there is an ultimate purpose in one's life. Though at times there are events which are cataclysmic with no apparent cause. משה teaches us to speak to הקב"ה even with words of anger and confrontation. In the quest for serious אמונה (faith), there are moments of a painful and angry quest for understanding.

Yet there is that special word which demonstrates the unique quality of the relationship between משה and הקב"ה. שלח נא – that word נא – "please," while משה essentially rejects the role of leader of כלל ישראל and speaks rather boldly with הקב"ה there is that word נא – "please."

It is משה's very intimacy and profound relationship, almost כביכול (were it possible) one of friendship, which compels and indeed allows משה to use the phrase שלח נא – "please send."

Not me; anyone just not me – נא – "please" is the word of a friend to a friend.

Anguished Spirit / קוצר רוח

וַיְדַבֵּר מֹשֶׁה כֵּן אֶל־בְּנֵי יִשְׂרָאֵל וְלֹא שָׁמְעוּ אֶל־
מֹשֶׁה מִקֹּצֶר רוּחַ וּמֵעֲבֹדָה קָשָׁה: (שמות ו:ט)

And Moshe spoke so to the People of Israel; but
they did not listen to Moshe because of their
anguished spirit and because of the cruel slavery.
(Shemot 6:9)

From this we see that a man is not held responsible for his actions
committed in his pain. (Midrash Hagadol)

מדרש הגדול
מכאן שאין אדם נתפש על צערו.

"And because of the cruel slavery" – this teaches us that anger
drives out knowledge. (Midrash Lekach Tov)

מדרש לקח טוב
"וּמֵעֲבֹדָה קָשָׁה," מלמד שהכעם מסלק את הדעת.

It is noteworthy that both Midrashim focus upon the impact of
physical stress and frustration, i.e., עבודה קשה (hard work) and כעם
(anger) upon the individual, and consequently upon the community. Hard work of an involuntary nature, and anger resulting
from physical and mental abuse, obstruct the objective thinking
of the victim.

A sense of frustration and futility demoralize the victim. This
is the message of these two Midrashim.

The Rabbinic insight from a psychological perspective is quite
contemporary. The tactic of the oppressor and the effect upon
the victim have not changed. The method is obviously more so-

403

phisticated. Yet the suffering of the victim remains and perhaps is more traumatic as a result of more sophisticated methodology. The ability of the individual to cope with physical and mental-emotional trauma has been demonstrated repeatedly. Yet as is evidenced from our Midrash, human suffering and trauma do always impact upon the thinking and judgment of the victim.

Go and Tell It / לך אמור

וַיְדַבֵּר ה' אֶל־מֹשֶׁה לֵּאמֹר: בֹּא דַבֵּר אֶל־פַּרְעֹה
מֶלֶךְ מִצְרָיִם וִישַׁלַּח אֶת־בְּנֵי־יִשְׂרָאֵל מֵאַרְצוֹ:
(שמות ו:י-יא)

And the Lord spoke to Moshe, saying. "Go in;
speak to Pharaoh king of Egypt [and tell him to]
send the Children of Israel from out of his land."
(Shemot 6:10—11)

Upon each word the Holy One, blessed is He, spoke to Moshe,
He told him to "go and tell it." From this our Sages inferred that
whoever hears something from his friend may not share it [with
others] until his friend tells him, "Go and tell it."

(Midrash Lekach Tov)

(מדרש לקח טוב)

עַל כָּל דִּבּוּר וְדִבּוּר שֶׁהָיָה הַקב"ה מְדַבֵּר אֶל מֹשֶׁה הָיָה אוֹמֵר לוֹ לֵךְ אוֹמֵר. מִיכָן
אָמְרוּ חֲכָמִים כָּל הַשּׁוֹמֵעַ דָּבָר מֵחֲבֵרוֹ אֵינוֹ רַשַּׁאי לְאוֹמְרוֹ עַד שֶׁיֹּאמַר לוֹ חֲבֵירוֹ
לֵךְ אֱמוֹר.

The מדרש is focused upon the specificity of this פסוק – ה' directs
מֹשֶׁה (in פסוק יא), לך אמור; הקב"ה tells מֹשֶׁה רַבֵּנוּ – "Go to פַּרְעֹה and this
is what you are to say to him." Thus concludes this מדרש.

You may not repeat what you hear unless you are so directed
by the source. The מדרש is concerned with the confidentiality of
information received.

The flow of language in contemporary society is free and undisciplined. Except when fear of libel becomes an issue or fear
of retribution instills some caution, modern society allows the
gift of language to be abused and desecrated. The human expe-

405

rience depends upon language to foster learning, the sacredness of interpersonal relationships, the preservation of profound and sacred thought, and the simple matter of communication. Yet it too often can be a vehicle of misunderstanding and pain.

We call the language of our people לשון הקודש, the "holy language," and so it has been called for millennia. Whether the use of contemporary Hebrew, i.e., עברית is always "holy" is yet another matter. Nonetheless, the very essence of Jewish civilization, the values, beliefs, history, pain and exultation, defeat and victory are all preserved in Hebrew, לשון הקודש, the holy language.

With one notable exception, the Talmud, with its Aramaic vocabulary, most of our philosophy, theology, history, law, poetry, and liturgy are recorded and preserved in Hebrew.

Perhaps above all when in 1948 the State of Israel was established, Hebrew, from its very first moment, was the State's official language, which successfully united its citizens. Jews from every land of the Diaspora – from Yemen to Germany – from Russia to America, all became fluent in Hebrew, the ancient and contemporary language of the Jew. In Israel, from the תנ"ך to the report of an Israeli soccer team all are in Hebrew. Whether Ashkenaz, Western Jewry, or Sefardic Jews from the Fertile Crescent, all come together in Hebrew. In prayer, study, and daily speech Hebrew is a uniting force of the universal Jewish people.

Language is a critical dimension of a people's culture, values, and unity. The Midrash has a very poignant comment about language.

> 'The tongue' (Mishlei 18:21). . . . Good comes from it and bad comes from it. When the tongue is good there is nothing better, and when it is bad there is nothing worse. (Vayikra Rabbah 33:1)

ויקרא רבה, לג:א

"לָשׁוֹן" (משלי יח:כא) ... ממנה הטובה וממנה הרעה כשהיא טובה אין טובה ממנה, וכשהיא רעה אין רעה ממנה.

Moreover, language is a force and source of unifying our people. The משנה in פרקי אבות says כל האומר דבר בשם אומרו מביא גאולה לעולם

(אבות ו:ו) – when you recited a worthy statement and identify the person who first made the statement, you bring גאולה – redemption to the world. You demonstrated (a) honesty, i.e., you are not the author of the statement; (b) you give honor and respect to the author; (c) you teach without seeking self-aggrandizement.

Faith and Trust / בטחון ואמונה

וַיִּקְרָא לְמֹשֶׁה וּלְאַהֲרֹן לַיְלָה וַיֹּאמֶר קוּמוּ צְּאוּ
מִתּוֹךְ עַמִּי גַּם־אַתֶּם גַּם־בְּנֵי יִשְׂרָאֵל וּלְכוּ עִבְדוּ
אֶת־ה' כְּדַבֶּרְכֶם: (שמות יב:לא)

And he (Pharaoh) called for Moshe and Aharon
by night, and said, "Rise up and get out from
among my people, both you and the Children of
Israel and go serve your Lord as you have said."
(Shemot 12:31)

It is a demonstration of Judaism's belief in a pragmatic approach
to a given problem, though in fact, the ultimate resolution may
be miraculous.

Chanukah is a perfect illustration. It could well have been a
miracle without the single jug of oil with which to light the Ner
Tamid.

The Purim miracle to save the Jews of Persia could well have
occurred without Esther becoming Queen.

The Sea of Reeds could have split without נחשן בן עמינדב first
jumping into the sea, as is reported in the Midrash.

The תורה is emphatic in its report of the confrontation of בני
ישראל with the "Sea of Reeds." The Children of Israel stood between the pursuing Egyptian army and the sea, which seemed to
suggest an insurmountable obstacle. Drown, be slain, or return to
enslavement in Egypt.

The miraculous escape through the sea which at first seemed
certain death was made possible by Nachshon Ben Aminadov
jumping into the sea, which only then split, allowing Israel to
escape.

The מדרש (מדרש רבה שמות כא:ח) states:

Rabbi Eliezer said: "The Holy One, blessed is He, said to Moshe: 'There is a time to pray extensively and there is a time to pray briefly. My children are in pain. The sea is closing in on them. The enemy is pursuing them and you are standing engaged in extensive prayer. Speak to the Children of Israel and tell them to move on'" (Shemot 14:15). Rabbi Yehoshua said: "The Holy One, blessed is He, said to Moshe: 'All that Israel has to do is to go forward, so let them go forward, let their feet step forward from the dry land to the sea, and you will see the miracles that I will perform for them.'" Rabbi Meir said: "G-d said to Moshe: 'There is no need for Israel to pray to Me. Just as I made dry land for Adam who was just one person' as it says, 'Let the waters under the heaven be gathered together' (Bereishit 1:9), how much more ought I to do so on behalf of a holy congregation that will soon say before Me, 'This is my G-d, and I will glorify Him'" (Shemot 15:2).

מדרש רבה שמות כא:ח

ר' אליעזר אומר, אמר לו הקב"ה למשה עת לקצר ועת להאריך בני שרוים בצער והים סוגר והאויב רודף ואתה עומד ומרבה בתפלה "דַּבֵּר אֶל־בְּנֵי־יִשְׂרָאֵל וְיִסָּעוּ" (שמות יד:טו). רבי יהושע אומר אמר הקב"ה למשה אין להם לישראל אלא ליסע בלבד "וְיִסָּעוּ" יסיעו רגליהם מן היבשה לים ואתה רואה נסים שאעשה להם. רבי מאיר אומר אמר הקב"ה למשה אין ישראל צריכין להתפלל לפני ומה אם אדם הראשון שהיה יחידי עשיתי יבשה בשבילו שנאמר "יִקָּווּ הַמַּיִם מִתַּחַת הַשָּׁמַיִם" (בראשית א:ט), בשביל עדה קדושה שעתידה לומר לפני "זֶה אֵלִי וְאַנְוֵהוּ" (שמות טו:ב) על אחת כמה וכמה.

These Midrashic texts demonstrate the Rabbinic view that 'ה demands and expects the community or the individual to act in response to a given situation, or opportunity, which is then the catalyst for 'ה to respond. Judaism's insistence upon human initiative is fundamental to its understanding of אמונה and בטחון – "faith" and "trust."

There is yet another direction to our view of the intervention of 'ה, which results in a נס (miracle). The Talmud teaches:

A person should not intentionally enter into a situation or venue which is determined to be dangerous, assuming that the intervention of a miracle will protect from all harm. Perhaps there will be no "miracle" to protect and save. (Babylonian Talmud Ta'anis 20b)

תענית כ:
לעולם אל יעמוד אדם במקום סכנה ויאמר עושין לי נס, שמא אין עושין לו נס.

Judaism expects a person to determine the situation to be confronted, consider all options, then choose the most appropriate response. Then our prayers should plead that our choice be correct.

The Jerusalem Talmud states אַשְׁרֵי אָדָם בֹּטֵחַ בָּךְ. (תהלים פד:יג)
"The Lord of Hosts: Happy is the person who has faith in You (Hashem)." (Psalms 84:13)
Rabbi Abuhoe quotes Rabbi Yochanan and his colleagues, "May this text [Psalms 84:13] never cease from your mouth." (Yerushalmi, Brachot 5:1)

ירושלמי ברכות פ"ה:א
רבי אבהו בשם רבי יוחנן וחברייא אמר, לעולם אל יהא הפסוק הזה זז מתוך פיך.

Once again these Talmudic texts emphasize the synthesis of faith in 'ה and human initiative. Faith, from the Torah perspective, does not preclude human choice, initiative, and action. On the contrary, both the experience at the Sea of Reeds and the absence of oil for the מנורה in the בית המקדש all demonstrative of the absolute necessity of human initiative as the catalyst for 'ה's interventions. In the case of the מנורה and the miracle of Chanukah, there was sufficient oil for one day, though it was obvious it would take another seven days to prepare oil for the Menorah to remain lit. Nonetheless, the Menorah was lit without assurance that it would remain lit. That was the miracle of Chanukah. The one day supply of oil lasted long enough for the Maccabees to make new oil. The act of faith in lighting the Menorah was the miracle.

The Advice of Yitro / עצת יתרו

וַיַּרְא חֹתֵן מֹשֶׁה אֵת כָּל־אֲשֶׁר־הוּא עֹשֶׂה לָעָם
וַיֹּאמֶר מָה־הַדָּבָר הַזֶּה אֲשֶׁר אַתָּה עֹשֶׂה לָעָם
מַדּוּעַ אַתָּה יוֹשֵׁב לְבַדֶּךָ וְכָל־הָעָם נִצָּב עָלֶיךָ
מִן־בֹּקֶר עַד־עָרֶב: (שמות יח:יד)

And when Moshe's father-in-law saw all that he
did to the people he said, 'What is this thing that
you do for the people? Why do you sit by yourself
alone with all the people standing by you from
morning to evening?' (Shemot 18:14)

Even משה רבנו who spoke to 'ה was chastened by יתרו, his father-
in-law.

It is not good what you [משה] are doing. (Shemot 18:17)

שמות יח:יז
לֹא־טוֹב הַדָּבָר אֲשֶׁר אַתָּה עֹשֶׂה.

You are not able to perform it yourself alone. Listen now to my
voice, I will give you counsel, and G-d shall be with you. (Shemot
18:18–19)

שמות יח:יח-יט
לֹא־תוּכַל עֲשֹׂהוּ לְבַדֶּךָ: עַתָּה שְׁמַע בְּקֹלִי אִיעָצְךָ וִיהִי אֱ-לֹהִים עִמָּךְ.

יתרו continues to admonish משה and then advises משה to apply ef-
ficiency to his leadership role and share his practical, logistical
powers with a host of leaders of different levels and responsibility.

How remarkable that משה accepts the admonition and indeed
the system suggested by יתרו. The תורה reports –

And משה chose able men out of all Israel and appointed male heads over the people – rulers of thousands, rulers of hundreds, rulers of fifties and rulers of tens. And they judged the people at all times: The hard cases they brought to Moshe but every small matter they judged themselves. (Shemot 18:25–26)

שמות יח:כה-כו

וַיִּבְחַר מֹשֶׁה אַנְשֵׁי־חַיִל מִכָּל־יִשְׂרָאֵל וַיִּתֵּן אֹתָם רָאשִׁים עַל־הָעָם שָׂרֵי אֲלָפִים שָׂרֵי מֵאוֹת שָׂרֵי חֲמִשִּׁים וְשָׂרֵי עֲשָׂרֹת: וְשָׁפְטוּ אֶת־הָעָם בְּכָל־עֵת אֶת־הַדָּבָר הַקָּשֶׁה יְבִיאוּן אֶל־מֹשֶׁה וְכָל־הַדָּבָר הַקָּטֹן יִשְׁפּוּטוּ הֵם: